PUBLIC AND PRIVATE

*Gender, Class, and the
British Novel (1764–1878)*

Patricia McKee

University of Minnesota Press
Minneapolis
London

Published by the University of Minnesota Press
111 Third Avenue South, Suite 290, Minneapolis, MN 55401-2520
Printed in the United States of America on acid-free paper

Library of Congress Cataloging-in-Publication Data

McKee, Patricia, 1945–
     Public and private : gender, class, and the British novel
(1764–1878) / Patricia McKee.
          p.   cm.
     Includes bibliographical references and index.
     ISBN 0-8166-2934-X (acid-free paper)
     ISBN 0-8166-2935-8 (pbk.: acid-free paper)
     1. English fiction — 19th century — History and criticism.
2. Social problems in literature.   3. Literature and society — Great
Britain — History — 19th century.   4. Literature and society — Great
Britain — History — 18th century.   5. English fiction — 18th century —
History and criticism.   6. Capitalism and literature — Great
Britain — History.   7. Production (Economic theory) in literature.
8. Consumption (Economics) in literature.   9. Social classes in
literature.   10. Sex role in literature.   I. Title.
PR868.S62M35   1997
823.009'355 — dc20   96-35350

The University of Minnesota is an equal-opportunity educator and employer.

For Don

Contents

Acknowledgments

Many of the ideas in this book have been worked out in class at Dartmouth College, and my first thanks are to the students who have studied and thought about British novels with me. I am also grateful to Dartmouth College for awarding me a faculty fellowship for work on this project.

Jay Clayton and John Brenkman each provided criticism crucial to the completion of the book. At Dartmouth, Chauncey Loomis read what seemed endless versions of the chapter on Austen. For their encouragement and criticism I am very grateful.

I want to thank the people at the University of Minnesota Press who have helped publish the book, especially Lisa Freeman for both her enthusiasm and her criticism and Tammy Zambo for her careful copyediting.

I am most grateful to Donald Pease, whose thinking and reading of this work at its various stages have made the greatest difference to it. The book is dedicated to him.

Introduction

In the chapters that follow, I will be examining representations of public and private life in British novels and, to a lesser extent, works of social and political theory written in the later eighteenth and nineteenth centuries. My primary focus is on knowledge: its production and its distribution and how these organize institutional, social, and psychological experience. The production of knowledge and self-knowledge defines to a great extent the experience of publicness and privacy in novels during this period. Knowledge becomes, moreover, a crucial means by which both public and private life are reordered in the course of a century to provide stable categories of experience.

The eighteenth-century public sphere appeared unstable to Tobias Smollett, for example, because of extraordinarily increased economic growth and because self-interest rather than reason motivated individuals' behavior in political and professional life. Capitalism was threatening to ideas of social order, Joyce Appleby has argued, until, in the course of the eighteenth century, theorists reconceived human nature and social order in terms that fitted them to the behavior of the new economy. Adam Smith's reconception of consumption, in particular, narrowed and stabilized concepts of individual interest by directing consumption toward self-improvement, revising self-interest from a force threatening to social order into a predictable component of social exchange. And the expanding market economy that could no longer be identified as a stable structure was saved from appearing chaotic by its reconception as a systematic if dynamic process, one comparable to natural physical systems.[1]

Such revisions of knowledge—knowledge of individuals and social systems both—will be the focus of my discussions of eighteenth- and nineteenth-century novels. Whereas in the eighteenth century patterns of increasing and open-ended productivity and consumption are seen to threaten stability because they occur as dynamic and interactive processes, by the later nineteenth century productivity and consumption come to be understood as distinct and stable categories of experience. Not only are these processes no longer threatening to social stability, they are known to be necessary to it. Production and consumption by now seldom intersect and seldom change or cause change. They become not only distinct processes but characteristic of distinct kinds of persons in distinctly separate spheres of social experience. The stabilization of experience once known to be unstable occurs through the development and distribution of different kinds of knowledge among men and women and within public and private life.

One reconception of production important to stabilizing ideas of both public and psychological orders during this period was the reconception of productivity as reproduction. Social and cultural reproduction are concepts that cover broad and various areas of experience, and such experience was evident to eighteenth-century and nineteenth-century novelists in several forms. For one thing, as Neil McKendrick has demonstrated, the consumer society that grew in eighteenth-century England depended on the lower classes copying the consumption of the upper class.[2] Such imitative consumption was what Smollett objected to as "levelling" individual and class differences. Later writers, especially Dickens, objected not only to the sameness of individuals within a consumer society but also to the reproductive character of public institutions that seemed to produce nothing but their own business.[3] Moreover, both Dickens and Trollope at midcentury clearly recognized what Pierre Bourdieu has theorized as the reproduction of social classes in patterns of taste and consumption.[4]

It is in particular the reproductive character of knowledge that I will be pointing to, in novels not only of Dickens and Trollope but of Shelley before them and Hardy after them. All of these writers depict knowledge as antiprogressive, so that the growth of knowledge effects more repetition than change. Dickens's attack on bureaucratic productions of knowledge-as-information, and the use of such information to maintain a status quo, is the most explicit of these depictions. In Hardy's novels, the reproductivity of social production eventually becomes its fixed character, largely because Hardy depicts reproductivity as natural. Whereas Dickens insists that the capacity of modern knowledge to do little more than reproduce its own terms is a situation requiring change, Hardy depicts knowledge as necessarily and naturally so limited by its own relativism as to be incapable of producing change.

In the novels I consider here, however, it is in private experience that social reproduction first appears and first begins to stabilize experience. As early as *The Castle of Otranto* (1764), individual desire is reoriented toward reproduction. Male desire is directed toward recovering a lost object. Female identity, as an object desirable to men, therefore depends on the ability to reproduce the lost object, to identify the female self in the image of another woman. This female constitution of personal identity, so fitting to the growth of imitative consumption, is cultivated by later novelists in the development of female character. And this is true even of authors, such as Dickens, who discourage reproduction in public spheres because it prevents change. It is as if female identity is required to take on certain elements of experience that men in the public sphere cannot afford.[5]

This reproductive representation of women in the Gothic novel begins a tendency in British fiction to depict women's psyches and women's knowledge very differently from those of men. For one thing, female knowledge, both self-knowledge and knowledge of others, is much less a knowledge of distinction and difference than is male knowledge. The female character tends to see herself as both subject and object; she sees herself as an image of someone else and thus interchangeable with someone else. Less productive of difference, female knowledge is also more immediate. Their experienced immediacy of subject and object seems to mean that women's understanding is less capable of the abstractions that increasingly become the hallmark of public, institutional knowledge, which is capable of reproduction because it remains abstracted from immediate and material experience. Women's reproduction, by contrast, is limited to the self as reproducible phenomenon. The fact that women are more immediately concerned in the reproduction of children certainly encourages their identification with social reproduction. What interests me here, however, is less women's roles as mothers than the ways that their psyches and their social lives, even as unmarried women without children, limit them to recognition as reproductions.

Differences between kinds of knowledge available to women and to men receive increasing attention in the later chapters of this study. Nancy Armstrong has argued that "the project of gendering subjectivity began to acquire the immense political influence it still exercises today" in the mid-nineteenth century,[6] and her assertion is supported by the texts I examine. My emphasis is on ways that distinctions of gender help to secure and maintain other distinctions — especially the separation of public productivity from personal consumption — useful to social order in the later nineteenth century. The capacity of proper men to produce both growth and regulation in public spheres is strengthened by the knowledge that consumption, with its emotional components of dependence and need, and reproduction, which would confuse the progressive character of knowledge in public spheres, are restricted to the private lives of women.[7]

In the private lives of women accumulates a variety of experience that cannot fit the order of public life: emotional confusion, imitative consumption, cultural reproduction. In private, moreover, such experience becomes increasingly inaccessible to public knowledge. Women come to exist in an unknowable realm. They are cut off from knowledge by the incommensurability of their experience with structures of knowledge, which occurs both because in their relation to the world around them women produce more confusions than distinctions, and because of women's own undifferentiated status as something other than distinguished individuals. Not practicing knowledge as differentiation, women also cannot be known by means of such knowledge.

But the obscurity of women's lives does not simply separate them from disciplines of knowledge. In addition, later-nineteenth-century knowledge in the public domain, including scientific and historical knowledge, may be said to cultivate realms of unknown and unknowable phenomena. Nineteenth-century novelists identify cultivations of obscurity and mystery existing together with, and in some cases inseparably from, cultivations of knowledge. Earlier novelists—Austen and Dickens—see cultivations of obscurity occurring in the interest and as the work of individuals. Later novelists, especially Hardy, represent obscurity cultivated together with knowledge, even by knowledge, and despite human interests and action. When the lives of women are identified as unknowable, therefore, they fit into a certain place in structures of knowledge: a place designated, indeed, as a sphere separate from public knowledge and public order, but a place that moreover assumes characteristics of realms of obscurity discovered, or produced, by disciplines of knowledge.

The production of knowledge in public spheres, therefore, eventually makes room for women in a very particular way. Women's lives are not merely separated from realms of public knowledge, they are known to be incompatible with knowledge, order, and regulation. This means that two different kinds of social order are necessary. If knowledge provides regulation in the lives of men who produce it and in the public spheres in which it is produced, the lives of persons beyond the reach of knowledge are ordered simply by being "kept down." Not only the lives of women but also the lives of working-class persons are located "beneath" those of men capable of knowledge and regulation. A hierarchy of social heights and depths appears, in which positions are not determined by traditional distinctions of upper and lower social classes but instead conform to degrees of knowledge. Heights of abstract idealism and depths of ignorance belong to knowledgeable, productive men, on the one hand, and emotional, consuming women as well as uneducated men, on the other.

What I am tracing in these chapters, then, are some of the ways that British literature was able to reform social experience through the eighteenth and nineteenth centuries by eventually reforming practices of productivity and consumption into stable dimensions of social order.

In the eighteenth century, capitalism, with its growth, its dependence on expanding markets and expanding personal desires, and its imaginative and creative potential, threatened British society with unpredictability and instability. For many writers the leveling of social classes was one of the most dangerous changes caused by rapidly increasing economic production and consumption. By the later nineteenth century, processes of production and consumption not only became predictable and stable, they also became a crucial means of restructuring social classes of persons. Much of this restructuring occurred through increasing distinctions between private and public realms of experience and between the kinds of knowledge produced and applied within those realms. It is a history of these distinctions, as represented by theorists as well as novelists, that I am proposing.

The reordering I have summarized here is not a phenomenon I will trace as a simply linear development. The novels I consider, even those written within a few years of each other, represent disparate perspectives on knowledge in public and private life. Austen's Emma Woodhouse, for example, is a clear exception to the tendency to deny women's productive use of knowledge; so is Dickens's Amy Dorrit, whose understanding projects historical depths into her present experience. Such disparities indicate both the debatable character of public and private experience and the variety of possibilities for their interrelation. Yet such alternatives in turn make more striking the general tendencies that emerge during this period.

Critical Views

My identification of such changes in representations of public and private experience owes much to earlier scholarship. To begin with, my sense of interrelations between institutional structures of public life and structures of subjectivity depends on earlier examinations by poststructuralist critics of interdependencies of public and private experience. Recent critics of English literature of the seventeenth and eighteenth centuries, for example, have argued that the representation of subjectivity during that period undergoes changes necessary to the increasing hegemony of "middle-class" ideology in public political life. Both Michael McKeon and Nancy Armstrong argue that assimilations or

internalizations occur, through subjectivity, of formerly public functions and structures of behavior and that this stabilizes social change.
These readings have been crucial to my understanding of the political
dimensions of narrative subjectivity.

McKeon provides an extensive history of internalizations of individual value in *The Origins of the English Novel*. He identifies a process
of public debate, carried out through early novels, that refigures questions of truth and virtue into conflicts of, on the one hand, romance
versus history and, on the other, aristocratic rank versus moral character. In both cases, the terms of conflict articulate and facilitate a complex but effective separation of external and internal experience. Virtue
becomes a moral quality rather than a value assigned by social rank:

> In the broadest terms, the transvaluation of honor that culminates in the
> seventeenth century is a process of separation and detachment comparable
> to that undergone by the compound unit "history-romance" during the
> same period. . . . Progressive ideology requires that it resolve itself into virtue
> on the one hand and aristocratic rank on the other, a discrimination that
> repudiates the automatic aristocratic signification of internals by externals.[8]

McKeon's discussion of the process by which aristocratic values were
reformed depends on an understanding of class ideology unlimited to
any particular group of persons:

> [I]t is perhaps the assimilationist and the supersessionist strains of middle-
> class ideology that define its very nature. Not yet (if ever) embodied within
> a delimited social class, middle-class ideology slowly suffused different seg-
> ments of the reigning status groups and gained its first expression through a
> network of beliefs that were themselves in the process of a critical mutation.[9]

This sense of middle-class ideology "suffusing" various social groups is
important to the history of the novel I am proposing. I argue that
nineteenth-century novelists impose increasingly definite classifications
on social groups in the course of the nineteenth century. But this occurs on the basis of peoples' knowledge and beliefs and can occur only
when various "external" criteria of social class no longer matter. McKeon
clarifies how much the power of middle-class ideology in the seventeenth and eighteenth centuries depended on an indefinition of classes
as it shifted individual worth to internal criteria.

In *Desire and Domestic Fiction: A Political History of the Novel,* Nancy Armstrong emphasizes, as does McKeon, how important internal values were to the gradual shift of power from aristocracy to middle class. Armstrong also identifies the middle class as more an ideology than a definite social group and thus can argue that domestic women were most influential in putting this ideology into power. For Armstrong, domestic female subjectivity, assigned increasing power in conduct books of the period, mediated the conflict between aristocratic and commercial values:

> In arguing for a new set of qualities to desire in a woman, these books... made her capable of authorizing a whole new set of economic practices that directly countered what were supposed to be seen as the excesses of a decadent aristocracy. Under the dominion of such a woman, the country house could no longer authorize a political system that made sumptuary display the ultimate aim of production. Instead, it proposed a world where production was an end in itself.[10]

Thus woman as domestic economist promoted the immateriality of capitalistic wealth. The domestic woman was to work not with her body but with her morals, the most important of which were regularity and regulation, particularly of the self: "The domestic woman executes her role in the household by regulating her own desire. On her 'feeling and principle' depends the economic behavior that alone ensures prosperity."[11] Thus female authority, in the domestic sphere of conduct books and of novels, carries political power because of its capacity to domesticate and emotionalize patterns of behavior needed within the public sphere.

It is the early work of Jürgen Habermas, however, in *The Structural Transformation of the Public Sphere,* that I have found most useful in theorizing relations between public and private spheres in eighteenth- and nineteenth-century Britain. For Habermas as for McKeon and Armstrong, a critical, reflexive subjectivity is the crucial characteristic of political life in eighteenth-century Britain. Like McKeon, Habermas attends to a public sphere constituted by debate; but his emphasis is on the common dependence of public and private spheres on a rational, autonomous subjectivity. Like Armstrong, Habermas sees the public sphere dependent on domestic life; but he does not differentiate male from female subjectivity as it develops within the domestic family.

Habermas's Public and Private Spheres

Habermas argues that eighteenth-century concepts of public and private spheres developed from earlier concepts and practices allowing for little participation and debate in public by private persons. He distinguishes the public spheres of the eighteenth century from political rule in the High Middle Ages in terms of representation:

> [Medieval] *publicness* (or *publicity*) *of representation* was not constituted as a social realm, that is, as a public sphere; rather, it was something like a status attribute. . . . As long as the prince and the estates of his realm "were" the country and not just its representatives, they could represent it in a specific sense. They represented their lordship not for but "before" the people.[12]

But during the seventeenth century a public came into being whose representativeness was a matter of debate. In public forums such as coffeehouses and later in the press, critical debate took place, "ignited by works of literature and art . . . [but] soon extended to include economic and political disputes" (33). The discussants in these debates represented, but did not *constitute,* the public: "Wherever the public established itself institutionally as a stable group of discussants, it did not equate itself with *the* public but at most claimed to act as its mouthpiece, in its name, perhaps even as its educator — the new form of bourgeois representation" (37).

The private persons who make up Habermas's eighteenth-century public entered it from the private life of the family. His concept of privacy is both economic and social, combining the privacy of property ownership and the privacy of intimate relationships. Habermas argues that subjectivity within the family was oriented toward an audience, both in that it developed within relationships and in that it was represented, read, and debated in "rational-critical debate in the world of letters" (51). The common characterization of individuals within the economy, the political realm, the world of letters, and the family consisted of their common autonomy, their common publicity, and their common representation as "human": "[T]here formed a public consisting of private persons whose autonomy based on ownership of private property wanted to see itself represented as such in the sphere of the bourgeois family and actualized inside the person as love, freedom, and cultivation — in a word, as humanity" (55).

Habermas thus identifies the stability of the public sphere with an ideology of individual autonomy understood to be exercised in the market, in the family, and in public debate alike. On the one hand,

> commodity owners could view themselves as autonomous. To the degree that they were emancipated from governmental directives and controls, they made decisions freely in accord with standards of profitability. In this regard they owed obedience to no one and were subject only to the anonymous laws functioning in accord with an economic rationality immanent, so it appeared, in the market. (46)

The rational autonomy of the property owner was reflected, moreover, in the character of family members:

> [A] private autonomy denying its economic origins... provided the bourgeois family with its consciousness of itself. It seemed to be established voluntarily and by free individuals and to be maintained without coercion.... The three elements of voluntariness, community of love, and cultivation were conjoined in a concept of the humanity that was supposed to inhere in humankind as such and truly to constitute its absoluteness: the emancipation... of an inner realm, following its own laws, from extrinsic purposes of any sort. (46–47)

Developing within the family, subjectivity "was always already oriented to an audience" (49), and this was also the case in eighteenth-century novels. Thus, "subjectivity... was related from the very start to publicity" (50). And the public sphere of debating individuals depended on the critically reflective subject developed in the family.

For Habermas the division that eventually ensued between public spheres and the sphere of intimate family life in England occurred with the expansion of the public sphere, in the early to mid-nineteenth century, to include more participants. The idea of public rule by reason and rational debate became difficult to sustain, because "along with its social exclusiveness [the public sphere] also lost the coherence afforded by the institutions of sociability and a relatively high level of educa-

tion." The public sphere lost coherence and "became an arena of competing interests fought out in the coarser forms of violent conflict. Laws
passed under the 'pressure of the street' could hardly be understood
any longer as embodying the reasonable consensus of publicly debating private persons" (131–32). Moreover, during the same period that
the capacity of public debate to rule became dubious, given conflicting
interests of an expanding "public," the liberal theory of a self-regulating
economy was also rendered dubious. Individual interests clearly were
able to gain enough power to interfere with free competition. And "[t]he
more society became transparent as a mere nexus of coercive constraints,
the more urgent became the need for a strong state" (144).

As state intervention in social and economic relations increased, state
and society permeated each other, resulting in what Habermas calls a
"Blurred Blueprint" (175). A similar blurring of the boundaries of private life occurred as the economic sphere of family life was "depriva-
tized" and "the 'world of work' was established as a sphere in its own
right between the private and public realms" (152). In effect, "the conjugal family became dissociated from its connection with processes of
social reproduction" (151–52) and became, increasingly, a social unit of
consumption.

In the course of the nineteenth century, then, public and private
spheres were separated as they lost their common denominator, a shared
reliance on a private and autonomous individual. The family lost autonomy as

> it lost its power to shape conduct in areas considered the innermost provinces
> of privacy by the bourgeois family. Thus, in a certain fashion even the fam-
> ily, this private vestige, was deprivatized by the public guarantees of its sta-
> tus. On the other hand, the family now evolved even more into a consumer
> of income and leisure time, into the recipient of publicly guaranteed com-
> pensations and support services. Private autonomy was maintained not so
> much in functions of control as in functions of consumption. (155–56)

The shaping of the conduct of individuals was thus taken over both
by the state and by mass media. But even the consumption of mass
media indicates a breakdown of the earlier interdependence of public
and private realms. Whereas the audience of literature in the eighteenth
century was public, the consumers of mass media were not:

To be sure, the individuated satisfaction of needs might be achieved in a public fashion, namely, in the company of many others; but a public sphere itself did not emerge from such a situation. When the laws of the market governing the sphere of commodity exchange and of social labor also pervaded the sphere reserved for private people as a public, rational-critical debate had a tendency to be replaced by consumption, and the web of public communication unraveled into acts of individuated reception, however uniform in mode. (160–61)

Through the consumption of mass media, Habermas argues, the "province of interiority" has been "hollowed out," because the consumption of culture no longer demands critical reflection or critical debate (162–63).

Consumption thus becomes the activity of public and private spheres alike. But the culture-consuming public no longer shares the experience of consumption through critical activity. Moreover, public consumption has gradually been fragmented into different interest groups, with intellectuals and "the public," for example, reading different things. What was a public sphere of autonomous persons engaging in rational debate becomes, in the twentieth century, disparate groups who do not come together to debate, nor to exercise through debate any institutional power, and who are increasingly separated in and by their patterns of consumption.

Finally, as the publicity of the public sphere becomes, in the twentieth century, controlled by advertising and "public relations," Habermas argues, it is to some extent "refeudalized" (200). One evidence of this is that consumption is classed. But Habermas's emphasis is on the return of an unexamined correlation between representation and authority in the reception of "public figures":

The aura of personally represented authority returns as an aspect of publicity; to this extent modern publicity indeed has affinity with feudal publicity. . . . The public sphere becomes the court *before* whose public prestige can be displayed — rather than *in* which public critical debate is carried on. (200–201)

With representative public debate completely displaced by the consumption of representations by the public, modern democratic society identifies its individuals as consumers rather than producers, dependent rather than independent individuals.

Revising Habermas's Public and Private Spheres

Critics have put Habermas's theory of the public sphere to various uses, and debate about his work has focused particularly on the adequacy of the dimensions he assigns to public life. Revisionist historians have argued that eighteenth- and nineteenth-century public experience was more heterogeneous than Habermas acknowledges and that his sphere of public debate was more exclusive than he admits.[13] As Nancy Fraser has said,

> [T]he problem is not only that Habermas idealizes the liberal public sphere but also that he fails to examine other, nonliberal, nonbourgeois, competing public spheres. Or rather, it is precisely because he fails to examine these other public spheres that he ends up idealizing the liberal public sphere.[14]

In the novels I discuss in the following chapters, there are certainly disparate conceptions of public life. *The* public sphere is difficult to identify; the term *public* is used in different ways and applied to different kinds of experience.[15]

For Habermas, the public sphere is distinct from the state and from market relations.[16] But I will be discussing both the state administration that developed in Britain in the early nineteenth century and market relations as public spheres of experience. Both the state and market relations alter Habermas's public sphere in the course of the nineteenth century, even to the extent that a state administration assumes powers once exercised by public debate in the determination of public policy. Habermas identifies these changes with a blurring of the boundaries of public and private spheres. I will nevertheless be identifying such confusions with particular effects on both public and private behavior.

Market relations, which Habermas treats as private enterprise, are crucial, in most of the novels I discuss, to both public and private behavior. Indeed, Dickens's depiction of public spheres of political and administrative institutions identifies them as processes of social production that work like commodity production. And most of the authors I discuss identify emotional life in terms that clearly suit the individual psyche to capitalist commodity consumption. Thus, market relations are apparent in the most public as well as the most private life.

My attention to gender also means departing from Habermas's concepts of both public and private life. For one thing, women have public experience in several of the novels I discuss. Especially in Jane Austen's
Emma (1816), women participate in a social community that is regu-
lated both by their private exercise of reason and by the discovery,
through reason as well as emotion, of their allegiance to a particular
social group. Moreover, the fact that a "consumer mentality" becomes
almost exclusively female in the later novels I consider means that the
social fragmentations that Habermas identifies with increased economic consumption in the late nineteenth century are experienced
most tellingly by women.

The same is true regarding psychological fragmentation. Habermas
is concerned with a social private life, but I assign much more importance to subjective or psychological than to familial privacy. One reason for this focus is that psychological differences between men in
public life and women in private life seem the most definite; they are
identified at such depths of experience as to be difficult to change. My
emphasis on subjectivity brings my work closer to that of McKeon
and Armstrong, and indeed to that of many literary critics who attend
to the privacy of individual characters in novels. My emphasis on subjective dimensions of private persons also owes much to Michel Foucault's argument that changes in public disciplines of knowledge in
the late eighteenth century were paralleled by changed conceptions of
the psyche.

Foucault's Depths of Knowledge

Foucault is the thinker whose work has been most influential in the
poststructuralist challenge to the separateness of private and public
life. It is particularly because of his identification of new depths of
knowledge at the end of the eighteenth century that Foucault's work
is important to my reading of private and public experience. Foucault's
depths give additional dimensions to Habermas's theory that both public and private spheres experienced fragmentation in the later nineteenth
century.

In *The Order of Things,* Foucault analyzes changes in structures of
knowledge that occurred when hidden, productive historical processes

were identified beneath the visible surfaces of economics, biology, and language. The introduction of these "depths" reconceived both the world to be known and the knowing subject as phenomena divided between visible surfaces and invisible depths in an "empirico-transcendental" tension. One evidence of hidden depths of knowledge that Foucault emphasizes is the disappearance from representation of relations between its parts: "representation has lost the power to provide a foundation... for the links that can join its various elements together."[17] Relations of parts of knowledge and of representation have become invisible.

From Habermas's perspective, such groundlessness of representation could be seen as consistent with its debatability, that is, as not a threat to the power of public opinion. But Foucault points to divisions within structures of knowledge that move it beyond the reach and rule of persons. Moreover, Foucault is considering knowledge as discipline, external to spheres of public debate. Habermas refers to early-nineteenth-century distinctions between knowledge and public opinion as indications of the dissolution of the public sphere. But Foucault suggests an additional, deeper division, between knowledge and individuals, as knowledge of transcendent depths of experience becomes inaccessible to consciousness. And because such division occurs both in the knowing subject and in objects to be known, there are hidden dimensions recognized in both subjectivity and the surrounding world that radically interfere with their integration.

Differences between Adam Smith's, David Ricardo's, and Thomas Malthus's economic theories provide Foucault with examples of new depths in the realm of public knowledge in the late eighteenth century. Whereas Smith posits the equivalent and exchangeable values of representations of labor as well as goods, Ricardo identifies labor as producing value: "The mode of being of economics is no longer linked to a simultaneous space of differences and identities, but to the time of successive productions."[18] Moreover, the historicity of production is not a linear progress. Finitude is introduced, as in Thomas Malthus's population theory of the 1790s, both to human increase and to natural supply. Production will increase population only by using up resources; growth, then, contains within itself both increase and increasing scarcity.

Once economists late in the century reimpose checks on growth by invoking natural scarcity, Foucault argues, the transcendental dynamic of economics suspends human effort between life and death: "*Homo oeconomicus* is not the human being who represents his own needs to himself, and the objects capable of satisfying them; he is the human being who spends, wears out, and wastes his life in evading the imminence of death."[19]

In the subjective realm, the changes Foucault theorizes are due to self-division. The constant struggle between subject and object within the self is particularly apparent in the historical conception of the romantic self. Alan Liu, another of the recent critics who identify internalizations of social practices in eighteenth-century England, describes the mimetic negation of family history that is necessary to Wordsworth's individuality:

> Like an adolescent in our modern acceptation, the self attended by its psychologies and philosophies negated the confining family form only by at last incorporating that form in its deep structure. . . .
> . . . "I" closet within myself the lingering drama of originary absence: the history of family rupture which is also the tragedy of my own breaking into self-consciousness.[20]

Here the psyche is made up of an irresolvable oedipal conflict between self and other. A prior and deeper experience determines, without regard to will, the structure of subjectivity, which is a self containing otherness in constant struggle. Beneath the surfaces of individual identity, a Malthusian reproduction occurs. The self reproduces its presence and its absent past as two inseparable products of a development that moves concurrently forward and backward.

Habermas emphasizes the development, in literature of the eighteenth century, of individual subjectivity in relation to an audience, in a dialogue of self and others. This is most evident perhaps in epistolary novels such as *Clarissa*. But Foucault's emphasis is on the tendency toward the end of the century to internalize that dialogue. Relations of self and other become increasingly imaginary, abstracted from social into psychological dynamics.[21]

For Foucault, one effect of these divisions in both public and private structures is a doubling of "man," who, Foucault says, "appears in his ambiguous position as an object of knowledge and as a subject that knows: enslaved sovereign, observed spectator."[22] These divisions can be identified as ontological decentralizations. With human consciousness being both knowing subject and subject to being known, consciousness is unable to claim itself as central director or initiator of knowledge. Moreover, with fields of knowledge — including "man" as well as economics, biology, and language — determined by hidden processes, the world is understood not only to include but to be determined by elements inaccessible to human consciousness.

Foucault's theory of such developments becomes even more compelling in light of nineteenth-century novelists' depictions of depths of knowledge. Dickens, in particular, describes historical transcendence moving "underground" as bureaucratic knowledge prevails in public life; and Dickens sees psychological depths repressed in parallel developments in private life. But, as with the work of Habermas, novels indicate that Foucault's theory is too limited to explain distributions of public and private knowledge. My revision of Foucault's "order of things" depends on recognizing first that the doubling of "man" that occurs with the division of knowledge into empirical surfaces and transcendent depths is, increasingly in the nineteenth century, a gendered experience.

Foucault's doubling is a male model of psychic reproduction similar to Freud's oedipal model, according to which the identification of child and father is repressed. To the extent that the child repeats the father, that experience of doubling is buried beneath the surface of consciousness. According to my reading of the female experience of doubling in novels written during the period Foucault covers in *The Order of Things,* doubling is not buried or contained. Women are depicted as likenesses of other women: in time, as when Frankenstein sees his fiancée turning into his dead mother; and in space, as when female characters in *East Lynne* repeatedly take each other's places. Because of this, women's knowledge, particularly self-knowledge, tends toward confusion rather than distinction. Whereas the oedipal model of identity produces individuation from others, with doubleness internalized, the female model produces identification with others, or doubling externalized.

It is this identification of women with each other, moreover, that is depicted as part of a general inability of women to produce the orderly distinctions necessary to orders of knowledge. And this depiction itself becomes the basis of a distinction of social order, according to which women belong under the control of men. Those persons incapable of confining their doubleness to depths of knowledge, then, themselves need to be confined and secured beneath persons more capable of order. According to this development, Foucault's empirico-transcendental divide becomes also a social divide. My readings of novels indicate social dimensions for structures of knowledge that are instrumental in organizing and classifying persons as well as things in nineteenth-century Britain.

1

Models of Stability: Production and Consumption in Humphry Clinker and The Castle of Otranto

Humphry Clinker is a work that clearly takes part in public debates occurring in eighteenth-century Britain. John Sekora has detailed the importance of Smollett's concerns in the novel to contemporary political debates both within Parliament and within "those common rooms of public philosophy, the political papers and pamphlets."[1] Male characters in the novel, moreover, discuss and debate public issues constantly. Jürgen Habermas's identification of the private constituents of the eighteenth-century public marks an integration of the two spheres that is of obvious concern to Smollett. In the eighteenth century, Habermas says,

> The bourgeois public sphere may be conceived above all as the sphere of private people come together as a public; they soon claimed the public sphere regulated from above against the public authorities themselves, to engage them in a debate over the general rules governing relations in the basically privatized but publicly relevant sphere of commodity exchange and social labor. The medium of this political confrontation was peculiar and without historical precedent: people's public use of their reason.[2]

Habermas argues that this public sphere lost its coherence and capacity to govern when, early in the nineteenth century, it was recognized as a sphere of competing interests rather than differing rational opinions. But already in Smollett's 1771 novel is evident a distrust of the public sphere, because it is made up of mixed classes and competing interests, and because interest rather than reason is seen to direct individual and public opinion both. Without questioning the dependence of the public sphere on individual opinion, Smollett questions the influence of reason on either.

Public debate in the press, as well as in private conversations about the arts and politics, has become simply partisan. In *Humphry Clinker,* Matthew Bramble writes,

> Considering the temper of the times, it is a wonder to see any institution whatsoever established for the benefit of the public. The spirit of party is risen to a kind of phrenzy, unknown to former ages, or rather degenerated to a total extinction of honesty and candour—You know I have observed, for some time, that the public papers are become the infamous vehicles of the most cruel and perfidious defamation: every rancorous knave...that can afford to spend half a crown or three shillings, may skulk behind the press of a newsmonger, and have a stab at the first character in the kingdom, without running the least hazard of detection or punishment.
>
> I should renounce politics the more willingly, if I could find other topics of conversation discussed with more modesty and candour; but the daemon of party seems to have usurped every department of life. Even the world of literature and taste is divided into the most virulent factions, which revile, decry, and traduce the works of one another.[3]

For Smollett, the character of the private individuals who make up the public sphere lacks the autonomy that reason might provide. Driven by interest into partisan rather than rational positions, persons in public life agree and disagree as part of a competitive struggle for power rather than as part of any rational government of public policy.

Moreover, Smollett sees this kind of behavior spreading into "every department of life." Without external or internal restraints on individual choice, both public and family life have been corrupted. Because individuals are seen, for the most part, to be incapable of exercising self-restraint, there are no limits to the indulgence of personal interests and appetites. And various kinds of unrestrained, laissez-faire economic production—of commodities, of fashions, of gossip and slander in newspapers—only encourage the indulgence of personal interest. Like Habermas, Smollett recognizes an interdependence of public life and private character, but he identifies it not in positive terms of autonomy but in negative terms of loss of control and loss of independence. And because private autonomy seems corrupted by unrestrained public production, Smollett finally insists, to maintain some sphere of rational order, on separating the rational individual from public life.

Those characters who do not effect such a separation experience a corruption of their family life, both their family property and their family relations. When Bramble visits his old friend Baynard, he finds that not only Baynard but also other men in the neighborhood are being "driven by their wives at full speed, in the high road to bankruptcy and ruin" (333). Neither wives nor husbands exercise reason or autonomy. Baynard's "unmanly acquiescence under the absurd tyranny" of his wife (332) marks his inability to judge or act according to principle, despite Bramble's insistence "that his [Baynard's] wife was unworthy of that tender complaisance which he had shewn for her foibles: that she was dead to all the genuine sentiments of conjugal affection; insensible of her own honour and interest, and seemingly destitute of common sense and reflection" (336).

The women's vanity is what drives their behavior. Their competitive consumption means, however, that they also lose all distinction and autonomy:

> The views of the ladies were exactly the same. They vied in grandeur, that is, in ostentation, with the wife of Sir Charles Chickwell, who had four times their fortune; and she again piqued herself on making an equal figure with a neighbouring peeress, whose revenue trebled her own. . . .
> All these three ladies have at this time the same number of horses, carriages, and servants in and out of livery; the same variety of dress; the same quantity of plate and china; the like ornaments in furniture. . . . I believe it will be found upon enquiry, that nineteen out of twenty, who are ruined by extravagance, fall a sacrifice to the ridiculous pride and vanity of silly women, whose parts are held in contempt by the very men whom they pillage and enslave. Thank heaven, . . . that among all the follies and weaknesses of human nature, I have not yet fallen into that of matrimony. (333–34)

As men are enslaved by conjugal affection, women are leveled by their vanity. For Smollett, autonomy is at risk in the family as well as in the public sphere. This is not to say that Smollett's ideal of humanity differs from that which Habermas assigns to the eighteenth century. On the contrary, "voluntariness, community of love, and cultivation"[4] are crucial to the humane individuals of *Humphry Clinker,* and they can be achieved in private. But they are at risk in many families in the novel, and they are wholly incompatible with public spheres of experience.

In Horace Walpole's Gothic depiction of family life, the case is different. Reaching back to "the darkest ages of christianity,"[5] Walpole sets *The Castle of Otranto* in a feudal period during which, according to both Habermas and Walpole, public spheres were not differentiable from private spheres of experience. Social disorder in the novel is due to the excesses of a single tyrannical prince, whose desire for an heir drives him to incest and murder. The emotional realm of family life thus conflates what would later become public and private concerns. In effect Walpole ignores public debate and, indeed, the exercise of reason as means of government. Yet, in the first preface to the novel, in which he dates it between 1095 and 1243, he does address the role of the novel in public opinion:

> Letters were then in their most flourishing state in Italy, and contributed to dispel the empire of superstition, at that time so forcibly attacked by the reformers. It is not unlikely that an artful priest might endeavour to turn their own arms on the innovators; and might avail himself of his abilities as an author to confirm the populace in their ancient errors and superstitions. If this was his view, he has certainly acted with signal address. Such a work as the following would enslave a hundred vulgar minds beyond half the books of controversy that have been written from the days of Luther to the present hour.
>
> The solution of the author's motives is however offered as a mere conjecture. Whatever his views were, . . . his work can only be laid before the public at present as a matter of entertainment. (3–4)

Identifying the novel with enslavement in its own period and entertainment in the present era, Walpole goes on in the preface to the second edition to say that he wrote it "Desirous of leaving the powers of fancy at liberty to expatiate through the boundless realms of invention" (7).

In either case, whether superstitious or fanciful, the story belongs to irrational realms of experience. This is evident from the opening scene, in which Manfred, the paterfamilias, sees "his child dashed to pieces, and almost buried under an enormous helmet" that drops out of the sky (17). Individuals here seem to have little influence on events. The force that causes things to happen as they do, working in ways no individual comprehends, has much in common with a divine power — its mystery, transcendence, and apparent omnipotence. But it also resembles laissez-faire capitalism, Adam Smith's "invisible hand," which exceeds human intention, reason, and action and so discourages human intervention in the world beyond personal relations and private enterprise. Walpole again conflates ancient and modern modes as he conjoins two superhuman public orders. The "powers that be" shift from divine to systematic without the transition being particularly noticeable, because Walpole recognizes the common character of old and new orders, in both of which ruling powers are accepted as impersonal, uncontrollable, and unknowable by individuals.

Yet Walpole is nevertheless able to identify means of personal autonomy within this fundamentally irrational world. For Walpole, the stabilizing mechanism of individual autonomy is not rationality but a form of desire. Seemingly sidestepping modern experience, he in fact faces head-on what the economic historian Joyce Appleby has identified as one of the most disturbing aspects of early capitalism, its dependence on passions traditionally requiring strict limitation:

> The idea of man as a consuming animal with boundless appetites, capable of driving the economy to new levels of prosperity, arrived with the economic literature of the 1690s.... Since man could satisfy his new wants only by increasing his purchasing power, what desire ultimately produced was an incentive to be more competitive in the market. From such a spring economic activity could function without outside direction.[6]

External controls were no longer necessary or useful; but internal control was no longer necessary or useful either. Rather, consumption had to be reconceived so that it could proceed without limits, to fuel growth in production and consumption both.

What was necessary to the legitimation of capitalism, Appleby argues, was "the constructive value given to consumption" in the work of Adam Smith. Whereas liberalism "asserted the right of each person to the enjoyment of himself and the fruits of his labor," capitalism required not individual freedom but individual drive. Theorizing "a human model in which the drive for economic self-improvement predominated," Smith's "conception of man was the antithesis of freedom, for

it presumed a compulsive market response."[7] Eventually, then, liberalism was restrained by limiting individual freedom to desires for self-
improvement that engaged persons in production and consumption.

Appleby emphasizes that for Smith, consumption is not a hedonis-
tic practice but rather a productive practice:

> Externally, it creates the effective demand which calls forth production sys-
> tems large enough for specialization and division of labor. Internally, the
> drive to truck and barter — to buy and sell — directs individual energies to-
> ward the market and away from other human satisfactions. . . . One im-
> proves through market power, but market power rests upon producing power.
> The more one produces, the more one can satisfy wants. . . . In Smith's
> model, people as producers and people as consumers act like an alternating
> electrical current, throwing a steady flow of impulses into the economy.[8]

Walpole's Gothic novel of 1764 can be seen taking part in such a re-
construction of desire, which he depicts finally as systematic and self-
regulating, providing an internal direction for its choice of objects that
stabilizes the driving force of economic growth and social change.

At the conclusion of *The Castle of Otranto,* the reader is told that
Theodore, the hero who in the final scene has both lost his beloved
Matilda and ascended to the throne, will eventually marry Isabella. This
cannot occur immediately; "it was not till after frequent discourses
with Isabella, of his dear Matilda, that he was persuaded he could
know no happiness but in the society of one with whom he could for
ever indulge the melancholy that had taken possession of his soul"
(110). The marriage occurs to allow Theodore to indulge his melancholy
by means of repeated representations of his lost love, who becomes
the stable though unreachable referent for the experience of love and
marriage.

Detached from actual, present objects, Theodore's desire is for feeling itself — the melancholy he indulges — and for the representations
of Matilda that provoke this feeling. The need for self-restraint apparently disappears with this formulation of desire. Smollett's Mrs. Baynard is out of control because she wants representations of herself as
an equal of her neighbors. Theodore wants representations that recover
a lost object. Self-indulgent, his representations are not acquired but

are produced in a process detached from objects for the gratification provided by the experience of representation per se.

Smollett's Bramble family withdraws, at the end of a tour of Great Britain, into an economically self-sufficient family estate; its productivity is both guaranteed and stabilized by its natural and material character. Walpole's fictional family achieves autonomy in mental productivity guaranteed and stabilized by reference to a dead woman. Here productivity is nonmaterial; it is an imaginative enterprise of representation.

Novels in Public Debate

Walpole explicitly detaches his fiction from political significance, identifying it for contemporary readers as merely imaginative and entertaining. But I will be considering *The Castle of Otranto* as if it were part of eighteenth-century public debates. Insofar as it can be identified as an argument, Walpole's novel can only be so inarticulately, beneath the surfaces of representation. Yet this is just where much of the progressive ideology of the eighteenth century is located by modern theorists.

In the eighteenth century, the historian J. G. A. Pocock suggests, conflicting ideologies resisted and supported changes whereby economic productivity became independent of land and whereby individual morality became independent of a common good:

> The "Machiavellian moment" of the eighteenth century... confronted civic virtue with corruption, and saw the latter in terms of a chaos of appetites, productive of dependence and loss of personal autonomy, flourishing in a world of rapid and irrational change.... What may be termed the ideology of the Country was founded on a presumption of real property and an ethos of the civic life, in which the ego knew and loved itself in its relation to a *patria, res publica* or common good, organized as a polity, but was perpetually threatened by corruption operating through private appetites and false consciousness....
>
> What may be termed the ideology of the Court, on the other hand,... had fewer magisterial exponents. We may synthesize it, however, as founded upon an acceptance of credit as a measure of economic value and of a psychology of imagination, passion, and interest as the mainsprings of human behavior. In the place of virtue it stressed the ego's pursuit of satisfaction and self-esteem, and was beginning to explore theories of how the diversities of passionate and self-interested action might be manipulated and coor-

dinated, or might magically or mechanically coordinate themselves, into pro-
moting a common good no longer intimately connected with the inner moral
life of the individual.[9]

The older Country ideology integrated the experience of individuals
and community and secured them in relation to each other. Here is
assumed an identification of autonomous individual egos with a common good similar to that which Habermas identifies in his rational
public sphere. But whereas this ideology assumed the need to repress
and control nonrational experience in individuals and public spheres
alike, the newer Court ideology approved individualistic pursuits of
passion, imagination, and interest—individual differences rather than
a common morality or rationality. This left unclear how a multitude
of individually oriented persons would function in relation to each
other.

Only the values of one of the ideologies Pocock discusses, the still-
dominant ideology of the Country, were fully articulated. The "ethical
vocabulary" of the Court ideology "was thin and limited by the lack
of any theory which presented human virtue as that of a *zoon poli-
tikon*."[10] The difficulty of positing the identity and behavior of the new
social institutions occurred partly because they were new but partly
because of the groundless, immaterial character of credit and desire.

Daniel Defoe, early in the eighteenth century, provides some clear
examples of language unable to posit or know experience in a world of
credit, though he celebrates rather than regrets such indefinition. Defoe, Isaac Kramnick suggests, "best described the sense of mystery…
evoked" by "the new world of public credit" in his *An Essay Upon the
Publick Credit* of 1710:

> Like the soul in the body it acts as all substance, yet it is itself immaterial; it
> gives motion, yet it cannot be said to exist; it creates forms, yet has it self
> no form; it is neither quantity nor quality, it has not whereness, or when-
> ness, site or habit. If I should say it is the essential shadow of something
> that is not, should I not puzzle the thing rather than explain it, and leave
> you and myself more in the dark than we were before?[11]

The extraordinary negativity of this description suggests the inarticulate-
ness Pocock ascribes to the ethical values of the Court ideology. Extreme
though it is, Defoe's description indicates kinds of difficulties the new

ideology posed because of its uncertainties and insubstantialities. In contrast to those who value land as a real basis for production, those who depend on credit depend on something literally nonexistent: as Defoe says, something for which no words exist.

Pocock's description of conflicting ideologies also suggests a shift that Michel Foucault identifies in his analysis of revolutionary changes in knowledge late in the eighteenth century. Foucault perceives a loss of grounds in the representation of knowledge, as relations among different elements of social and economic life move into unrepresented depths:

> What came into being with Adam Smith, with the first philologists, with Jussieu, Vicq d'Azyr, or Lamarck, is a minuscule but absolutely essential displacement, which toppled the whole of Western thought: representation has lost the power to provide a foundation ... for the links that can join its various elements together. No composition, no decomposition, no analysis into identities and differences can now justify the connection of representations one to another.[12]

What links the parts of representation together "resides henceforth outside representation," moving into "the very heart of things."[13] Such a change is suggested by Adam Smith's identification, in *The Wealth of Nations* (1776), of the direction of economic behavior by an "invisible hand."

Like Defoe, Smith invokes a disjunction between the familiar and immediate experience of private individuals, on the one hand, and the society at large, on the other. For Smith, the public interest and the common good are better off ignored by individuals:

> As every individual ... endeavours as much as he can both to employ his capital in support of domestick industry, and so to direct that industry that its produce may be of the greatest value; every individual necessarily labours to render the annual revenue of the society as great as he can. He generally, indeed, neither intends to promote the publick interest, nor knows how much he is promoting it. ... [H]e intends only his own security; and ... he intends only his own gain, and he is in this, as in many other cases, led by an invisible hand to promote an end which was no part of his intention. Nor is it always the worse for the society that it was no part of it. ... I have never known much good done by those who affected to trade for the publick good.[14]

The "invisible hand" that directs economic behavior ignores the individual will, and the individual will ignores the public welfare. A public good is reached only by invisible and circuitous means and regardless of individual intention or knowledge. Smith not only accepts the unknown character of the public good, he also sees the uncertainty as beneficial.

Smollett's alliance, however, is clearly with the older of Pocock's ideologies. Smollett also identifies a public sphere of rational government such as Habermas theorizes, though for Smollett the time is already past when such a sphere functioned successfully. Identifying himself with the old and against the new, Smollett is concerned in his last novel with the restoration of a past social and economic order; but such restoration can occur only in private life. Smollett not only posits this order, he attempts to materialize it in terms of a return to nature. Matthew Bramble's recovery of bodily health is only one version of the cure Smollett offers for national as well as individual ills. By means of repeated analogies between bodily and social orders, Smollett can claim to ground his critique of social life, and this in itself is crucial to the value of that critique. Nature is used as an unchallengeable standard and foundation of value.

Smollett's Natural Grounds

In a sense, the grounds for natural order in *Humphry Clinker* are the lands of Scotland, where the travelers find a more "natural" life than in England. For one thing, whereas the English are all mixing together, particularly by frequenting London and Bath and other towns, the Scots, remaining in their various native habitats, remain different. The healthy differences in persons that Smollett acknowledges identify persons as parts of some larger whole — a social group or a natural environment — rather than as detached individuals. Thus, many differences among the Scots are due to place: "The people of Glasgow have a noble spirit of enterprise" (284); "The Lowlanders are generally cool and circumspect, the Highlanders fiery and ferocious" (291). And there are natural reasons for some of these differences. The Lowlanders work harder in part because the ground in the Lowlands is fertile and productive, whereas the Highlanders, like the Highlands, are "amazingly wild" (290) and difficult to cultivate.

Just as the Scottish character is grounded in the land, grounds serve as limits to other kinds of productivity. Detailing the natural landscape as well as kinds and habits of wildlife and plants native to particular areas of Scotland, Smollett provides a natural variety unavailable in the gardens of eighteenth-century England that James H. Bunn describes, where "imports suppressed into latent ground the native features of the place."[15] Cultivation is advocated by Matt Bramble, but along strictly native lines: "[A] company of merchants might, with proper management, turn to good account a fishery established in this part of Scotland — Our people have a strange itch to colonize America, when the uncultivated parts of our own island might be settled to greater advantage" (294). Such cultivation is identified as both native and natural, cultivating nature to serve natural needs.

According to these grounds, production and consumption do not work in tandem. On the contrary, it is necessary to keep them distinct to maintain productivity. Natural productivity, on the one hand, depends on the cultivation and use of natural resources; it is limited by what is available in nature. Artificial productivity, on the other hand, is limited only by imagination; it is theoretically unlimited. Yet for Smollett, artificial or inventive productivity does not occur independently of natural resources, it destroys them. Crucial to his attack on groundless social production is his insistence that it perverts and abuses nature.

Smollett uses nature to restrict the leveling effects of competitive and imitative consumption such as that practiced by Mrs. Baynard, who aims to wipe out differences between herself and her neighbors. At Bath, the dangers of "mixing" are discussed often by Matthew Bramble in his letters and conversations. At one point, Jeremy Melford reports a disagreement about his uncle's insistence that "the mixture of people in the entertainments in this place was destructive of all order and urbanity" (80). The men agree to test the assertion by observing a "general tea-drinking" at which "every table is to be furnished with sweet-meats and nosegays" (81):

> There was nothing but justling, scrambling, pulling, snatching, struggling, scolding, and screaming. The nosegays were torn from one another's hands and bosoms; the glasses and china went to wreck; the tables and floors were strewed with comfits. Some cried; some swore; and the tropes and figures of Billingsgate were used without reserve....
>
> ...Indeed, [Matthew's] victory was more complete than he imagined; for, as we afterwards learned, the two amazons who singularized themselves most in the action, did not come from the purlieus of Puddle-dock, but from the courtly neighbourhood of St. James's palace. One was a baroness, and the other, a wealthy knight's dowager. (82)

In the competition for the nosegays, all other means of distinction and all means of order are lost. Social distinctions of speech and manners evaporate, and things as well as people fall out of place as physical disorder follows social indistinction. What directs activity here is apparently sheer, unrestricted self-interest: all the women want nosegays and will do anything to get them.

Yet the strongest support for Matthew's attack on "mixing" comes with reference to his bodily experience of the baths. After several visits he doubts their healthy effects, and then he begins to doubt too the benefits of the pump waters:

> I am now as much afraid of drinking, as of bathing; ... it is very far from being clear with me, that the patients in the Pump-room don't swallow the scourings of the bathers. I can't help suspecting, that there is, or may be, some regurgitation from the bath into the cistern of the pump. In that case, what a delicate beveridge is every day quaffed by the drinkers; medicated with the sweat and dirt, and dandriff; and the abominable discharges of various kinds, from twenty different diseased bodies, parboiling in the kettle below. (75)

This attack on mixing identifies, in both the plumbing system at Bath and the digestive system of the human body, a malfunction—regurgitation—that leads to a confusion of consumption and discharge. The body offers natural and material limits on consumption and production as part of its natural distinction between the two processes. As in the balance-of-trade economic theory that prevailed in the early eighteenth century, Smollett's material referents here insist that consumption and production are properly independent.[16]

To allow unrestricted consumption is, for Smollett, to cultivate disaster, because, left unrestricted, self-interest will consume anything. Ultimately, this means that even the means of production will be consumed. This is the danger Mrs. Baynard poses to her husband's property:

> To shew her taste in laying out ground, she seized into her own hand a farm of two hundred acres, about a mile from the house, which she parcelled out into walks and shrubberies, having a great bason in the middle, into which she poured a whole stream that turned two mills, and afforded the best trout in the country. The bottom of the bason, however, was so ill secured, that it would not hold the water which strained through the earth, and made a bog of the whole plantation: in a word, the ground which formerly paid him one hundred and fifty pounds a year, now cost him two hundred pounds a year to keep it in tolerable order.... There was not an inch of garden ground left about the house, nor a tree that produced fruit of any kind. (331–32)

All for the sake of showing her taste, Mrs. Baynard destroys the productive capacity of the land, forcing her husband to go to market for food and feed. According to natural production, land is cultivated and produces a return on the investment. But Mrs. Baynard's display of taste produces no return because it consists merely of representations. To show her taste, or, as the passage quoted earlier indicates, to show her equality with her neighbors, Mrs. Baynard is primarily concerned with representations of her self. For Smollett, such production of representations merely consumes resources.

According to a different economic theory, one more sympathetic to capitalism, such consumption as Mrs. Baynard and her cocompetitors practice would fuel production of commodities such as furniture, carriages, food, and feed. But Smollett's emphasis is on the cost of artificial production: such consumption perverts natural productivity and human character, because it is motivated by vanity. Most important, perhaps, such competitive or imitative consumption as Mrs. Baynard practices has no necessary limits. And without any limits on invention and production, Smollett sees no way to secure any values at all. Unlike Smith, Smollett does not recognize any internal, psychological limitation on consumption. Similarly, he sees no means of restricting such consumption to the private sphere.

Representation in Public Life

The public sphere is for Smollett as corrupted as the Baynards' private life because it also is dominated by individual interest rather than reason. When Matthew Bramble reads the London papers, he finds representations of political figures so partisan as to preclude rational debate or consensus. The object of such representation is identified not as consensus or government but as productivity and profit. Because of this, it is not possible to dispute effectively what is published:

> Suppose [a victim of slander] should prosecute the publisher, who screens the anonymous accuser, and bring him to the pillory for a libel; this is so far from being counted a punishment, *in terrorem*, that it will probably make his fortune. The multitude immediately take him into their protection, as a martyr to the cause of defamation, which they have always espoused — They pay his fine, they contribute to the increase of his stock, his shop is crowded with customers, and the sale of his paper rises in proportion to the scandal it contains. (134)

Here liberalism causes the public — not a thinking public but a mob — to defend any published statement on the principle of freedom of the press. Production here is groundless and increases without limits by means of invention. Not only is such publication profitable to the publisher, it is also profitable to the government, because "the duty upon stamps and advertisements has made a very considerable addition to the revenue" (135).

The loss that concerns Smollett here is not truth so much as the use of public opinion to cultivate virtue and govern moral character:

> To what purpose is our property secured, if our moral character is left defenceless? People thus baited, grow desperate; and the despair of being able to preserve one's character untainted by such vermin, produces a total neglect of fame; so that one of the chief incitements to the practice of virtue is effectually destroyed. (136)

Because public representations of individuals no longer are grounded on character or behavior but are instead invented, individual morality also has increased freedom to follow individual interests.

For Adam Smith, such a loss of moral referentiality was answerable by internalizing others' judgment. In his *Theory of Moral Sentiments*

(1759), Smith relocates social morality within the depths of individual conscience, allowing for an internal mediation, even an internal production of social relations. Relations no longer acted out between persons are transferred to the psyche; mental negotiations of sympathy replace public relations with others. Both the sufferer and those who sympathize with the sufferer experience suffering indirectly:

> As they [the sympathizers] are constantly considering what they themselves would feel, if they actually were the sufferers, so he [the sufferer] is as constantly led to imagine in what manner he would be affected if he was only one of the spectators of his own situation. As their sympathy makes them look at it, in some measure, with his eyes, so his sympathy makes him look at it, in some measure, with theirs, especially when in their presence and acting under their observation.[17]

This experience is an imaginative mediation of social relations. But Smith detaches the subject not only from the experience of suffering but also from those who observe the suffering. His "impartial spectator" — the internalized moral judge — is not to be confused with other actual persons. Indeed, as David Marshall emphasizes, the impartial spectator may allow the subject to ignore others, "as we enter into a private relation with an ideal spectator who allows us to bypass, so to speak, the eyes of the world."[18] Others' judgment is not merely mediated but produced. This impartial spectator is not a representation of others' judgment so much as an ideal imagined by the self, impersonal in its detachment from reactions of others or of the self.

For Smollett, however, public standards of judgment are not internalized. The multiple narrators in *Humphry Clinker* make clear that people vary in their capacity to observe and judge. Each letter writer sees things differently. Some of these differences are resolved in the course of the novel. Jery, for example, learns to agree with his uncle increasingly often. But other differences cannot be resolved. It seems likely, for example, that Letty, Jery's sister, will remain, at least for some time, much more easily impressed, excited, and amused by things than will the older Matthew or the more thoughtful Jery. And Tabitha, Matthew's sister, remains too vain and stupid to agree with her brother about anything. Smollett's depiction of Tabitha as well as Lismahago as "originals" (390) marks his willingness in certain cases to cultivate the detachment of curiosity rather than judgment, and in these cases he seems closer to Laurence Sterne than to Adam Smith.[19]

But for Smollett, because such cultivations of detachment break up rather than consolidate common ground, they are incapable of ordering public or private life. In the courts, when Humphry is accused of robbery, the damage that individual interests inflict on public order is most marked. Individual interests are so disparate as to interfere not only with justice but also with communication. Humphry's accuser, himself a thief, seeks not justice but credit for himself by turning others in. And the justice's "severity to Clinker was no other than a hint to his master to make him a present in private" (185). But the "innocent" Humphry also misleads people, because his own judgment is based on the precepts of Methodism. Refusing to confess, he "declared, that he looked upon confession to be a popish fraud, invented by the whore of Babylon" (180). Still, Humphry feels guilty: "'God forbid,'" Humphry says, "'that I should call myself innocent, while my conscience is burthened with sin.' 'What then, you did commit this robbery?' resumed his master. 'No, sure (said he) blessed be the Lord, I'm free of that guilt'" (180). In such a situation, Smollett suggests, few spectators are capable of understanding what others are doing. The "judgment" of most characters is directed by interest rather than conscience; and even guilty consciences, as Humphry makes clear, may judge differently.

Gendering Judgment

From Smollett's perspective, an assumption of standardized individual judgment is yet another leveling perspective that threatens natural distinctions and order. One distinction he is particularly concerned to maintain is that between men and women, as my discussion of his characters has perhaps already indicated. Unless, like Letty, their behavior is directed by men, women in the novel consume resources and produce no returns. Indeed, the cure for their artificial behavior is a return to nature, a restoration of natural resources and of natural productivity. Identifiable to a great extent with Milton's Eve, Smollett's women, when given free rein, exercise boundless appetites and demonstrate infidelity, vanity, love of change for the sake of change, and uselessness.

Female behavior thus takes on the dangerous characteristics of a lais-sez-faire commercial economy.

For Smollett, a female economy — that is, exchanges entered into by women unrestrained by men — is utterly cut off from the natural econ-omy. Women's consumption is based not on need but on competition, resulting in the predictable leveling associated with imitative buying. This is the case with Mrs. Baynard and her friends, whose views are "exactly the same" and who all have "the same number of horses, car-riages, and servants in and out of livery; the same variety of dress; the same quantity of plate and china" (334). Like the "deficient" females in conduct books of the period whom Nancy Armstrong identifies with corrupt aristocratic behavior, these dangerous women are identified with display and decoration, no longer restricted to a particular social level.[20] As "equal figures," they perpetuate a merely formal equality and thereby increase the indistinction of persons and ranks. The van-ity of women is identified with the vanity of an economy in which production and consumption are both groundless and which there-fore experiences not growth but only inflation. Whereas men cultivate nature and participate in a natural cycle of returns, women's produc-tion is inventive and unnatural, returning nothing.

One major form of restoration in the novel is the return of long-lost sons — Matthew Bramble's, Mr. Brown's, Mr. Dennison's, and Mr. Bay-nard's — to their fathers. Another is the restoration of lost estates to men. With both proper relations women interfere. Matt Bramble and his "natural son," Humphry, were unable to get together earlier because when Bramble fathered the child, he was using his mother's name, as her heir (359). Because of Matthew's change of name, Humphry was unable to find him.

Most graphically, women are destructive of proper male relations in the story Lismahago tells of being captured with a young man named Murphy by the Miami Indians:

The intention of these Indians was to give one of them as an adopted son to a venerable sachem, who had lost his own in the course of the war, and to sacrifice the other. . . . Murphy, as being the younger and handsomer of the two, was designed to fill the place of the deceased, not only as the son of the sachem, but as the spouse of a beautiful squaw, to whom his predecessor had been betrothed; but in passing through the different whigwhams or villages of the Miamis, poor Murphy was so mangled by the women and children, who have the privilege of torturing all prisoners in their passage, that, by the time they arrived at the place of the sachem's residence, he was rendered altogether unfit for the purposes of marriage. (228)

These castrating, as well as cannibalistic, women are joined to other women in the novel who are more interested in gratifying their appetites for "unnatural" and useless things than they are in natural reproduction. Lismahago's family has been corrupted by the heir marrying "the daughter of a burgeois" (311); Matt Bramble is plagued by the appetites and infidelities of Tabby Bramble; and Baynard is almost destroyed by his wife. Only when she dies near the end of the novel can his estate be restored to working order.

Mrs. Baynard's corruption of her husband's estate is marked by her obsession with fashion, the uselessness of her interior decoration (the chairs too richly upholstered to sit on, the floors too highly polished to walk on, and so on), and her perversion of the natural landscape for decorative purposes. After she has died, Matt sets all this to rights:

> I ordered the gardener to turn the rivulet into its old channel, to refresh the fainting Naiads, who had so long languished among mouldring roots, withered leaves, and dry pebbles — The shrubbery is condemned to extirpation; and the pleasure ground will be restored to its original use of corn-field and pasture — Orders are given for rebuilding the walls of the garden at the back of the house, and for planting clumps of firs . . . at the east end, which is now quite exposed to the surly blasts that come from that quarter. (385)

Under cultivation by a man, the property will again produce natural food and shelter and will eventually meet all the needs of Baynard, who is now so much in debt because of his wife's spending and the unproductivity of his land that he can barely support himself and his son. The latter, kept home and spoiled by his mother, is only now sent to school to cultivate his mind.

Individualizing Disorder

Smollett works in *Humphry Clinker* to restore to human experience integral relations of spiritual and material and of social and personal life. Returned home to Brambleton Hall and restored to good health, Matthew Bramble is in control of his property and at the head of his family, now extended to include a new brother-in-law, Lismahago, and his newfound "natural" son, Humphry. *The Castle of Otranto* opens with a very different picture of family life. Manfred, the ruling prince, in possession of a dynastic house that doesn't belong to him, sees his son smashed into pieces by the giant helmet on the day of the wedding that was to bring his regime stability and continuity. If Smollett works to discover and cultivate natural relations among the parts of the commonwealth, the family, and the body, all three phenomena come apart in Walpole's novel.

Yet Walpole also is concerned with restorations. Returning to the distant past, he addresses throughout his Gothic novel the need to make returns and effect restorations. But Walpole converts nostalgia into an operative element of progressive rather than conservative thought. For Walpole, nostalgia functions as an entertainment of a return to the past, as a representation, in his novel for example, of an idealized past. Such restorative representations, moreover, constitute the means by which his hero, Theodore, achieves emotional autonomy at the end of the novel.

On the one hand, there is a restoration of public order at the end of *The Castle of Otranto*. A supernatural vision directs the return of the usurped throne to Theodore, the heir of Alphonso. This is an aristocratic return of the kind that Smollett endorses as a return to nature and to an "original" patriarch. However, on the other hand Theodore's subjective life is given security through a different pattern of usurpation and restoration, one that occurs in representative terms. In Walpole's domestic replay of usurpation, Isabella takes the place of the dead Matilda as Theodore's wife. This usurpation is allowed to stand, though only as a partial displacement; Theodore marries Isabella so that he can concentrate his emotions on his loss of Matilda. Thus he moves into a realm of representation. The absence of his object of desire means that available women such as Isabella are mere substitutes for that object; and so are the representations of Matilda that Theodore shares with Isabella. But because he is able to return constantly, in memory, to his original love, Theodore's emotional life is stabilized and secured by Matilda's death, even as that death allows him to accept substitutes in her place.

The aristocratic return depends on body: Theodore's body gives the sign, in a birthmark, that his blood is Alphonso's. There is no bodily integrity in the usurpation of Matilda's place by Isabella. Smollett uses the body as a standard of natural systems. Walpole uses the body as a figure of excess. According to the prophecy that haunts Manfred, "*the castle and lordship of Otranto should pass from the present family, whenever the real owner should be grown too large to inhabit it*" (15–16; Walpole's emphasis). Materializing in parts, the giant body whose helmet falls on Conrad undergoes a disintegration identifiable with representation itself. It appears only in pieces and parts, unable to surface in full. Physical objects do not provide grounds for experience in Otranto; instead, lost or partial objects, in their very absence, secure experience. Theodore, the "real owner," will, as the prophecy says, outgrow the castle. Only partly contained and only partly represented by the castle, he will become permanently absented from it by his melancholy. Both subjectively and objectively, in mind and body, dispersal sets in.

But, in pieces and parts, experience stabilizes. Various disconnections and disintegrations that occur in Walpole's novel contribute to the psychological stability found at its end. The most important of the separations that Walpole identifies by means of Gothic experience is a separation between individual experience and what can be called "the powers that be." Whatever it is that directs and determines the course of affairs in this novel is not known or understood by individuals. Not only does this preclude the possibility of Habermas's public sphere governed by reason, but furthermore, neither of the alternative "governing" characters Walpole has to offer—the usurper Manfred or the true heir to the throne, Theodore—seems able to rule his kingdom with any good results.

On the one hand, there is Manfred, who has only a usurped right to his reign and who is so obsessive, passionate, and self-interested that he is neither publicly nor privately responsible. In this novel, and to some extent in the Gothic generally, "unnaturalness," uncertainty, and lack of control—dangers identified by Smollett, among others, with an increasingly commercial society—are internalized within an individual human being. According to this transposition, the most dangerous characteristics of the public sphere are assigned to an individual, who now takes the blame for social disorder. Manfred's character makes a strong case for the need to internalize repression.

The preferred ruler in the novel, on the other hand, is able to rule himself but stays pretty much to himself. Theodore, who is moved only by calm and beneficial passions, is put in his rightful place on the throne at the end of the novel, at the same time that he drops all concern with public life. His calm and kindness seem to depend on extreme detachment. His primary interest is always sympathetic personal relations, but his sympathies are finally experienced only at one remove. The sympathy for which he marries Isabella at the end of the novel provides him with a wife who reflects his own feelings but who has in fact no part in them, because their object is the dead Matilda.

Cultivating Detachment

Crucial to the detachment of characters from public spheres of experience is the disconnection Walpole effects between human action and events. Characters in *The Castle of Otranto* are detached from events in part by passivity; but what human action there is also seems useless. Manfred, though clearly the villain, doesn't really do much in the novel. He is thwarted both by his passions and by enemies human as well as supernatural (indicated at one point by "a door clapped-to with violence by an invisible hand" [24]). Jerome, his antagonist, can't do much either, partly because of ignorance and partly because his reason, too, is overcome by passion:

> Jerome's mind was agitated by a thousand contrary passions. He trembled for the life of his son, and his first idea was to persuade Isabella to return to the castle. Yet he was scarce less alarmed at the thought of her union with Manfred. He dreaded Hippolita's unbounded submission to the will of her lord: and though he did not doubt but he could alarm her piety not to consent to a divorce, if he could get access to her; yet should Manfred discover that the obstruction came from him, it might be equally fatal to Theodore. He was impatient to know whence came the herald, ... yet he did not dare absent himself from the convent, lest Isabella should leave it, and her flight be imputed to him. He returned disconsolately to the monastery, uncertain on what conduct to resolve. (60)

Jerome is unable to take any decisive action. Yet even as individuals are disabled from action, the novel is full of action, with new characters showing up and unexpected things happening one after another.

This activity is largely unintended by any individual. As in the preceding description, the situation is often one in which the behavior of a lot of characters is unintentionally and unpredictably interdependent. Jerome can't decide what to do because anything may set off something else. His virtual laissez-faire attitude, though assumed, in a sense, by default, is the predominant sense of events in the novel. Things happen, that is, by a coincidence or confluence of people and events that somehow come together and seem to work out right, though no one can foresee this and no one is capable of the overview that could foresee it. Unlike Smollett's characters, Walpole's characters are unable to put together their observations and experience to produce any knowledge, let alone direction, of the world around them.

This inability to interact effectively with the world around them isolates Walpole's characters. And to a great extent the reader is also isolated. With no preparation and little context in which to understand such phenomena, the reader confronts the absurd prophecy in the first paragraph of the novel and the helmet crushing Conrad in the second. The reader has little to do but "watch" the action. In fact, Judith Wilt suggests that the novel's merits and influence lie "in half a dozen memorable tableaux, frozen moments of action."[21] In a sense, of course, all readers are observers. But in an epistolary novel such as *Humphry Clinker*, characters as well as readers read, so that the reader is included in part of the action. In contrast, *The Castle of Otranto* disconnects from its readers. Its Gothic setting and characters, of course, are unfamiliar; and its lack of detail further marks a lack of the formal realism that Ian Watt identifies with early novels.[22] Moreover, there is little point in thinking about the opening prophecy, because it can be understood only in light of subsequent events; the reader must wait and see.

The most important experience made available to readers seems to be sensation: frights, shock, and thrills, which are internal reactions rather than feelings for objects. Sometimes, moreover, these are of a kind that cannot be represented. "Words cannot paint" a character's astonishment or horror or other feelings, which "must be conceived" by the reader because they can't be represented (22, 26, 54). In such cases, readers are isolated in their conceptions, though Walpole, like Smith, seems to assume that various persons can share feelings by such means. As for more "serious" passions, of the kind that drive Manfred in his mad pursuit of a male heir, these are both "entertained" and rejected by the novel. The Gothic, for all the thrills it seeks in playing with such emotions, is usually careful to let readers know that those passions won't do.

Characters, and readers too, are cut off from one another and from events by misunderstanding as well as by inaction. When, at the beginning of the novel, the helmet falls on Manfred's son, not only is the event inexplicable, but so is Manfred's reaction to it:

> He fixed his eyes on what he wished in vain to believe a vision; and seemed less attentive to his loss than buried in meditation on the stupendous object that had occasioned it.... All who had known his partial fondness for young Conrad, were as much surprised at their prince's insensibility, as thunderstruck themselves at the miracle of the helmet. (17)

Nobody knows or says much, and when Manfred does speak, he is ignored; the servants don't do what he tells them (17), and his daughter also disobeys his orders (20). Partly by choice and partly not, Manfred is isolated in a private existence in which self takes over.

But Manfred isn't the only character who suffers what appears to be a narcissistic confusion about the world around him. Throughout the novel and among all the characters, as is characteristic of Gothic works, failures of knowledge and communication cause mistaken identities with dangerous consequences. Jerome and Theodore do not know they are father and son until Theodore takes off his shirt and exposes "the mark of a bloody arrow" (54); and so Jerome is responsible for his son being condemned to death (52–53). Isabella's father, Frederic, comes along to save her from Manfred's persecutions, but Theodore, who has already rescued her and "who took him for one of Manfred's captains," almost kills him (74). Isabella's father is also one of the knights who visit Manfred but keep their visors down; Manfred questions them "but was answered only by signs" (63). Yet even if Frederic's visor were lifted, his daughter would not know him, because they have been separated since she was a child.

Other characters know things that they won't tell but that would clear up a lot of misunderstanding if they did: Isabella won't tell anyone of Manfred's incestuous proposals to her; Theodore keeps quiet about his love for Matilda; and Jerome hasn't talked for years about his own past, so that no one has any idea of his identity. There are a lot of silences among the characters, and even when people do speak, understanding may not follow. At one point, for example, people hear a servant shriek, "Help! Help! The princess is dead!" (53). Because both the mother, Hippolita, and the daughter, Matilda, are princesses, some take the one and some the other for dead. The servant has "misread" the situation altogether, though; neither is dead.

This disconnection of word from stable referent is perhaps the most important detachment in *The Castle of Otranto*.[23] Much of the experience in the novel cannot be communicated by language. On the one hand, the increasing individualization of experience means that emotions become incommunicable: "words cannot paint" them. On the other hand, the increasing individualization suggests an endless variety of possible referents. Multiple referents — multiple princesses, daughters, fathers, as well as conceptions of characters' emotions — are acknowledged; and their multiplicity also challenges the capacity of representation to differentiate experience. Smollett insists that rationality can figure out meaning even when representation seems inadequate; thus, Matthew knows what Humphry means when he says he is not innocent. But Walpole allows failures of representation to generate confusion in all his characters and often in his readers too.

Detachments of Desire

Particularly with family identities, Walpole makes it difficult to tie down meaning. Whereas in *Humphry Clinker* various sons are recognized and restored to their fathers with great satisfaction and conclusiveness, in *The Castle of Otranto* children resist identification with long-lost parents. Neither Isabella nor Theodore is willing to obey newly discovered fathers: "Theodore, like Isabella, was too recently acquainted with parental authority to submit to its decisions against the impulse of his heart" (90). Authorizing meaning from deep inside the individual, such a move effectively disperses the government of meaning among all individuals equally. But it also buries this self-government in feelings that others do not share.

Shared feelings are in fact the cause of much dissension in the novel, because when characters feel the same thing for the same object, they are in competition for it. Both Smollett and Walpole pose problems for a theory of sympathetic understanding in which persons share feelings and judgments. Smollett would identify Adam Smith's sympathy as dangerously leveling; Walpole identifies one danger of such leveling in the competitions among characters who desire the same things. One solution to such competition, of course — a solution in keeping with the character of capitalism — is to produce multiple objects. This solution would not satisfy Smollett, because it only increases leveling, but it would convert competition into a productive rather than a destructive social mechanism. Yet if the object of desire is a person, the difficulties of reproduction are greater.

In *The Castle of Otranto,* one argument that attempts to resolve conflicting claims occurs between Manfred, who wants Isabella, and Jerome, who is hiding Isabella in sanctuary. Hippolita, Manfred's wife, listens:

> It is my duty to prevent [Isabella's] return hither, said Jerome. She is where orphans and virgins are safest from the snares and wiles of this world; and nothing but a parent's authority shall take her thence. I am her parent, cried Manfred, and demand her. She wished to have you for her parent, said the friar; but heaven, that forbad that connexion, has for ever dissolved all ties betwixt you: and I announce to your highness — Stop! audacious man, said Manfred, and dread my displeasure. Holy father, said Hippolita, it is your office to be no respecter of persons... but it is my duty to hear nothing that it pleases not my lord I should hear. (47)

There are too many fathers and lords here, all in competition for the same authority. Apparently not resolvable by rational means, this conflict of interests is settled only when a vision comes out of the sky at the end of the novel to name Theodore as the ruler of Otranto. According to this solution, competition is ended.

But among the women in the castle, a different competition takes place. In the course of the novel, both Isabella and Matilda fall in love with Theodore and then become suspicious and jealous of each other.

But they "naturally" withdraw their "interference" in each other's love
and engage instead in a "contest of amity":

> He saw you first, and I am far from having the vanity to think that my little
> portion of charms could engage a heart devoted to you. May you be happy,
> Isabella. . . . My lovely friend, said Isabella, whose heart was too honest to
> resist a kind expression, it is you that Theodore admires; I saw it; I am per-
> suaded of it. . . . This frankness drew tears from the gentle Matilda; and
> jealousy, that for a moment had raised a coolness between these amiable
> maidens, soon gave way to the natural sincerity and candour of their souls. . . .
> At length, the dignity of Isabella's virtue reminding her of the preference
> which Theodore had almost declared for her rival, made her determine to
> conquer her passion, and cede the beloved object to her friend. (85–86)

In this resolution of conflict, Isabella gives up the object of her and
Matilda's desires, represses her own desire, and resigns from competition.

Neither of the preceding disputes is resolved by means of common
principles of reason or common feelings of sympathy. What the characters have in common causes competition. Yet the second resolution
suggests how Walpole retransforms competition into a form of sympathy that becomes the binding relation of the marriage that occurs at
the end of the novel. What Isabella eventually has in common with
Theodore is the experience of losing a beloved object.

When Isabella and Theodore marry, each regains a beloved object
at one remove, or at second hand. Isabella regains Theodore; but he
doesn't want her and marries her only because those "frequent discourses
with [her] of his dear Matilda" convince him that she will help him
remember his first choice (110). Not in possession of him, Isabella has
only mediated access to him, through memories and representations
of another woman. Theodore, similarly, has only mediated access to
Matilda, whom he regains as a representation, as well as to Isabella,
who is for him also a representation. In this marriage, characters focus
representations and imagination not, as in Smith's theory of sympathy, on feelings but on an object of desire that is reproduced by these
means. Unlike reason or Smith's sympathy, in which thoughts and feelings are standardized, Walpole's sympathy calls up a lost object of desire as the standard of representation.

By identifying desire with a lost and unattainable object, Theodore's experience effects both a stability and a productivity unavailable to the old regime. With Theodore's melancholy and nostalgia in force, he is protected from the exchangeability of persons in social relations by his relative indifference to everything but his lost love. Yet, not only accepting Isabella as a substitute but also accepting the world as a place in which only substitutes are available, he enters into exchange as a condition of his emotional existence.

The desirable but unrecoverable object is understood to lie behind the images that represent her and to precede such substitutions in time. Walpole thereby "grounds" not production but consumption, providing depths behind and beneath objects of consumption that preclude the leveling and "mixing" of experience that Smollett deplores. These depths mean that a man distinguishes between the superficially and partially satisfying woman who is available to him and the unavailable woman who is the object of his "deepest" desires. As in the doubling of "man" that Foucault locates late in the eighteenth century, Walpole identifies depths beneath representations of desire in which desire transcends representation as well as both the temporal and spatial present. For the woman, however, these depths provide neither subjective depth nor the stability that the man acquires in his detachment from available objects. As objects of desire, women apparently exist on only one level at a time: they are the superficial representations of objects, or they acquire "depth" by dying. The women in this novel, while alive, experience doubling not by containing it but by recognizing that other women are their doubles. The doubling of women marks not their depth but their superficiality and, therefore, their exchangeability.

But although women are subject to representation and containment, men, doubled beneath the surfaces of representation, cannot be represented or contained. At the end of Walpole's novel, then, the prophecy — that *"Otranto should pass from the present family, whenever the real owner should be grown too large to inhabit it"* (15–16; Walpole's emphasis) — is fulfilled. After Theodore, the real owner, is abstracted in melancholy desire from his surroundings, part of him is always elsewhere. Thus dispersed, he is also stabilized, experiencing desire as a constant return. Such internal stability guarantees public stability, as it guarantees that individuals will remain confined to a new conception of "proper channels."

Experiences that in the public sphere are decisive and revolutionary are depicted as constant and stabilizing when moved into a private realm of emotional relations. Manfred, devoted heart and soul, mind and body to political power, always exceeds permissible behavior. Infringing on others' territories, stepping over the lines that separate his own from others' concerns, his behavior is not confined to "proper channels." Theodore, with his interests divided between his rule of Otranto and his love for Matilda, internalizes the separations that Manfred cannot realize externally.

The shift from public instability to private stability is clearly gendered. Theodore is allied with women in the novel, both personally and politically. He is always sensitive to their needs and interested in their concerns. And although he is the male heir of Alphonso, he comes to the throne in a female line, by way of Alphonso's daughter. Unlike Smollett's returns to nature via "proper channels," Walpole's return of the throne to Theodore occurs through women. Moreover, women are crucial to the shift from grounded exchange and production to groundless productivity and exchangeability, perhaps because they are already, by convention, exchangeable. For Manfred, any woman will do, as long as she produces a son. For Theodore, any woman will do, as long as she allows him to concentrate on his memories of Matilda. The shift from a male product to a female return as the objective of male desire does not change the exchangeable value of women, but changes the orientation of male desire from the irreplaceable male to the replaceable female, from natural reproduction to a production of representations, a process identifiable as a systematic balance of production and return. Theodore is returned to Isabella after she gives him up, even as his thoughts keep returning to Matilda. The internal production of images and memories that alone can satisfy Theodore after Matilda is dead suggests a radical revision of productivity that stabilizes productivity from the inside.

2

Productions of Knowledge:
Emma *and* Frankenstein

According to Jürgen Habermas's analysis, part of the strength of British social organization in the eighteenth century lay in the common reliance of public and private spheres on individuals understood to be rationally and emotionally autonomous. That the autonomy of such individuals was primarily due to their owning property was obscured, Habermas argues, by the "fictitious identity" of property owners with "human beings pure and simple."[1] This fiction was seen through in the nineteenth century as propertyless persons began to claim rights to participate in debates about public policy. Public opinion was then reconceived, by the Mills, for example, as a power that must be limited. The ensuing demotion of public opinion and the simultaneous promotion of a bureaucratic public administration, according to Habermas's argument, meant that critical debate by rational men was no longer the means of determining public policy. The autonomous individual became increasingly irrelevant within the public sphere.

But despite the demotion of rational debate as a means of regulating public policy, reason remained crucial to public and private experience alike, not as a means of debate but as a means of knowledge. Public administration governed competing interests by means of knowledge. And in the private lives of individuals — specifically, as Jane Austen represented them in *Emma* (1816) — interests were both served and governed by knowledge. In both public and private spheres, the governing capacity of knowledge depended on its productive character. Reason became increasingly recognized as a productive process, more important for the different values it could produce than as a stable set of common values.[2] Yet Austen nevertheless suggests that reason can produce communal order. With a dimension of government different from the dimension of public administration, Austen identifies public order with social class and individual place; and she identifies reason capable of producing social order as a set of discriminations of persons and places.

Administrations of Reason

According to Habermas, the public sphere of the eighteenth century, in which autonomous private subjects produced public policy by means of rational criticism and debate, lost social coherence and exclusiveness in the nineteenth century. As this happened, rational debate became incapable of governing competing interests:

> Conflicts hitherto pushed aside into the private sphere now emerged in public. Group needs that could not expect to be satisfied by a self-regulating market tended to favor regulation by the state. The public sphere, which now had to deal with these demands, became an arena of competing interests fought out in the coarser forms of violent conflict. Laws passed under the "pressure of the street" could hardly be understood any longer as embodying the reasonable consensus of publicly debating private persons. (132)

Both because reason seemed replaced by interest in those who participated in public debate, and because reason seemed replaced by circumstances as the dictator of public policy, a strong administrative state apparatus became increasingly desirable in the nineteenth century.

To reconceive individuals in the public sphere exercising interests rather than reason would seem to disperse a group formerly unified by the exercise of common principles of reason. A similar dispersal is suggested by the increasing reliance of public policy in the nineteenth century on particular circumstances — "the pressure of the street" — that makes consistency and principle, at best, secondary considerations. But the identification of disparate interests in the public sphere was met by Jeremy Bentham's conception of bureaucratic administration as an institution that worked according to principles of human interest and required the participation of interested individuals. Self-interest, rather than posing a threat to common principles of reason, took the place of reason as what persons had in common. No longer to be repressed, interest became not only, as for Adam Smith, the driving force of individual behavior, but also a power to be cultivated, rationalized, and used in the organization of public administration.

Jeremy Bentham and James Mill, as Sidney and Beatrice Webb point out in their study *English Local Government* (1922), believed that individuals needed to be educated to observe self-interest as an institutional mechanism:

> What was needed to complete this all-embracing principle of individual self-interest was knowledge, by which term Jeremy Bentham and James Mill meant, not the observation and analysis of facts, but a series of logically accurate deductions from a single law of human nature, namely that every man will follow his own interests as he understands them: a law as certain and as uniform in its operation in human society as the law of gravitation in the physical universe.[3]

Moreover, Bentham saw it necessary to administer this law, since he did not believe that the "free play of individual self-interest would automatically, without social contrivances of one sort or another, produce the greatest happiness of the greatest number."[4]

By means of education and administration, self-interest became a law. Self-interest, when rationalized, seems to distinguish the individual but does so in common terms that make individuals both productive of and subject to systematic governing procedures:

> Far from dispensing with law and public administration, what Bentham desired was that his uncouth formula, "the duty-and-interest-junction-principle," should dominate the whole field of government, which he always recognised as indispensable. This explains his obsession in favour of "farming" [i.e., employing independent contractors to perform] . . . every function in which this plan was conceivable, whether the execution of public works, the conduct of a prison, the setting to work of the unemployed, or even the maintenance of orphan children. But he could not ignore the fact that the contractor would himself seek his own pecuniary advantage; and to

prevent this militating against the public interest, Bentham devised an equally bewildering array of checks, from the "central inspection chamber," perpetually surveying the radiating corridors and workshops of the Panopticon, to the "life-warranting principle," by which the prison or Poor Law "farmer" had to pay a forfeit . . . for every death above the previous average that took place among those committed to his charge.[5]

In this administrative organization, self-interest plays a crucial role. Dependent on the interests of individuals to check one another, the system both cultivates disparate interests and stabilizes its workings by means of their mutual checks and balances.

For a brief period in the early nineteenth century, then, individual interests were thought to enter the public sphere in orderly fashion, even as a means of ordering administrative procedure. They could do so, it seems, because of the governing capacity of knowledge. Austen also depicts, in *Emma,* interests governed by knowledge in private life. Reason is demonstrated to serve individual interests in the private lives of characters and, in the very process of serving those interests, to produce knowledge capable of governing competing interests in the public community.

This change in the public use of reason in the early nineteenth century, from a medium of criticism and debate to a means of producing knowledge, parallels the dispersal of interests in Bentham's administrative sphere. When the perspectives of judgment have been dispersed among various interests and circumstances, the discriminations useful to critical judgment multiply. Rather than adding to differences in debate, such discriminations add details to knowledge. The dispersal of the referents of judgment becomes an infinite resource of knowledge, which can be produced ad infinitum. It is by means of this transformation of knowledge and judgment that bureaucracy becomes not just a means of administration but a self-producing means of administration.[6] And it is by similar means that the individual self produces order in private life, both within the individual psyche and in relations with others.

The ordering capacity of such productivity is what Foucault has theorized in his discussion of institutions of discipline in the eighteenth and nineteenth centuries. Discipline, Foucault writes, refers individual actions to a whole that is at once a field of comparison, a space of differentiation and the principle of a rule to be followed. It differentiates individuals from one another, in terms of the following overall rule: that the rule be made to function as a minimal threshold, as an average to be respected. . . . The perpetual penality that traverses all points and supervises every instant in the disciplinary institutions compares, differentiates, hierarchizes, homogenizes, excludes. In short, it *normalizes*.[7]

According to Foucault's analysis, discipline occurs as a productive process and increases constraints on behavior and character in the process of knowing persons. What is produced are the relations of likeness, difference, and order that critical judgment uses to see persons, and things, relative to one another. The very abandonment of any common principles of evaluation makes possible the proliferation of information that knows only relatively. Government by such processes is a matter of knowledge rather than opinion; it is policy for managing differences rather than negotiating them. Public policy, therefore, requires not agreement among different interests but instead their discrimination, which produces more and more detailed differentiations as more complete knowledge.

In *Emma,* too, knowledge governs experience *as* a productive process. Austen makes clear that reason can no longer govern social relations as a means of debate. The development of competing interests — notably emotional and economic interests of love and marriage — is governed instead by their rational discrimination. Reason both produces desire and effectively governs consumption in the novel by producing sufficient discriminations among interests to allow for everyone's satisfaction.

In *Emma* is evident, then, a private sphere in which rational and interested persons both produce and consume. A contemporary work, however, makes evident the division of private life from social production that Habermas identifies with the experience of the nineteenth century. In *Frankenstein* (1818), which Mary Shelley wrote in 1816, the year *Emma* was published, knowledge does not function as a process of discrimination capable of governing persons, but instead reproduces, both within and among persons, irresolvable conflicts of interest. Shelley's internal division effects a privatization of individual knowledge and reorders the individual psyche as a consuming mentality without productive capacity.

Debilitating Debate

In the previous chapter I suggested changes in eighteenth-century depictions of reason and interest that demoted rational debate and promoted representations of desire as means of government. In *Humphry Clinker,* the public sphere in which Matthew Bramble meets and converses with strangers indicates "[t]he dimension of the polemic within which," Habermas says, "the public sphere assumed political importance during the eighteenth century" (52). In Smollett's novel only men participate in rational debate, flawed though the process often is by individual interests. The model for government remains rational order, but this model is followed only in the private sphere of Matthew Bramble and his friends. In *The Castle of Otranto,* Horace Walpole also identifies a public sphere of political power made up exclusively of men, and they argue repeatedly with one another, usually about Manfred's abuses of power. As in *Humphry Clinker,* however, reason is unable to govern interest among these characters, and their arguments do not produce a public policy of government. The ruler of Otranto is replaced according to the direction of supernatural signs unaffected by men's debates.

But in *The Castle of Otranto,* women also argue with one another, in the private sphere of the family. Their arguments are resolved emotionally rather than logically, with the repression of self-interest by love and generosity. Unlike Smollett's women, Walpole's Isabella and Matilda demonstrate independence: if theirs is not the autonomy of reason, they nevertheless demonstrate a capacity to govern their interests voluntarily. At the end of the novel, in a working compromise of male and female models of behavior, Theodore is put on the throne with his interests limited to his melancholy memories of Matilda, memories he indulges in conversations with Isabella, who also represents Matilda in words and memories. Conversation between a man and a woman at the end of the novel thereby produces not rational policy or emotional control, both of which function by the repression of interest, but representations of desire that direct interest toward absent objects.

Thus, conversation becomes not a medium of debate that works as a means of governing, but a medium of desire that is satisfied, though only in part, by the representation and recovery of lost objects. These representations of desire do not reach toward agreement among persons by means of the common terms of reason. Rather, they achieve agreement in their common referent, the lost object of desire, which is understood to be the object common to representations of memory and conversation.

Women first enter debate in *The Castle of Otranto* as irrational participants, dealing less in reason than in emotion. But more important than the female's representation of emotion is her own capacity to be represented. Men in rational debate represent not themselves but a particular perspective or argument located within the common, impersonal terms of reason. Women represent themselves, with feelings that are personal interests; women can therefore be represented, and exchanged, as objects. Women both exchange themselves in representation and are rendered exchangeable in ways men are not. Finally, therefore, Isabella can become an object of desire to Theodore as a representation of Matilda, by representing Matilda in conversations with him.

In Austen's *Emma,* once again rational debate doesn't work. Arguments occur, usually between men and women, but repeatedly deteriorate into recognitions of interest and prejudice unalterable by reason. Austen retains reason as a means of government, but such government occurs as a process very different from a public sphere of critical debate. Critical thought in Austen's novels is productive of discriminations that govern behavior by knowing it. Differences among persons generated by means of critical reflection are not to be resolved; they are to be elaborated in as much detail as possible to constitute individual identity *in* detail. The rational representation of self and others by detailed discriminations, moreover, allows the desires of the self and the desirability of others to be discovered. Here, as in *The Castle of Otranto,* the medium of debate becomes a medium of desire, but their common identity lies in their productive capacities. There is no fixed referent for desire, which increases with the increasingly elaborated representations that attribute to objects more and more character and characteristics. Desire works with reason to produce the differences among persons that allow them to be known as individuals.

Debating Interests

The inadequacy of rational debate in *Emma* is repeatedly evident. Early in the novel, for example, Mr. Knightley enters into an argument with Mrs. Weston, Emma's former governess and companion, about the value of Emma's new friendship with Harriet Smith. But there is little real debate, and neither character sees the other as reasonable in what there is of it. Mrs. Weston says that Mr. Knightley is not "a fair judge in this case": "perhaps no man can be a good judge of the comfort a woman feels in the society of one of her own sex, after being used to it all her life." Mr. Knightley, on the other hand, says that Mrs. Weston has a "charm thrown over [her] senses" so that she cannot see Emma as she is.[8] Common terms of reason seem unavailable. At the end of their discussion, moreover, Mrs. Weston indicates that their opinions don't matter: "[I]t cannot be expected that Emma, accountable to nobody but her father, who perfectly approves the acquaintance, should put an end to it, as long as it is a source of pleasure to herself" (25).

Here social debate is rendered ineffectual by several criteria. For one thing, reason is not sufficient as a means of reaching agreement; according to Mrs. Weston, persons need more experience in common than reason can provide. For another thing, all people do not observe reason: Mrs. Weston seems to Mr. Knightley unable to judge because of her feelings for Emma. And social debate cannot govern Emma's behavior if she seems, to Mrs. Weston and herself, to be unaccountable to the debaters. Representation is no longer a medium of rational debate but a means of producing differences that rational debate cannot resolve.

Repeated arguments between Mr. Knightley and Emma also seem ineffectual. Particularly in their debate about Frank Churchill's conduct, a debate in which the reliability of common principles is itself debated, the uses of argument are suspect. Frank has not come to visit his father and new stepmother. Though he has repeatedly promised to come, he has kept canceling his planned visits at the last moment because "he could not be spared" by his adopted parents, the Churchills (97). Mr. Knightley argues that Frank is at fault for not doing what everyone knows is right: "There is one thing, Emma, which a man can always do, if he chuses, and that is, his duty" (99). Moreover, "It ought to have been an habit with him by this time, of following his duty, instead of consulting expediency" (100). Emma insists that Frank cannot act so independently of the Churchills, because his welfare depends on inheriting their money. Circumstances thus may alter, or at least make impracticable, any absolute standard of conduct. "He may have as strong a sense of what would be right, as you can have," Emma argues, "without being so equal under particular circumstances to act up to it" (100).

Emma does not deny common principles, but she moves toward a relative or circumstantial judgment, according to which every case may be different. Austen, on her part, does not deny that circumstances may affect judgment. Mr. Knightley himself rebukes Emma after the incident at Box Hill, when she has hurt Miss Bates's feelings, on the grounds of Miss Bates's situation. And Emma seems to be "rendering justice" when she decides that, if she considers Jane Fairfax's "history, indeed, her situation, as well as her beauty," she cannot justify disliking Jane (112).

In Frank's case, then, what is the situation? Frank's situation is not known. As it later becomes known, however, the situation is much more complex than Emma suggests, to a degree that would probably alter both Emma's and Mr. Knightley's opinions about it. Frank, secretly engaged to Jane Fairfax, has misrepresented the situation, blaming on the Churchills what is in fact his own unwillingness to come to Highbury before Jane arrives. Arguing that his circumstances justify his conduct, Emma has nevertheless misjudged Frank, because he has misrepresented himself and his circumstances. Mr. Knightley's arguments seem equally invalid. Given knowledge of Frank's situation, Mr. Knightley too would probably doubt that Frank should visit his father. It is not clear what principle of duty would apply in such a situation, because no dutiful person would get himself into it. Frank's situation renders both Emma's and Mr. Knightley's judgments insufficient.

Yet there is another situation in this scene, and that is the situation between Emma and Mr. Knightley themselves. That their situation affects their judgment is indicated first by the fact that Emma is not

saying what she thinks about Frank and eventually by the fact that she
is more interested in judging Mr. Knightley than Frank Churchill. Having just had to tell Harriet that Mr. Elton after all does not care for
her, Emma is "not at this time in a state of spirits to care really about Mr.
Frank Churchill's not coming, except as a disappointment at Randalls."
She begins to discuss Frank with Mr. Knightley only because "it was
desirable that she should appear, in general, like her usual self" (98):

> She then proceeded to say a good deal more than she felt, of the advantage
> of such an addition to their confined society in Surry; the pleasure of look-
> ing at some body new; . . . and ending with reflections on the Churchills
> again, found herself directly involved in a disagreement with Mr. Knight-
> ley; and, to her great amusement, perceived that she was taking the other
> side of the question from her real opinion, and making use of Mrs. West-
> on's arguments against herself. (98)

Actually in agreement, Emma and Mr. Knightley nevertheless get into
a heated dispute in which Emma declares, "We shall never agree about
him [Frank]" (101), calls Mr. Knightley prejudiced, and declares her
own prejudice in favor of Frank, thereby making Mr. Knightley so an-
gry that he, too, seems unable to deal in principles: "To take a dislike
to a young man, only because he appeared to be of a different disposi-
tion from himself, was unworthy the real liberality of mind which she
was always used to acknowledge in him" (102).

To resolve this dispute, what matters most is not reason, duty, or
principle on the one hand, nor Frank's situation on the other; it is the
situation of the dispute itself. At some point in their argument, Mr.
Knightley and Emma stop dealing with the apparent object of dispute
and begin to deal almost exclusively with their own relationship. Yet it
is not clear in this scene when they are expressing their own differences and when they are expressing different opinions about Frank. It
is eventually clear that Mr. Knightley's opinion of Frank is determined
by his feeling for Emma and that Frank himself is a matter of total indifference to him, but Austen says this only after Emma's and Mr.
Knightley's feelings for each other have been admitted:

> He had found her agitated and low. — Frank Churchill was a villain. — He
> heard her declare that she had never loved him. Frank Churchill's character
> was not desperate. — She was his own Emma, by hand and word, when

they returned into the house; and if he could have thought of Frank Churchill then, he might have deemed him a very good sort of fellow. (298)

With judgment affected by feelings to this extent, there is little but feeling functioning. Reason itself is a blind in the earlier scene, enabling Mr. Knightley to express his emotions under cover of judgment. This means that there are three characters in this situation practicing deceit. Though they do so at different levels of consciousness, Frank, Emma, and Mr. Knightley all deceive others to forward their own interests.

This examination of the relative character of the situation in which the argument occurs alters rather wildly its meaning. Both the principled and circumstantial positions become blinds to obscure interests, thereby making it impossible for Emma or Mr. Knightley to recognize that each is doing something similar to what Frank is doing. The greatest fault of rational debate in the novel is that it covers up the emotional interests that really drive characters' thoughts and actions. To negotiate competing interests, individuals' representations must be seen through; it is not the object represented, but the subject doing the representing, that must be identified.[9]

After this happens, however, what is recognized are the competing interests, and therefore the implied exchangeability, of individuals. In the preceding argument, Emma is more willing to acknowledge this than is Mr. Knightley. She puts herself in another's place, implying her own exchangeability, as she does repeatedly in the novel. But it is in Emma's interest, as she eventually recognizes, not to be exchangeable. And what she learns is to practice discrimination, a form of reason that can distinguish among competitors. What Austen effects, then, is a reform of representation and reason both. As interests enter into debate, representation functions as a sign of both subject and object. Thus entered into exchange, the self can nevertheless achieve distinction by means of discrimination, a productive form of reason that produces knowledge as difference.

Knowing Interests

Austen's alliance of interest and knowledge occurs first in the individual's need to learn what her interests are. Like Bentham, Austen, in her depiction of desire as a phenomenon to be discovered, suggests that individuals must learn to recognize their interests. Changes entailed in this discovery of desire can be suggested by looking back to such novels as *Moll Flanders* (1722) and *Tom Jones* (1749). In those eighteenth-century works, self-knowledge is assumed; it is others' knowledge of the self, or lack of it, that poses the greatest problems for heroine and hero. But, with Austen's fiction most emphatically, self-knowledge becomes the crucial, if unrecognized, aim of the novel's central character. "Till this moment," as Elizabeth Bennett says to herself at the turning point of *Pride and Prejudice* (1813), "I never knew myself."[10]

In Austen's work, the discovery of individual desires occurs as both a social and a psychological process. Desires must be represented to be recognized; and they are represented both by other persons, acting like mirrors in which one's own desires are reflected, and by internal, rational reflection on one's own behavior.

In *The Castle of Otranto,* as I argued in the previous chapter, some form of withdrawal is necessary in the face of competition among characters for an object of desire. A character may withdraw her desire from competition; or — and this is the novel's final solution to the difficulty — the object of desire may be withdrawn from availability. After Matilda dies, only representations of her are available, and they can be readily produced by means of representation. In *Emma,* competition is also productive, though it seems to cost less; no one dies or is eventually disappointed in love.

Indeed, in Austen's novel, competing interests among characters do not pose obstacles to desire, but seem rather to generate desire. It is only by seeing another person experience desire for Mr. Knightley that Emma recognizes her own desire for him. As for Mr. Knightley, "He had been in love with Emma, and jealous of Frank Churchill, from about the same period, one sentiment having probably enlightened him as to the other" (298). This is one form of representation on which desire depends, so that characters seem to experience their desires as reproductions of others' desires. Whereas Walpole's Gothic characters eventually experience desire at second hand, Austen's characters seem to experience desire at second hand right away, although other characters' representations of those desires make possible the discovery of emotions that existed prior to their representations.

In *Emma,* desire is experienced only reflectively, in the face of another person's desire, because it depends on a recognition of exchangeability. Only when Emma recognizes that she could lose Mr. Knightley to Harriet, who would then take her place, does Emma recognize her own desire. When Emma has heard that Harriet hopes to marry Mr. Knightley,

> A few minutes were sufficient for making her acquainted with her own heart.... It darted through her, with the speed of an arrow, that Mr. Knightley must marry no one but herself! (280)

> ... How to understand it all! How to understand the deceptions she had been thus practising on herself, and living under! — The blunders, the blindness of her own head and heart! (283)

> Till now that she was threatened with its loss, Emma had never known how much of her happiness depended on being *first* with Mr. Knightley, first in interest and affection. — Satisfied that it was so, and feeling it her due, she had enjoyed it without reflection; and only in the dread of being supplanted, found how inexpressibly important it had been. (285)

When she no longer takes him for granted, Mr. Knightley becomes for Emma exchangeable, subject to loss, and she herself becomes replaceable too. "Reflection" here is an internal, rational process of taking a second look at things. It also is a recognition of likeness or equivalence, of Emma's own capacity to be mirrored in another person. It is her own value as well as Mr. Knightley's that she learns not to take for granted, but rather to see in reflection.

The process of reflection occurs with the recognition of blindness and as the means of looking again at what has deceived or blinded one in the first place. Producing differences by means of rational processes of comparison and discrimination, reflection always reveals, or even produces, an "otherness" in things that are not what they were initially taken for granted to be. Not only does Emma recognize that Harriet may supplant her in Mr. Knightley's affections, she also recognizes that Mr. Knightley belongs in the place in her own affections where she has put Frank Churchill. She sees, moreover, that if she had thought to compare the two men earlier, she would not have misplaced them:

> How long had Mr. Knightley been so dear to her?...When had he suc-
> ceeded to that place in her affection, which Frank Churchill had once, for a
> short period, occupied? — She looked back; she compared the two — com-
> pared them, as they had always stood in her estimation, from the time of
> the latter's becoming known to her — and as they must at any time have
> been compared by her, had it — oh! had it, by any blessed felicity, occurred
> to her, to institute the comparison. — She saw that there never had been a
> time when she did not consider Mr. Knightley as infinitely the superior....
> She saw, that in persuading herself, in fancying, in acting to the contrary,
> she had been entirely under a delusion, totally ignorant of her own heart.
> (283–84)

Once comparison is instituted as the discriminating process of identification, Emma can tell differences between the two men.

Such discrimination doesn't merely record, it produces differences;
and Emma now has the means of increasing Mr. Knightley's value and
her own happiness. Even at the end of the novel, she continues to appreciate him by comparing him to Frank Churchill:

> [F]alling naturally into a comparison of the two men, she felt, that pleased
> as she had been to see Frank Churchill, and really regarding him as she did
> with friendship, she had never been more sensible of Mr. Knightley's high
> superiority of character. The happiness of this most happy day, received its
> completion, in the animated contemplation of his worth which this com-
> parison produced. (332)

Such appreciations of value emphasize the productive capacity of discrimination. More important than what in particular Emma is blinded
to in the novel is her recognition of the need for constant critical reflection. Reflection not only avoids blindness, it can also endlessly increase perception, as long as nothing is taken for granted; every identification must be criticized to be assured.

This productive capacity of critical reflection means for Mr. Knightley that his criticisms of Emma are suddenly recognized as a blind for
love. Misunderstanding criticism as a negative process, he has not perceived how it produces value in the elaboration of knowledge rather
than in the reform of objects. Though he has meant to change Emma
by correction, his criticisms of her in fact accumulate value for her:

> "I do not believe I did you any good. The good was all to myself, by mak-
> ing you an object of the tenderest affection to me. I could not think about

you so much without doating on you, faults and all; and by dint of fancy-
ing so many errors, have been in love with you ever since you were thirteen
at least." (318–19)

Mr. Knightley does not actually confuse Emma with another person,
but his criticism, like Emma's imagination, identifies an "other" Emma
whom he sees as exchangeable with her. As with Emma's comparison
of Mr. Knightley and Frank Churchill, Mr. Knightley's critical discrimination between his ideal and Emma herself comes close to producing
an object of desire. Discrimination serves as a means by which an object accumulates attributes and characteristics and achieves distinction
in these details.

Reflective Relations

Like Gothic heroes before her, and like her contemporary, Frankenstein,
Emma is isolated, having lost her only friend to marriage. Like them,
too, she exercises virtually absolute power and seems unable to submit
to anyone or anything (24). And, further like those characters, who
wish to perpetuate themselves by creating human beings in their own
likenesses, Emma attempts to form another person — Harriet Smith —
in her own image. Emma thereby initiates the first of many confusions of subject and object in Austen's novel. She is attracted to Harriet both because of Harriet's qualities and because of the qualities in
herself that Harriet brings out:

> She was not struck by any thing remarkably clever in Miss Smith's conver-
> sation, but she found her altogether very engaging . . . and yet so far from
> pushing, shewing so proper and becoming a deference, seeming so pleas-
> antly grateful for being admitted to Hartfield . . . that she must have good
> sense and deserve encouragement. Encouragement should be given. Those
> soft blue eyes and all those natural graces should not be wasted on the infe-
> rior society of Highbury. . . . *She* would notice her; she would improve her;
> she would detach her from her bad acquaintance, and introduce her into
> good society; she would form her opinions and her manners. It would be
> an interesting, and certainly a very kind undertaking; highly becoming her
> own situation in life, her leisure, and powers. (13–14)

Harriet is the object of Emma's interest and kindness, yet it is clear
that Harriet is more interesting as she reflects Emma. Increasingly, as

the passage proceeds, Emma the subject becomes also the object of her "undertaking," as if she were considering not so much Harriet but herself in the mirror Harriet provides.

To Emma's confusion of self and other Austen adds many mistaken identities, leading to a situation resembling Shakespearean comedy, as Emma recognizes, or even Gothic novels such as *The Castle of Otranto,* in which people are hard to tell apart. Mr. Elton thinks he's courting Emma, who thinks he's courting Harriet. Emma thinks Harriet is fond of Frank Churchill because of a kindness he did her, when in fact Harriet is fond of Mr. Knightley because of a kindness *he* did her. Mr. Knightley and the Westons think Emma is fond of Frank, who has seemed to be courting her; but it is really Jane Fairfax whom Frank loves, and Emma cares not for Frank but for Mr. Knightley.

This means that characters often seem to be in the place of someone else and subject to extraordinary exchangeability. There are various reasons for such confusions. Frank is particularly attentive to Emma to cover up his engagement to Jane. But it is not only to hide the truth that characters act parts. Mr. Knightley is particularly attentive to Harriet because, as a friend of Robert Martin, who loves her, Mr. Knightley is interested in her welfare. In a sense, he acts for Robert Martin. Harriet may also serve as a kind of stand-in, for Emma. Just as Emma imagines herself in various scenes of courtship with Frank (178–79), she seems to put Harriet into scenes of courtship that she herself is unwilling to experience firsthand. Emma is, in her imaginative matchmaking, a creator of fictions.[11] But the various exchanges of roles in the novel also resemble the experience of the "mirroring body" of consumer behavior. It is as if Emma is "trying on" different parts, different identities, as she confuses herself with others and about others. What she sees of herself reflected in others' representations are images available to her for consumption and reproduction.[12]

Reproduction is particularly evident when whole scenes in the novel are replayed, with different characters in the same parts. After she learns about Jane and Frank, Emma finds herself reenacting a scene in which, as in the argument earlier with Mr. Knightley, she takes a part that someone else played in the first version, and someone else takes the part she played:

In spite of her vexation, [Emma] could not help feeling it almost ridiculous, that she should have the very same distressing and delicate office to perform by Harriet, which Mrs. Weston had just gone through by herself. The intelligence, which had been so anxiously announced to her, she was now to be anxiously announcing to another. Her heart beat quick on hearing Harriet's footstep and voice; so, she supposed, had poor Mrs. Weston felt when *she* was approaching Randall's. Could the event of the disclosure bear an equal resemblance!—But of that, unfortunately, there could be no chance. (277–78)

In fact, of course, there is an equal resemblance. Emma expects to severely disappoint Harriet with news of Frank's engagement to Jane. But Harriet, like Emma with Mrs. Weston, professes no personal interest in Frank Churchill, and Emma, repeating Mrs. Weston, expresses disbelief in her indifference.

For Austen, however, such mirrorings are "blind" reflections. Such reproductions of likeness can be countered by critical reflection, which discriminates among likenesses and produces enough detailed discrimination to prevent their reproduction. The superior characters of the novel are, eventually, more productive than reproductive. Moreover, Austen repeatedly requires, from readers as well as characters, discriminations of apparent likenesses.

When Emma tells Harriet that she will never marry, for example, Harriet responds by imagining her "to be an old maid at last, like Miss Bates!" At this Emma makes what is for her an easy distinction between rich and poor old maids, but when she forecasts, "I shall often have a niece with me," Harriet repeats the association Emma has rejected: "Do you know Miss Bates's niece?" (58, 59). Mr. Knightley presents Emma with yet another likeness she would rather deny: Jane Fairfax, as "the really accomplished young woman, which she wanted to be thought herself" (111).

Mrs. Elton presents still another reflection of Emma. Her patronage of Jane Fairfax echoes Emma's patronage of Harriet and realizes the least attractive qualities of the heroine unambiguously. When Mrs. Elton says of marrying and coming to live in Highbury, for example, "Blessed with so many resources within myself, the world was not necessary to *me*" (187), she calls up Emma's earlier words to Harriet about not marrying: "If I know myself, Harriet, mine is an active, busy mind, with a great many independent resources" (58). Mrs. Elton, too, takes Emma's place in Highbury society when, as a bride, she is given precedence at dinner parties.

Distinguishing Emma from Mrs. Elton can produce other discriminations, between, for example, the kinds of distinction the two women desire for themselves. Near the end of the novel, Emma goes to visit Jane Fairfax, whose engagement to Frank has just been made known to the Westons and to Emma but has not been made public. She finds Mrs. Elton there too, and in possession of the secret:

> [Emma] soon believed herself to penetrate Mrs. Elton's thoughts, and understand why she was, like herself, in happy spirits; it was being in Miss Fairfax's confidence and fancying herself acquainted with what was still a secret to other people. Emma saw symptoms of it immediately in the expression of her face; ... she saw her with a sort of anxious parade of mystery fold up a letter which she had apparently been reading aloud to Miss Fairfax, ... saying, with significant nods,
> "We can finish this some other time, you know. You and I shall not want opportunities. ... But not a word more. Let us be discreet — quite on our good behaviour. — Hush!" (312–13)

Mrs. Elton, in on the secret but unaware that Emma also knows, uses her knowledge to distinguish herself from Emma. Like all of Austen's characters, she is dependent on others for her sense of self. But she is dependent on Emma's lack of what she herself has. She finds in others' lacks or needs proof of her own superiority. Emma, on the other hand, learns to see in others' needs a reflection of her own needs and then to locate superiority in discriminations among reflected identities. Emma includes where Mrs. Elton excludes.

Possession and lack offer absolute distinctions, producing haves and have-nots. This is a form of distinction sought not only by Mrs. Elton but also by Frank Churchill, who also likes to make a "parade of mystery" — at the word game, for example, when he gives Jane "blunder" and "Dixon." Frank's likeness to Emma is probably the most important in the novel. Like Mrs. Elton and like Emma early on — when, for example, "She was not much deceived as to her own skill either as an artist or a musician, but she was not unwilling to have others deceived" (28) —

Frank attempts to keep others blind to his real thoughts and feelings and flirts with Emma "to blind the world" to his engagement with Jane (303).

Also like Emma, Frank is repeatedly in the same situation, as if replaying a scene in which he does one thing to cover up another. Frank takes pleasure, as Emma guesses at the end of the novel, in "tricking us all" (330). Even as he denies this, he corroborates it by tricking Jane into another pretense as he recalls the blunder he made regarding Mr. Perry (331–32). A double consciousness is repeatedly characteristic of Frank, as doubleness is repeatedly characteristic of the situations in which he "finds" himself. This may be initially due to an external situation, to his need to be, since adopted by the Churchills, in two places and in two families at once. But Frank reproduces, in repeated tricks and blinds, distinctions between parts of himself and between self and others that depend on withholding something.

Emma can also be said to cover up her true situation, because she finds that she has all along been in love with Mr. Knightley. And she, too, uses others. Harriet has acted as a blind for her, just as Frank has acted as a blind for Mr. Knightley, in the sense that Harriet and Frank have acted out feelings that belong to Emma and Mr. Knightley but are inexpressible by them. Yet Emma and Mr. Knightley do not keep secrets. They are as blind as others to what they are doing until they later reflect on their behavior; thereafter they discriminate between, rather than confuse, persons.

Emma and Mr. Knightley's openness distinguishes them from the secrecy practiced by Frank and Mrs. Elton: "Oh! if you knew how much I love every thing that is decided and open!" as Emma says (318). Frank and Mrs. Elton represent relations between self and others by employing terms that provide absolute distinctions, between possession and lack. Emma and Mr. Knightley codify relations of self and others by processes of discrimination that are more diverse and productive. The differences produced are differences told. In its openness such discrimination produces knowledge rather than secrecy and, moreover, a body of knowledge as an increasingly subtle survey of individual differences.

Discriminating Class

As she depicts characters dependent on others and on reason for representations of their own desires and for individual distinction, Austen's emphasis is on a stability of both self and community. She insists on the need for rational discrimination to sort out competing interests and on the capacity of discrimination to govern both production and consumption. The capacity to survey differences among persons puts persons in their places. Though characters recognize their exchangeability, those capable of reflection arrive at a sense of belonging that is not exchangeable, and do so by means of discrimination.

For Austen, discrimination puts persons in their places vis-à-vis each other through discriminations as well as identifications. This process of comparison acknowledges attachments to persons and places but also discriminates persons from one another on the basis of those attachments. This is in contradistinction to the sense of displacement Jon Klancher identifies with the English middle class in the early nineteenth century. Klancher sees middle-class identity as an irresolute, constantly displaceable critical perspective that cultivates no grounds whatever for identity. Identity lies only in detachment, having no place but instead being in "perpetual self-displacement."[13] But for Austen, to "institute the comparison" between persons effects a binding sense of place for persons in community.

Moreover, discrimination becomes a mark of class in *Emma*: it is not only a means of sorting out competing interests but also a means of distinguishing superior from inferior persons, who tend to confuse rather than discriminate. Discrimination is both a means and a mark of good taste. As both the means of producing discriminations of class and place in the community, and the mark of upper-class taste, rational discrimination becomes a means of producing order in the hands, or really the minds, of the upper class. People are placed in the novel by means of discriminations that place them relative to others; thus, their places are produced as part of binding relations of persons. The fact that the production of these ordering discriminations belongs to the upper class is another mark of the security of their orderliness.

Yet the representative uses of discrimination in *Emma* occur along with a reconception of the self as representation, a reconception that coincides with the needs of a growing economy to increase production and consumption. Both external and internal processes of reflection enter the self into exchange. Parts of the self are recognized in others, played by others as parts and representations of the self. Because of this, and because of the need to discover one's desires, parts of the self are understood as acquisitions. Not only objects of desire but desire itself is something of which one comes into possession. Entered into exchange, moreover, parts of the self seem to be subject to both production and consumption in processes of representation and knowledge. Thus in *Emma* can be seen an increased exchangeability of selfhood that suits the private self to its eventual role as consumer of public productions.

Frankenstein

In the course of the nineteenth century, Frank Churchill's secrecy became more characteristic of depictions of private life than did Emma Woodhouse's openness. And with *Frankenstein,* Mary Shelley contributed much to the identification of secrecy with private life. Depicting depths of the psyche that surface only with destructive effects on self and others alike, Shelley cuts off psychological depths from social production and insists on the need to hide them. For Shelley, knowledge is not productive of discriminations but can only reproduce irresolvable antagonisms, both within the self and between self and others.

In *Emma,* individuals recognize their doubleness as reproducible character. Doubleness is seen in others who reflect parts of the self, as if in a mirror, and it is produced by reflective thinking that identifies equivalences in self and other. This reproducible doubleness gives way to an increasingly productive knowledge, yielding discriminations among persons. As in *The Castle of Otranto,* characters learn a detachment from others and also from parts of the self. A competitive doubleness, in which two persons share the same space and want the same object, is distributed over time and space and among various representations of objects so that conflicts are dispersed.

Frankenstein's monster, however, is produced by a process that reverses the differentiating productivity of these earlier novels. Frankenstein produces not discrimination but combination. Digging up parts of dead bodies from graves, Frankenstein puts them together to form a body that cannot take part in representation or reproduction, a body with no likeness in others and, therefore, no exchange value. Unable to recognize himself in the representations of literature, the creature is also terrified of his reflected image in a pool, which he recognizes only as "the monster that I am."[14] With no reflection of himself in others, his own reflection cannot produce anything other than he is. Working against the dispersion and distribution that characterize institutionalized productivity, Frankenstein combines parts so as to preclude their exchange. Subject to no differentiation, representation, or reproduction, the monster reverses the processes by which desire is recognized and experienced in *Emma* and turns desire for an object against the subject, into self-loathing.

Like the Gothic patriarch — Manfred in Walpole's Gothic novel, for example — Frankenstein rebels against common identity and wishes to return to a hierarchy of clear and exclusive distinctions between persons. He separates himself from parents, from lover, from friends to experience no dependence. Whereas Frankenstein praises his own parents for their "deep consciousness of what they owed towards the being to which they had given life," he imagines himself as a parent owing nothing to his offspring: "[M]any happy and excellent natures would owe their being to me. No father could claim the gratitude of his child so completely as I should deserve theirs" (33, 52–53). This return to an old-fashioned, one-way economy is repeated in Frankenstein's creation of life from pieces of corpses. Rather than create children with a woman, Frankenstein wants absolute power and credit. This he finds, moreover, not exactly in creating life but in making life from death. Power is understood as the negation of some other power, as getting rid of the competition.

Shelley therefore tends to present her readers with double meanings that are in absolute and irresolvable conflict; Frankenstein and his monster are one such pair. Representation in various passages in the novel indicates similarly conflicting meanings wherein the "hidden" meaning conflicts with the surface meaning in a life-and-death struggle. In the following passage, for example, a covert statement competes with the overt description of the creation of the monster. Beginning with Frankenstein's "confinement," the passage represents the creative process of scientific discovery as the "double" of reproduction by sexual intercourse:

> My cheek had grown pale with study, and my person had become emaciated with confinement. . . . One secret which I alone possessed was the hope to which I had dedicated myself; and the moon gazed on my midnight labours, while, with unrelaxed and breathless eagerness, I pursued nature to her hiding places. Who shall conceive the horrors of my secret toil as I dabbled among the unhallowed damps of the grave or tortured the living animal to animate the lifeless clay? . . . I collected bones from charnel-houses and disturbed, with profane fingers, the tremendous secrets of the human frame. In a solitary chamber, or rather cell, at the top of the house, . . . I kept my workshop of filthy creation. . . . The dissecting room and the slaughter-house furnished many of my materials; and often did my human nature turn with loathing from my occupation, whilst, still urged on by an eagerness which perpetually increased, I brought my work near to a conclusion. (53)

Frankenstein has taken the place of a woman, experiencing confinement and labor himself. He substitutes his filthy and revolting "secret toil" for sexual intercourse, as "with unrelaxed and breathless eagerness" he "dabbled among the unhallowed damps of the grave or tortured the living animal." "[U]rged on by an eagerness which perpetually increased," but loathing his occupation, he experiences desires in a conflict that is not resolved.

Competition and conflict are absolute rather than dispersed in this process. The overt meaning of the passage pits life against death, as Frankenstein only gains his ends by the torture and death of others. The struggle to the death is also implicit. The substitutions of the passage are repressive substitutions in which one thing is negated altogether in giving place to another. Woman is one phenomenon that disappears in this way. More generally, the whole process of substitution works in terms such that only one element survives. This is in part because the ostensible or surface meaning seems to have no meaning except the obfuscation of the hidden meaning. The monster may have been created, whether by Frankenstein or by Shelley, to displace certain inadmissible feelings of its creator, or as a cover-up. Its surface meaning obviously made up, the story of Frankenstein's monster has no reality for the reader except as a story, a metaphor, a dream; the latter, in fact, was the form in which, according to Shelley, the novel first occurred to her, as Walpole also claimed was true with *The Castle of Otranto*. In Austen's *Emma*, this kind of story is told by Emma before she differentiates her interests from those of others, or by Frank when he wishes to blind others to his secrets. But Frankenstein cannot move beyond the blind. Turned against himself by conflicting surfaces and depths of desire according to which he loves his fiancée and family but does nothing to prevent his monster from killing them, Frankenstein is confronted not only with conflicting directions of desire but also with conflicting aims of reason. With the creation of the monster, he confronts the reversal of his rationality, his means of progress and production, into a destructive power. Rather than differentiation, what results from Frankenstein's work is a recognition of the reversible character of all phenomena. Anything can turn against itself, and oppositions rather than discriminations are produced by knowledge.

Thus Frankenstein and his monster end up chasing each other around the North Pole. Shelley makes a distinction between them an impossibility but also their only desire, with an irresolvable relation that engages both in an obsessive reproduction of their own conflict. Circling around one pole rather than suspended between poles of difference, these two beings are difficult to identify according to any of the normalizing practices, such as comparison and differentiation, that Foucault identifies with discipline. Frankenstein and his monster are at an end of meaning, right at the limit of meaning, around which they circle, going nowhere.

Reproducing Conflict

As I have argued earlier, the identification of conflicting interests in the early-nineteenth-century British public did not necessarily indicate disorder. For one thing, if the expression and exercise of various interests were viewed as parts of knowledge, then they could be seen to add to a comprehensive understanding of society. Moreover, if expressions of various interests constantly checked each other, they could be seen as, in effect, stabilizing. Various interests could be exercised as part of both economic growth and political stability.

Malthusian economics, however, predicted another kind of checking mechanism on economic growth. In his 1798 *Essay on Population,* Thomas Malthus argues that there are natural limits to growth that preclude the progressive economy theorized by Adam Smith. Population growth, spurred by economic well-being, will eventually exceed natural limits, Malthus argues, and will then be checked by wars, famine, and pestilence. Gertrude Himmelfarb summarizes Malthus's revisions of Smith's ideas as follows:

> In place of an industrial economy cooperating with nature to bring about a "natural progress of opulence," he had nature and industry working at cross purposes, with industry creating more mouths to feed and nature providing less food to feed them. In place of a "progressive state" in which wages and population increased simultaneously, he postulated an inverse relationship between the two—an inverse relationship, in effect, between survival and natural passion, so that it was only by doing violence to themselves, by thwarting human nature, that the poor could exist.[15]

Elements such as nature and industry that had, for Smith, worked together now work against one another, not reaching toward any new condition but in a sense canceling each other out, with the effect of keeping the economy in constantly "checked" motion.

Unlike the checks and balances of Bentham's government administration, the dynamics of a Malthusian economy are nonprogressive. An elemental conflict within nature—between natural desires and natural resources—means that all progress is naturally checked. Malthusian theory is also dramatic and exciting, since it pits nature against itself at revolutionary extremes. Natural cross-purposes do not merely cross but absolutely oppose each other, for one thing. Moreover, there is forecast an apocalyptic moment in the future when natural conflict will come to a crisis: productivity will be turned against itself and will cause destruction.

The revolutionary character of experience here lies in the capacity of any element of experience to turn against itself. Malthus was not alone among his contemporaries in this perspective. Fred Botting, discussing *Frankenstein* in the context of public debates about the French Revolution in Britain in the 1790s, identifies the danger of the Revolution in its unstoppable character, its continuously revolutionary effects:

For many, the hopes for liberty invested in the Revolution were dashed because it was seen to perpetuate the injustices it set out to overthrow. . . . [I]n the name of liberty the Revolution had overthrown tyranny, only to repeat the tyrannical modes of rule that had been overthrown. Disposing of monstrous tyrants, the emergence of revolutionary violence and injustice marked the moment when the Revolution made a monster of itself.[16]

Discussing this revolutionary pattern as one of "unarrestable rotation," Botting argues that readings of the Revolution, including those of Mary Shelley's parents, William Godwin and Mary Wollstonecraft, were unable to locate any point at which change might stop, or any principles that could withstand change. Botting sees the character Frankenstein as a revolutionary who cannot put a stop to the revolution he initiates: "The revolving momentum, inaugurated by the dream turning to nightmare, plays on through the rest of the text in a fraught dialectic of desire and lack, authority and subjection, autonomy and interdependence."[17]

These conflicts are characteristic of the "strange empirico-transcendental doublet" that Foucault identifies with "man" in late-eighteenth-century thought, and Frankenstein's interest in anatomy suggests the reconception of biological science that Foucault has identified at the turn of the nineteenth century, as biology shifted its attention from plants to animals:

[T]he animal maintains its existence on the frontiers of life and death. Death besieges it on all sides; furthermore, it threatens it also from within, for only the organism can die. . . . Hence, no doubt, the ambiguous values assumed by animality towards the end of the eighteenth century: the animal appears as the bearer of that death to which it is, at the same time, subjected; it contains a perpetual devouring of life by life. It belongs to nature only at the price of containing within itself a nucleus of anti-nature.[18]

But because his fascination with the "incessant transition" between life and death leads Frankenstein to produce a body whose surfaces reveal the depths of death in life, this model of knowledge is collapsed in Shelley's novel.

Frankenstein's Reproductions

Unlike Austen's central characters, Frankenstein is not interested in representing experience in words and images; he wants to produce a living human being. His means of doing so are, to begin with, books; but to discover the secret of human life, he reasons, he must also study death: "I became acquainted with the science of anatomy: but this was not sufficient; I must also observe the natural decay and corruption of the human body" (50). Unable to differentiate life from death, Frankenstein studies the conversion of one into the other and vice versa:

> I beheld the corruption of death succeed to the blooming cheek of life; I saw how the worm inherited the wonders of the eye and brain. I paused, examining and handling all the minutiae of causation, as exemplified in the change from life to death, and death to life, until from the midst of this darkness a sudden light broke in upon me—a light so brilliant and wondrous, yet so simple, that...I was surprised...that I alone should be reserved to discover so astonishing a secret. (50–51)

What Frankenstein wants to reproduce is simply change, the difference between life and death. He "knows" this difference, finally, not by learning from representation but by revelation or inspiration. When he succeeds in embodying this difference, moreover, the effect is to obliterate the means by which representation orders difference and change.

Emma learns to produce orderly discriminations among persons that distribute knowledge, as Foucault suggests, across an imaginary field. Mr. Knightley is differentiated from Frank Churchill in part by discriminations between kind and unkind behavior. Produced in time and in an imaginary space, discriminations between kindness and unkindness increase the difference between the two. There is no point at which one turns into the other; instead, variations on each increasingly qualify one by the other. The stability of such discrimination lies in its gradual dispersal of opposition. But rather than dispersing differences, Frankenstein wants them as close as possible. He wants to reproduce, one could say, the point at which kindness becomes unkindness.

That point does not exist in an evaluation or understanding of human behavior. But in actual time and space, one can come close to such points, as Frankenstein does with his sudden revelation. In a second, a person may switch from being kind to being unkind; or in a second, one may turn from dealing with a kind person to dealing with another, unkind person. In such cases, as in representation, time and space are media in which difference occurs. But when Frankenstein reproduces that point, which has no temporal or spatial dimension, in a body that takes up time and space, he collapses each medium of change and order into a single moment and a single space.

With dead parts that are nevertheless alive, a body is created by sticking together fragments of other bodies. Frankenstein brings Foucault's depths to the surface. But this does not mean experiencing time as history. If history is denied by the spatialization of time in Foucault's doubling of man, as Homi K. Bhabha has argued, history remains spatial when it surfaces in *Frankenstein*.[19] Time is collapsed, in fact, into an even smaller space, because it is present at two "ends," birth and death, at the same time. Not only is time collapsed, but space is also filled in. Like a vampire, as Joan Copjec explains, the living dead monster "confronts us with an absence of absence" rather than with a presence.[20] There is no room in the monstrous identity for difference to appear.

In a sense, *Frankenstein* confirms that only representations can be produced and consumed in a progressive, or growing, economy. If Frankenstein is stymied in his attempts at material production because he rules out representation and reproduction, he is more successful in the images he produces in his dreams. These images, unlike the monster, are subject to reproduction and are female. Persons are seen as images of one another when Frankenstein dreams that Elizabeth, his fiancée, turns into his mother's corpse:

> I thought I saw Elizabeth, in the bloom of health, walking in the streets of Ingolstadt. Delighted and surprised, I embraced her, but as I imprinted the first kiss on her lips, they became livid with the hue of death; her features appeared to change, and I thought that I held the corpse of my dead mother in my arms; a shroud enveloped her form, and I saw the grave-worms crawling in the folds of flannel. I started from my sleep with horror; . . . I beheld the wretch — the miserable monster whom I had created. (57)

Here the difference between life and death is not reproduced. Unlike the monster's body, these images of women's bodies do not collapse the difference of that opposition but collapse instead the difference between their own bodies. One body turns into another body and then, in fact, into still other bodies as worms consume it. "Progress" occurs in reverse, one might say, but although the imagined progression in time and space moves toward death, it involves changes in time and space. Production and consumption do not conflict with each other.

In most literary depictions, monsters are also images. As Botting's discussion of public debate about the French Revolution indicates, political threats of "the masses" were depicted in terms of monstrosity, and this continued in Victorian writing.[21] But in *Frankenstein*, monstrosity is produced in a "living dead" male body. It is only "living dead" females who are images. They are immaterial on two counts: as images and as images of bodily disintegration that the monstrous body precludes. Such a female is "living dead," then, only in the sense that she appears as one and then is seen to be the other; she does not contain life and death but changes from one to the other, losing consistency as she does so. This depiction confirms the opposing character of differences that Shelley repeatedly invokes: the male has absolute consistency and the female none.

Representations of women as living dead, even, like Elizabeth, as undergoing bodily disintegration before men's eyes, reappear in Victorian novels.[22] As objects breakable into parts, women, unlike the male monster who combines parts, are figured as part-objects subject to consumption. These women are also crowded, however. Like Matilda and Isabella in *The Castle of Otranto* who are characterized by exchangeable parts, the bride and the mother of Frankenstein have to share a single space, even a single body, in his eyes. This female combination does not pose the threats that the monster embodies, because its parts are identified as exchangeable, and so it easily comes apart.

This gendering of objects of desire identifies women as commodities subject to reproduction by representation and subject to distribution. In women's bodies combination is dispersed, and the secret difference between life and death is distributed openly over time and space. Frankenstein's desire here is not turned against itself but directed toward objects that turn from life to death and for which he can therefore feel both love and loathing. The woman's body as part-object means that desire as well as objects of desire can be dispersed into partial phenomena.

Shelley's model of production and consumption is effective only in private life and "private" enterprise, realms in which desire can be ex-

perienced as conflict. Because Shelley understands desire to be in conflict and to desire conflict — the desire of differences between objects
rather than of the objects themselves — neither the representation nor
the distribution of desire provides satisfaction. And this is suitable to
the marketplace, because the consumer is committed to continued consumption by the partial satisfaction that commodities provide. But this
form of representation cannot work in Habermas's public debates or
in Austen's discriminations among persons in a community, because
although it disperses desire, it does so only in conflicting terms. Frankenstein produces a monstrous male body, a living dead creature who kills
his family; images of living dead female bodies that die and are eaten;
and a story in which his life is destroyed by his productivity. These
products "feed" a desire for conflict, violence, and violation that can
be legitimately experienced only in private.

Mary Shelley thus produces a narrative that insists on a sharp division between public and private life. Personal desire and personal consumption are experienced in an economy that functions as an "under-
side" of rational exchange. The legitimate dispersion of interests in
representations of reason is mirrored in the legitimate dispersion of
desires in the production and consumption of commodities. But the
latter dispersion, like the depths of Foucault's doubled man, experiences conflict and violation in images that are not allowed to surface
in public. Shelley's continuous reproduction of conflicting surfaces
and depths, like her reproduction of conflict in desire, is restaged again
and again in the same spatial relations. *Frankenstein* replaces history, as
a production of potentially revolutionary differences, with an opposition that stabilizes differences in a fixed structure of distinctions whose
revolutionary potential is experienced only in private.

3

The Emptied Subject of Public Knowledge:
The Old Curiosity Shop

In Charles Dickens's *The Old Curiosity Shop* (1840–41), Nell likes to sit at a window of her grandfather's house, watching the street and survey-ing the London landscape. Unlike Austen's Emma, Nell is unable to feel much connection to the neighbors she observes:

> None are so anxious as those who watch and wait, and at these times, mourn-ful fancies came flocking on her mind, in crowds.
>
> She would take her station here at dusk, and watch the people as they passed up and down the street, or appeared at the windows of the opposite houses, wondering whether those rooms were as lonesome as that in which she sat, and whether those people felt it company to see her sitting there, as she did only to see them look out and draw in their heads again. There was a crooked stack of chimneys on one of the roofs, in which by often looking at them she had fancied ugly faces that were frowning over at her and try-ing to peer into the room, and she felt glad when it grew too dark to make them out, though she was sorry too, when the man came to light the lamps in the street, for it made it late, and very dull inside. Then she would draw in her head and look round the room to see that everything was in its place and hadn't moved; and looking out into the street again, would perhaps see a man passing with a coffin on his back, ... which made her shudder and think of such things until they suggested afresh the old man's altered face and manner, and a new train of fears and speculations. If he were to die— if... one night, he should come home, and kiss and bless her as usual, and after she had gone to bed and had fallen asleep and was perhaps dreaming

pleasantly, and smiling in her sleep, he should kill himself and his blood come creeping, creeping on the ground to her own bed-room door—These thoughts were too terrible to dwell upon, and again she would have recourse to the street. . . . By degrees [the lights in the houses] dwindled away and disappeared . . . and all was gloomy and quiet, except when some stray footsteps sounded on the pavement.[1]

Nell's mind does not produce the rational comparisons and discriminations by which Emma discovers her relations to others. Instead, Nell remains in an isolated imaginative and emotional state, receiving images, when she looks at the chimneys or the man with the coffin, that carry her mind farther away from the people around her.

This scene suggests that Nell's consciousness depends on objects both to validate and to initiate mental images. Nell neither originates nor even directs her thoughts. Because of this, her observations here remain visual, superficial, and fragmented—observations without comprehension. Even the images produced by her own imagination are involuntary; and they terrify her, in part, because they represent phenomena beyond her control. These images, moreover, which "flock on her mind," produce changes in her—her sorrows, her fears—that she alters only by turning her head to look at other things. Watching the street, her mind veers away from the objects in it as she imagines ugly faces, on seeing the chimneys, and then images of her grandfather's death, on seeing the coffin. Then, to check her imagination, she has "recourse to the street" again. That objects provide relief from her imagination is particularly clear in a passage Dickens cut from the original manuscript, in which Nell, after seeing the man with the coffin, "was obliged to go close up to an old oaken table . . . and turn up its cover to convince herself that there was no corpse or coffin there" (686). Reassured that there is nothing but another surface underneath, Nell returns to the other surfaces around her.

In this process Nell's consciousness seems a passage through which images travel, a conduit rather than a generative or active power of any kind.[2] It is as if Nell's observation is a systematic process that occurs through her, rather than a series of actions governed by her; she reflects passively, like a mirror. She does not represent her experience in any orderly form but depends for a sense of order on seeing "that everything was in its place and hadn't moved." Moreover, as her consciousness seems to receive more impressions than she generates, Nell's mind not only watches but also is watchable in its behavior, both because her mental activity is imagery and because her emotions are determined by imagery. This surveying subject is equally subject to surveillance as subjectivity surfaces and displays its workings.

The Force of Circumstances

Nell's inability to take part in or otherwise affect the scene in front of her is shared by most of the characters of *The Old Curiosity Shop,* who spend an extraordinary amount of time watching and waiting. This 1841 novel seems thereby to confirm a great change that Jürgen Habermas identifies in private life during the nineteenth century: its withdrawal from social productivity, resulting in the identification of the private individual as consumer. For Dickens, this change occurs because patterns of public production and personal consumption alike assume the human being to be a passive subject in a world directed by circumstances and forces beyond human control.

To Dickens, social reproduction appeared not only to empty subjectivity of power but also to cause individuals to reproduce, even by choice, a sense of subjective emptiness. Dickens does not directly represent the public sphere of government debate or government administration in this novel. Nevertheless, he identifies within productions of "private enterprise" in the novel a form of knowledge comparable to knowledge produced in the public sphere in the 1830s and 1840s.

In Habermas's analysis of the nineteenth-century British public sphere, administrative regulation of competing interests became necessary as "the pressure of the street," rather than rational debate, increasingly dictated public policy.[3] In fact, one issue publicly debated in the 1830s was the very capacity of persons to determine public policy rationally, under the pressure of circumstances. The empirical, even expedient character of parliamentary behavior in the 1830s meant for Benjamin Disraeli, looking back in 1843, that government was acting on the basis of no underlying principle, law, or standard:

In 1834 England, though frightened at the reality of Reform, still adhered to its phrases; it was inclined, as practical England, to maintain existing institutions; but, as theoretical England, it was suspicious that they were indefensible.

No one had arisen either in Parliament, the Universities, or the Press, to lead the public mind to the investigation of principles; and not to mistake, in their reformations, the corruption of practice for fundamental ideas.[4]

This separation of practice from any stable law, grounds, or principle is observed by the historian David Roberts too. "Very few in the two decades after 1833," he writes, "embraced wholeheartedly a centralized, paternalistic state, one that would regulate labor, clean towns, educate the poor, control the Church, commute tithes, supervise asylums, and manage lighthouses. And yet from 1833 to 1854 Parliament created such a state." Roberts identifies "presumptuous empiricism" as "the mood that explains the growth of administration from 1833 to 1854": "Each reform was passed to meet an observed fact not to accord with a principle. The result, most naturally, was a helter-skelter series of statutes and agencies, unrelated and uncoordinated."[5] Government could itself seem governed by no unifying concept but merely by circumstances.

But the increasing pressure of immediate circumstances on reason was not only a political phenomenon. Thomas Carlyle, in 1829, objected to Jeremy Bentham's thought because Bentham ignored "the great truth that our happiness depends on the man that is within us, and not on the circumstances which are without us."[6] Carlyle saw the force of circumstances threatening the power and distinction of individual men and turning society into a mechanical process:

Speak to any small man of a high, majestic Reformation, of a high, majestic Luther, and forthwith he sets about "accounting" for it; how the "circumstances of the time" called for such a character, and found him, we suppose, standing girt and road-ready, to do its errand; how the "circumstances of the time" created, fashioned, floated him quietly along into the result; how, in short, this small man, had he been there, could have performed the like himself! For it is the "force of circumstances" that does everything; the force of one man can do nothing. Now all this is grounded on little more than a metaphor. We figure Society as a "Machine," and that mind is opposed to mind, as body is to body; whereby two, or at most ten, little minds must be stronger than one great mind. Notable absurdity![7]

For Carlyle, the circumstantial understanding of individual behavior promotes an equivalence and exchangeability among persons and renders the individual powerless. The mind is identified quantitatively rather than qualitatively, and society is similarly conceived as a mechanical organization.

In 1839 and 1840, John Stuart Mill explored differences between, on the one hand, the knowledge of fact and observation on which Bentham's reforms depended and, on the other hand, Coleridge's intuitive knowledge. Much later, in his *Autobiography* of 1869–70, Mill clarified that reform depends on disregarding intuition and other innate human qualities:

> The practical reformer has continually to demand that changes be made in things which are supported by powerful and widely spread feelings, or to question the apparent necessity and indefeasibleness of established facts. . . . There is therefore a natural hostility between him and a philosophy which discourages the explanation of feelings and moral facts by circumstances and association. . . . In particular, I have long felt that the prevailing tendency to regard all the marked distinctions of human character as innate, and in the main indelible, and to ignore the irresistible proofs that by far the greater part of those differences, whether between individuals, races, or sexes, are such as not only might but naturally would be produced by differences in circumstances, is one of the chief hindrances to the rational treatment of great social questions, and one of the greatest stumbling blocks to human improvement.[8]

This "practical" turn on intuition, given the circumstances of the times, marks the fundamentally Benthamite character of Mill's thought. Even when most sympathetic to intuitionist or "internal" grounds of truth, Mill remains devoted to the "external" bases of truth he sees as necessary to reform.

Thus it became recognized that the force exerted by circumstances on public policies of reform was neither temporary nor a mere interference with policy, but instead was necessary to policies of reform. Carlyle's criticism of 1829 indicates that if for some in the public sphere the pressure of circumstances caused confusion, others were beginning to recognize adaptation to circumstances as itself a systematic and predictable process of behavior. During the early Victorian period, as Dickens recognized, what could appear as merely expedient action, directed by neither reason nor policy but dictated by circumstances, became de facto policy, institutionalized as such while knowledge was reformed into a circumstantial phenomenon. Even in *Emma,* as characters argue about the degree to which circumstances should affect judgment, it is clear that knowledge of circumstances has begun to challenge reason for the power to explain behavior. And in the public sphere of administration that, due to centralizations and parliamentary reforms, increased in size during the 1830s and 1840s, the knowledge upon which government was based was knowledge of circumstances, acquired by a systematic accumulation of information rather than by reason, wisdom, or any other subjective means.

The circumstantial content of such knowledge was reinforced by the formal institutionalization of knowledge as an increasingly independent, self-sufficient system of production. Knowledge was beginning to be identifiable, as Alexander Welsh has suggested, as "knowledge in the abstract." The authority of such knowledge is not personal or intellectual but, on the contrary, is marked by its independence of individual minds. As Welsh says, such information "cannot remain intrinsic to one mind but must be separable and potentially exchangeable," existing, as it were, in storage somewhere and capable of existing whether anyone "knows" it or not. Knowledge becomes identified as independent of the human mind both because it is made up of external and material facts and because statistical knowledge is collected without regard to its usage but for the sake of knowledge itself, as a perhaps unknown potential.[9] Moreover, much "internal" experience must be eliminated for knowledge to be gained. As if the mind brings the wrong equipment to the enterprise at hand, habits of thought, beliefs, and assumptions must be actively repressed in order to know. This may be relevant to the fact that so much of the "progress" made by early administrators of social reform was a matter of collecting information rather than doing anything else.[10]

The concept of knowledge as an institution in relation to which persons are essentially passive consumers marks a great difference from Adam Smith's economy. Detached as both systems are from individual control, the earlier conception depends nevertheless on the active and energetic participation of individuals, whose energy fuels the system as a whole. The body of knowledge that began to grow by leaps and bounds in the early nineteenth century has a curiously inert character; moreover, it is much more independent of individual action than is the productivity of Smith's laissez-faire capitalism. The nineteenth-century accumulation of knowledge, unlike the accumulation of wealth for Smith, was a process that occurred impersonally, a process with which personal desires and interests and other motives of human action could only interfere.

The independence of this institution of knowledge was corroborated by the information it collected and produced. In what is perhaps the most familiar body of nineteenth-century knowledge — evolutionary natural history — Charles Darwin and others asserted that circumstances determine natural adaptations, which occur circuitously and without reference to human or divine control. Although Darwin's work developed from a tradition of "theological naturalists" for whom the study of nature revealed God's design of the universe and man's centrality to that design, it eventually, as Loren Eisley says,

> left man only one of innumerable creatures evolving through the play of secondary forces. . . . Mechanical cause had replaced Paley's watch and watchmaker. It was not possible to argue from special design to the Deity. If this were true it could also be observed that men no longer were forced to wonder privately by what road the parasitism and disease which had troubled Darwin came to exist in the world. . . . These, too, were part of the evolving life-web. . . . Man could learn from the secondary laws which had brought them into being how they might be controlled.[11]

There is a utilitarian flavor to this conception, given its emphasis on fact as opposed to belief and on improvement of the circumstances of existence. This is true for Darwin's concept of change as well. Constant adaptation to environment, ruling out any sense of a final design, became the status quo for him in a world in which he saw all creatures determined by their particular circumstances rather than by God or man. Darwin's concern with this concept of change was virtually exclusive, Eisley argues, causing him "to forget or ignore the interior organizing ability of the body" and other internal causes of change.[12]

Visualizing Knowledge

Early Victorians who studied the interior of the human body also contributed to a "decentralization" of natural experience. For one thing, as Jonathan Crary has clarified, physiology reconceived the human being *as* a body and thereby displaced and diversified the powers of the human mind among various senses and organs. Thus, vision, the faculty on which Crary focuses his attention, becomes an exclusively physical process, directed not by will or by any other subjective power but produced as physical responses to external stimuli. Moreover, persons become objects of knowledge that is itself produced not in centralizing terms but by the systematic differentiation of the parts of their own physical systems: "By the 1840s there had been both (1) the gradual transferral of the holistic study of subjective experience or mental life to an empirical and quantitative plane, and (2) the division and fragmentation of the physical subject into increasingly specific organic and mechanical systems."[13]

This process of productive differentiation works somewhat analogously to the production of differences in Austen's *Emma* discussed in the previous chapter. But here differentiation is claimed as an empirical rather than rational phenomenon, and it is unaffected by personal action or choice. The production of knowledge in which physiology and other disciplines take part has the normalizing effects Foucault identifies with the surveillance of knowledge. The differentiation of organs and other physiological functions standardizes human differences by identifying all bodies as similar units unrelated to, though like, those around them. With vision reconceived as physical reception, or what Crary calls "a neutral conduit" transmitting rather than forming impressions, the physiology of vision suits both the individualist romantic aesthetic of Ruskin's "innocent eye" and the standardizing practices of scientific discipline.[14] In effect, subjectivity is emptied out, brought to the surface, and made subject to codification and standardization.

All of these developments in fields of knowledge depend on objective rather than subjective abilities, and therefore they distance knowledge from subjective influence. Moreover, for Dickens the reproductive character of such knowledge also distances it from the reality of objects. "Objective" knowledge delimits things as well as persons to characteristics that are stable and repeatable, and in doing so it fragments both objects and subjects. Knowledge becomes a self-sufficient, reproductive process only insofar as it is abstracted from both subjective and objective experience.

Identifying knowledge with the observation of objects and external conditions means, in *The Old Curiosity Shop*, that persons come to rely on objects for security, as Nell does in the passage quoted earlier. This subjective dependence on objects is encouraged, moreover, by producers of commodities in the novel. These characters are, for the most part, producers of traveling shows and sideshows. In their production of knowledge as commodity, the Punch-and-Judy show, the freak shows, and the traveling wax museum all produce images that are consistent and repeatable. But their effect on persons is a fragmentation, both of groups and of individual consciousness. These productions never get together in one place for very long; they travel around the country, meet at races and other public gatherings, then disperse again. They compete with and attack each other. Sharing little common ground, they fragment their "public" too, by producing different shows to suit different audiences.

Yet their aim is always reproduction, not only in that they keep their displays "always the same," as Mrs. Jarley says of her wax figures (272), but also in that they produce recognizable images, or what people already know. For Dickens, insofar as knowledge is a matter of representation — of objects, of circumstances, of facts — it is incapable of changing objects, conditions, and facts. Yet such reproduction and representation are the only means of security and continuity that knowledge provides. Individuals know objects but know no power to change or control them. Because of this ignorance, and because of a need for security, persons come to reproduce the very objectification of knowledge that alienates them from deeper levels of experience. This is apparent in the passage I discuss at the beginning of this chapter. In *The Old Curiosity Shop*, reproductive practices of both persons and institutions cut them off from what Dickens identifies as deeper connections and relations: specifically, from historical continuities that exist beneath the surfaces of experience.

Although such depths are at work in the passage in which Nell watches and waits, their effects are not visible. For one thing, as time passes, in the passage cited as well as in the novel as a whole, Nell is gradually exhausted. Her time and energy are worn away as the day "wears out" and the lights in the houses and the footsteps on the street "dwindle away." The passage of time that on the surface is simply successive is, beneath the surface, cumulative and consequential: resources are used up and disappear. Moreover, as the images on the street move into gloom, Nell's mind also produces gloomy images that threaten her with loss and creep toward death. There seem to be both subjective and objective depths at work that wear out life. Because of this, the passage suggests the "empirico-transcendental" doubling that Foucault identifies in early-nineteenth-century experience.

On the one hand, in this scene there is a superficial succession of images, one after another. But on the other hand, this surface of experience is countered by both a natural move toward the end of the day, a social movement behind closed doors as the day ends, and a subjective projection toward the close of life. All of these movements are closings or dwindlings of something present. Temporal and spatial projections toward points closed off from sensual perception, these changes remain hidden in the depths, with no ability to surface as conscious or knowable processes. Both in *Emma* and in *Frankenstein,* despite the novels' differences, depths surface; psychological depths are reflected and recognized in other persons, and covers and blinds used by persons are seen through. But in *The Old Curiosity Shop* it becomes questionable whether hidden phenomena can become evident, because of the limited capacity of subjectivity and knowledge to receive or produce any but surfaces of experience.

Like Foucault's early-nineteenth-century *"homo oeconomicus,"* Dickens's Nell "spends, wears out, and wastes [her] life in evading the imminence of death."[15] But for Dickens her exhaustion, as well as the exhaustion of her resources, is not due to facts of life, to facts of limited time, limited space, and limited natural resources. It is due instead to conventions of knowledge that impose such limits *as* facts. The production of conventional knowledge in *The Old Curiosity Shop* depends on a medium of representation abstracted from time and space, as well as from imagination, all of which are, for Dickens, means of producing knowledge.

Reproduction as Fragmentation

For Dickens, history depends on recognizing absent phenomena, which need recognition because they influence what exists in temporal and spatial presence. A sense of history thus depends on putting together rather than dispersing parts of experience. Because contemporary conventions of knowledge tend to rule out both practices, there is little connective sense of change over time. Connections are made instead within present time and space, in the identification of circumstances as causes and of differences as parts of wholes. Moreover, reproductive processes consume the resources on which the experience of change depends. Time, space, and subjective energy get used up in reproducing surfaces and images.

But the greatest cause of repetition, and the most powerful source of fragmentation, in the society of *The Old Curiosity Shop* is the profitability of representation. For production and consumption to increase without being limited by material need, the exchangeability that confronts consumers must be more than an exchangeability of objects. Representation fosters economic growth as it identifies value in abstract rather than material qualities. Just as the productivity of knowledge depends on dispersals of matter into pieces and parts, economic productivity depends on a diversification of parts that accrue value independently of things.

As William Leiss has argued, in modern consumer society both objects and subjects are fragmented into various characteristics and various desires and needs. Value is not identified in things at all but in relations between partial characteristics of things and other things, or parts, that are otherwise unrelated. Thus, in modern times a menthol cigarette can be valued, according to its advertisement, because it represents the fresh air of a country idyll.[16] According to such ludicrous but apparently effective representative substitutions, both objects and subjects are fragmented into various characteristics and various desires

and needs, which are separated and recombined in ways wholly independent of subjects and objects.

Jean-Christophe Agnew explains that in these exchanges the subject's
needs — "like the characteristics they take as their objects — become
infinitely divisible and divorced from any cognitively stable context":

> Neither the commodity nor the consumer remains definable in terms of
> some steady or persisting nucleus of traits or needs. The result, according to
> Leiss, is a . . . seemingly random movement of detached and fragmentary
> motives and goods through a radically defamiliarized material and symbolic
> landscape. "All that is solid," as Marx put it, "melts into air."[17]

According to this argument, the commodity value has become detach-
able from any actual object and floats free in a system of purely exchangeable characteristics.

Objects are no longer objects but "highly complex material-sym-
bolic entities" with imputed attributes as well as objective characteristics.[18] The identification of a commodity not only abstracts the object
from its materiality but also removes it from any fixed place and sets it
down somewhere else, so that it can assume attributes of other desirable but unrelated things. This is the case with the menthol cigarette
to which advertisers attribute the value of fresh air by representing it
in country scenes. Agnew argues that advertisers sell not things but
representations or repositionings of things that are desirable because
of these displacements. Moreover, the field into which the commodity
is displaced — the "background" in the advertisement of the cigarette —
may also suffer fragmentation, insofar as its characteristics are represented by commodities.[19]

Taken further, the abstraction of experience necessary to modern
consumption becomes a wholly visual affair whose function is not to
consume at all, but to produce desires. According to such theories of
consumption, as Arthur W. Frank has suggested, the human body becomes a mirror reflecting objects, and objects are seen as reflections of
the human body. Consumption becomes a process of imagery and
simulation:

> The paradox of the mirroring body's consumption is that it need not, as it
> were, be consummated. As the body sees the object it immediately aligns it-
> self in some fit with that object; its desire is to make the object part of its

image of itself. Thus the object becomes a mirror in which the body sees itself reflected. . . .

Consumer culture then shortens the time and space between desire and consummation. For the ultimate mirroring body, it is enough simply to walk through the shopping malls, to see what is there, perhaps to "try on some things." The object need not be purchased because it has already been consumed in the initial gaze. . . . What counts is the endless producing and reproducing of desire, of the body in the world's image and the world in the body's image.[20]

Collapsing differences in time and space, practices of consumption also collapse differences between subjects and objects. Both lose their material character and are experienced as parts and signs of each other, or, more exactly, as parts and signs of an infinite variety of combined effects.

Although the degree of abstraction in this consumption of images is understood as a twentieth-century phenomenon, Dickens sees early signs of it in 1841. More in keeping with his contemporaries is his insistence on the capacity of invisible phenomena to alter these signs. In the story of Nell and her grandfather, Dickens depicts the reproductive character of private life in persons who have no capacity to control their own experience. But he also insists on the potential of individuals to reform knowledge and produce change in both public institutions and private life.

Collapsing Time and Space

In *The Old Curiosity Shop,* Nell's experience is driven by circumstances. This happens in part because she cannot imagine how consequences might be altered. As when she is looking out the window in London, her imagination, taking off from the images in front of her, is driven by physical impressions. When, later in the novel, she recognizes that her grandfather will steal to get money for gambling, Nell is again forced, Dickens suggests, to act as she does:

What could the child do, with the knowledge she had, but give him every penny that came into her hands, lest he should be tempted on to rob their benefactress? If she told the truth (so thought the child) he would be treated as a madman; if she did not supply him with money, he would supply him-

self; supplying him, she fed the fire that burnt him up, and put him perhaps beyond recovery. (314)

All of Nell's hypotheses here are based on "the knowledge she had" —
what she already knows — with the effect that the future is collapsed
into the past and the present. Productivity undergoes a similar collapse.
Able only to reproduce what she already knows, Nell can make no difference to her grandfather's habits. She supplies what he consumes,
but what he consumes consumes him.

A similar collapse occurs when Nell changes direction and goes into
the manufacturing city even though she earlier decided to avoid cities
for reasons of health and anonymity. She takes a ride on a barge, not
knowing where it is going, because she must escape the more immediate threat of the men her grandfather has been gambling with (408).
The pressures of expediency confine her, limit her choices, turn her
against her purposes. At such times she is unable to perceive any difference between present and absent times or spaces. Her mind seems
to lack a capacity to conceive differences, and this seems due to various externalizations of knowledge in her society.

Thus it happens that, to return for a moment to the passage in which
she watches at the window, when Nell shudders at the sight of the coffin, she reassures herself by looking under the tablecloth. Her references are from objects to objects, from surfaces to surfaces. This refer-
ential process collapses the differences between things as one thing is
referred to another in order to check or limit its qualities. Though
the effect of this is differentiation, it severely limits the potential for
change.

It is not only Nell who experiences such limits, and they are evident
even when more differences are produced by an observer. The initial
narrator, for example, on first seeing Quilp, sees much more in him
than Nell tends to notice about people:

> The child was closely followed by an elderly man of remarkably hard
> features and forbidding aspect, and so low in stature as to be quite a dwarf,
> though his head and face were large enough for the body of a giant. His
> black eyes were restless, sly, and cunning; his mouth and chin, bristly with
> the stubble of a coarse hard beard; and his complexion was one of that kind

which never looks clean or wholesome. But what added most to the grotesque expression of his face, was a ghastly smile, which, appearing to be the mere result of habit and to have no connexion with any mirthful or complacent feeling, constantly revealed the few discoloured fangs that were yet scattered in his mouth, and gave him the aspect of a panting dog. His dress consisted of a large high-crowned hat, a worn dark suit, a pair of capacious shoes, and a dirty white neckerchief.... Such hair as he had, was of a grizzled black, ... hanging in a frowzy fringe about his ears. His hands ... were very dirty; his finger-nails were crooked, long, and yellow.

There was ample time to note these particulars, for besides that they were sufficiently obvious without very close observation, some moments elapsed before any one broke silence. (65–66)

The knowledge produced here is both specific and various; many different details are elaborated. But the effect of the description is to fragment human experience. Specifically, subjectivity is cut off from consideration. Wholly externalized, this description not only is limited to physical images but also explicitly denies connections between external and internal phenomena. Quilp is seen with a smile that expresses no internal feeling; and the narrator need make no internal effort to observe what is before his eyes. The survey of Quilp's parts does not connect them to one another either; they are discrete parts, making no sense and no whole. Part man, part dwarf, part giant, part dog, Quilp appears a freak; yet at the same time he appears as a known entity, particularized in all his parts.

Freaks become the most knowable persons in the novel because they are subject to extreme physical differentiation and are easily recognizable according to the extensive differences that mark them. These differences are physical and not historical. Such a survey notes no changes in things; it limits differences to the terms of systematic production, and the production of the detailed survey is what takes time. Time itself, reconceived in "ample" supply to produce the survey taken, makes no difference to the phenomena represented but is used to know them. Time is thus used up, and space, too, is implicitly filled up. Knowledge requires more and more details and could be increased by more detailed observations, but these details and observations would all exist within the same space.

Innocence and Monstrosity

Taking up time and space so that there is no room for the differences subjectivity can make, practices that externalize knowledge also tend to collapse the possibilities of human character into two categories: the innocent and the monstrous. When the initial narrator first sees Nell, she makes an impression on him very different from that made by Quilp. Lost on the streets of London, Nell asks the older man to take her to her home:

> For my part, my curiosity and interest were at least equal to the child's, for child she certainly was, although I thought it probable from what I could make out, that her very small and delicate frame imparted a peculiar youthfulness to her appearance. Though more scantily attired than she might have been she was dressed with perfect neatness, and betrayed no marks of poverty or neglect. (45)

Nell goes on to speak with the man "with no appearance of cunning or deceit, but with an unsuspicious frankness that bore the impress of truth" (45–46). With much less physical detail than this narrator provides on meeting Quilp, and much more sense of Nell's internal characteristics, this first impression is comprehensive of character as well as appearance. In place of details, the description consists of generalizations common to Nell's various parts; she is clean, neat, youthful, true, and therefore has consistency, whereas Quilp has endless differentiated parts with no integrity or unity.

Of a piece, Nell is nevertheless, like Quilp, seen as a means of producing interest when she is seen in part, as part of an image. Aware of the dependence of his own interest on externals, the initial narrator cannot help but imagine Nell as part of the curiosity shop:

> We are so much in the habit of allowing impressions to be made upon us by external objects, which should be produced by reflection alone, but which, without such visible aids, often escape us; that I am not sure I should have been so thoroughly possessed by this one subject, but for the heaps of fantastic things I had seen huddled together in the curiosity-dealer's warehouse. . . . I had her image, without any effort of imagination, surrounded and beset by everything that was foreign to its nature. . . . If these helps to my fancy had all been wanting, and I had been forced to imagine her in a common chamber, with nothing unusual or uncouth in its appearance, it is

very probable that I should have been less impressed with her strange and
solitary state. As it was, she seemed to exist in a kind of allegory; and having these shapes about her, claimed my interest so strongly, that . . . I could
not dismiss her from my recollection. (55–56)

Nell's innocence requires grotesque circumstances to become interesting.
Relative to these surroundings, her value increases for the observer because of the difference between her innocence and their grotesqueness.
This is something quite different from the observer's being interested in Nell. The external difference that generates interest depends
on a contrast as clear as that between the coffin and the table that Nell
checks to be sure it contains no coffin. It is an unchanging difference.
Moreover, because it is external and unchanging, it has allegorical possibilities; it seems to represent something else. The allegorical possibilities depend on the externalization of Nell's situation, as they project
meaning away from her. She becomes pure sign, symbolic insofar as
she maintains an internal selfsameness that offers no interference with
the extension of meaning beyond her.

In this case of identification, then, there is a great difference opened
up between what is seen and what it means. The allegorical capacity
of Nell's image allows the observer's imagination an open field in which
to produce meaning. But there is no room for Nell to do so. She is a
means of generating interest in superficial, objective terms, insofar as
she doesn't change, she makes apparent no internal difference or conflict, and she makes no difference in her situation. Moreover, the subjective dimension of meaning that is opened up has no historical dimension and is meaningful only in detachment from the time and space
of Nell and the curiosity shop.

If Nell's innocence is her selfsameness, Quilp's monstrosity lies in
his excessive difference. The fragmented quality of his physical appearance is such that it cannot be contained or integrated by any principle;
he is nothing overall, but he is bits of many things. Similarly, his behavior is erratic, unpredictable, and nonsensical: he shows up everywhere,
having no apparent sense of direction or purpose that would explain
or integrate his actions. Yet Quilp also approaches the allegorical because of the consistency of his grotesqueness and the lack of any rational or historical explanation of his character.

Nevertheless, the allegorical potential of *The Old Curiosity Shop* does not develop. The novel clearly tends toward allegory, as Steven Marcus's discussion "The Myth of Nell" makes clear. Marcus suggests that "Dickens was seized more strongly than ever with the idea of purity" and so "resorted to the radical polarities of representation which compose the shape of the book — the chief of which are the characterizations of Nell and Quilp."[21] But at the end of the third chapter, the initial narrator disappears from the novel, to "leave those who have prominent and necessary parts in it to speak and act for themselves" (72). From this point forward, multiple characters provide parts of the narrative, which becomes comprehensive by its inclusion of these parts more than by a composition of polarized differences.

Society under Surveillance

Most of the characters in the novel participate in a surfacing of experience that cuts them off from both temporal and spatial depths. This is particularly evident in the watching that characterizes both public and private relations. Characters in *The Old Curiosity Shop* spend a lot of time watching each other. Quilp eavesdrops on Nell and her grandfather and spies on his own wife; the "Marchioness" spies on her employers, the Brasses; the Brasses spy on their lodger; Nell spies on her grandfather gambling with the gypsies. Kit stands in the street watching over the house in which Nell is left alone every night. Nell is also watchful at night, as she sits at the window in London and as she later follows and watches her grandfather. All these observers tend to confine their attention to "external" perceptions. Theirs is a society under surveillance and on display.

Many things, even people, are put on show in the novel. In the Punch-and-Judy shows; the traveling players' shows; the freak shows; the waxworks exhibit, where Nell is employed to show the wax figures; and finally the church, which Nell also shows to visitors, Dickens identifies how knowledge is produced as show. The reproduction of show involves temporal and spatial collapses. But, through the theatrical metaphor, Dickens also opens up time and space, moving behind the scenes and into history.

What goes on behind the scenes in the novel tends to preclude knowledge but to invite curiosity. Curiosity is pitted against knowledge in *The Old Curiosity Shop* according to a shift of representation whereby Dickens attaches subjective to objective values. Both a commodity and an internal form of interest in the novel, "curiosity" bridges gaps between physical and mental experience, between individuals, and between times and places. Dickens cultivates curiosity because curiosity itself cultivates attachments that are not produced in modes of social reproduction in the novel. As an alternative to knowledge, moreover, curiosity is not wholly a private experience but a means of attaching private to public life. Knowledge depends on show and produces facts rather than interest, objective rather than subjective gains. Curiosity moves observers behind the scenes, to look into things, and generates and sustains interest in things.

The first showpeople Nell meets in the novel are Mr. Short and Mr. Codlin, in a graveyard into which Nell wanders with her grandfather after a long day's walking:

> It was not difficult to divine that they were of a class of itinerant showmen — exhibitors of the freaks of Punch — for, perched cross-legged upon a tombstone behind them was the figure of that hero himself. . . .
>
> In part scattered upon the ground at the feet of the two men, and in part jumbled together in a long flat box, were the other persons of the Drama. . . . Their owners had evidently come to that spot to make some needful repairs in the stage arrangements. . . .
>
> "Why do you come here to do this?" said the old man. . . .
>
> "Why you see, . . . we're putting up for the night at the public-house yonder, and it wouldn't do to let 'em see the present company undergoing repair."
>
> "No! . . . [W]hy not?"
>
> "Because it would destroy all the delusion, and take away all the interest, wouldn't it? . . . Would you care a ha'penny for the Lord Chancellor if you know'd him in private and without his wig? — certainly not." (180–81)

Scattered in parts in this scene, Punch is easily recognizable but nevertheless hidden from view by his "exhibitors." What must be kept behind the scenes is the process of "repairs," which will make possible the figures' public representation as changeless characters.

Assuming that they—indeed any public person—cannot afford to be seen except "in character," Tommy Codlin assumes that the public will care for a Punch or a Lord Chancellor only if those figures consistently reproduce the same figures. This is to suggest that freaks are ideal public figures because of their highly diversified appearance, as long as they do not change. According to the same policy, Mr. Vuffin, who exhibits giants, keeps them out of public view when they are old: "Once get a giant shaky on his legs, and the public care no more about him than they do for a dead cabbage stalk" (204).

Public appearances for Mr. Codlin and Mr. Vuffin limit visibility to the same things repeatedly produced. Mr. Short blames Mr. Codlin's attitude, and the fact that he can no longer act, on the fact that he is now the money collector for the show: "When you played the ghost in the reg'lar drama in the fairs, you believed in everything—except ghosts. But now you're a universal mistruster" (183). Always "a-calculating" how much profit he and Mr. Short will make, Mr. Codlin cannot concentrate on playing his role because he watches the audience during performances, "particularly the impression made upon the landlord and landlady, which might be productive of very important results in connexion with the supper" (185).

Like Nell as she watches and waits at the window in London, Mr. Codlin is divided between an imaginary projection and attention to the objects in front of him. Made what Crary calls a "neutral conduit" by his skepticism, however, he is fragmented into a part-object, his eye, which receives an impression of the impression made on the audience. Productivity is understood by him as an external process to be watched and waited for, and requires from him no subjective capacity but only his body going repeatedly through the motions of his role. Both subject and objects are converted into surfaces and images.

Early the next morning, Nell goes back into the graveyard, where she sees "a feeble woman bent with the weight of years" at the grave of "a young man who had died at twenty-three years old, fifty-five years ago":

> "Were you his mother?" said the child.
> "I was his wife, my dear."
> She was the wife of a young man of three-and-twenty! Ah, true! It was fifty-five years ago.

"You wonder to hear me say that ... You're not the first. Older folk than you have wondered at the same thing before now. Yes, I was his wife. Death doesn't change us more than life, my dear."

... [N]ow that five-and-fifty years were gone, she spoke of the dead man as if he had been her son or grandson, with a kind of pity for his youth, growing out of her own old age, ... and yet she spoke about him as her husband too, and thinking of herself in connexion with him, as she used to be and not as she was now, talked of their meeting in another world as if he were dead but yesterday, and she, separated from her former self, were thinking of the happiness of that comely girl who seemed to have died with him. (188–89)

Here the evidence of the senses is inadequate to the truth. According to Nell's reading of the surfaces, the old woman must be the dead man's mother. But comprehension of her depends on the years that have passed between his death and the present. Because of these years, the woman feels as much like his mother as his wife, separated from herself as she is separated from him. The distances that have opened up over time are perceived only by imagination. There is a certain freakish quality to the woman's identity as given here, a monstrous excess of parts she has played as wife and mother to the same man. But these cannot be made evident, and the woman evokes no public interest.

The next show that Nell joins up with is Mrs. Jarley's waxworks, in which dead persons, reproduced in wax, are exhibited to the public. Like Mr. Codlin's, Mrs. Jarley's show is calculated to confirm a correspondence between truth and the evidence of the senses, so that objects, rather than subjects, are responsible for producing truth:

"That," said Mrs. Jarley, in her exhibition tone, ... "is an unfortunate Maid of Honour, in the Time of Queen Elizabeth, who died from pricking her finger in consequence of working upon a Sunday. Observe the blood which is trickling from her finger. ...

"That, ladies and gentlemen, ... is Jasper Packlemerton of atrocious memory, who courted and married fourteen wives, and destroyed them all, by tickling the soles of their feet when they was sleeping. ... Observe that his finger is curled as if in the act of tickling, and that his face is represented with a wink, as he appeared when committing his barbarous murders." (283–84)

Mrs. Jarley represents the bodies of wrongdoers so as to expose all at once the knowledge later acquired of some past and secret transgression. On the one hand, the representation objectifies history, insisting that knowledge of different times is available in visible form. On the other hand, it insists that the public figure is fully known and without secrets. These figures are public by virtue of exposure, the conversion of their secret lives into evident and knowable character, which entails seeing into hidden places and past times and displaying both. Recognition of persons here is not assumed, as in the case of Punch and the Lord Chancellor. Rather, recognition is produced as part of the show: the story is told by the exhibitor and then corroborated by the evidence of the wax figures. Mrs. Jarley exhibits a perfect correspondence between history and fact, of a kind unavailable to the woman in the graveyard because her body has changed beyond recognition since she was twenty. Part of the superiority of Mrs. Jarley's show to Punch and Judy, she tells Nell, is simply that there is no change or movement in it: "No low beatings and knockings about, no jokings and squeakings like your precious Punches, but always the same, with a constantly unchanging air of coldness and gentility" (272).

Yet there are changes in the exhibit, analogous to the repairs made to Punch and Judy behind the scenes, for Mrs. Jarley, like Mr. Codlin, doesn't trust her audience to appreciate the show. She changes the identity of various figures, for example, for the visit of Miss Monflathers,

> by altering the face and costume of Mr. Grimaldi as clown to represent Mr. Lindley Murray as he appeared when engaged in the composition of his English Grammar, and turning a murderess of great reknown into Mrs. Hannah More — both of which likenesses were admitted by Miss Monflathers, who was at the head of the head Boarding and Day Establishment in the town, ... to be quite startling from their extreme correctness. Mr. Pitt in a nightcap and bedgown, and without his boots, represented the poet Cowper with perfect exactness: and Mary Queen of Scots in a dark wig, white shirt-collar, and male attire, was such a complete image of Lord Byron that the young ladies quite screamed when they saw it. Miss Monflathers, however, rebuked this enthusiasm, and took occasion to reprove Mrs. Jarley for not keeping her collection more select. (288)

In fact interchangeable with a few adjustments, the wax figures connote, for those behind the scenes, no individual integrity but instead the exchangeability of images of identity. And this characteristic of the wax figures seems, like the repairs in the graveyard, also representative of public figures and their private lives. Both wax and public figures are, in their public reproductions, apparently consistent, whereas behind the scenes they experience great insecurity of identity, so extreme here that Byron can quickly become Mary Queen of Scots.

Such changeability is caused by the limitation of character to apparent attributes. However, the limitation of identity to apparent attributes precludes any observation of the insecurity, because it is never made apparent. Motivated by mistrust rather than belief, these productions can be likened to the social reproduction of factual knowledge by virtue of the skepticism they assume and, indeed, produce.[22]

Innocence and Monstrosity in Private Life

If public knowledge surfaces in display, private experience in *The Old Curiosity Shop* remains an experience of multiple parts that cannot fit onto a single plane or into a single moment without becoming monstrous. The private subject, such as the old woman in the graveyard, experiences her own identity as multiple and shifting. This process of identification uses subjectivity rather than objects to produce meaning. Unlike the survey of Quilp's parts taken early in the novel, this survey of the woman's past indicates parts whose interrelation over time is necessary to make them comprehensible.

The present does not provide any understanding of the old woman's experience. By standing near her husband's grave, she is able to reproduce the same physical relation to him at any moment throughout her life. But because his body, her body, and her mind have all changed over time, there have been various relations between him and her, recognizable only in time and subjectivity. One part of her has been "in connection with" the dead husband and seems "to have died with him." Another part has grown old and is "separated from her former self" as well as from her husband. The relations provided here negotiate changes in persons as well as in parts of persons. Such recognitions preclude monstrosity, because the different identities the woman recognizes in herself exist at different times. This process also precludes the "innocent eye" of an observer who perceives only with the senses. Rather than being innocent, the old woman is responsible for subjectively making, in memory and imagination, the history that she knows.

Innocence and monstrosity become interdependent and necessary to each other in *The Old Curiosity Shop*, as in *Frankenstein*. Nell is innocent in part because, to "protect" her innocence, her grandfather tells her little about his financial troubles and nothing about his secret gambling. She is used to carry letters about money back and forth between the grandfather and Quilp, but she doesn't know what is in them. A "neutral conduit" in these exchanges, Nell is useful to both the grandfather and Quilp, and contributes to the grandfather's loss of all his money and possessions because her innocence prevents her interference in their business.

It is also, in part, because of her innocence that it takes Nell so long to "see" that her grandfather himself is not an innocent victim of the monstrous Quilp, but a person both innocent and monstrous and more dangerous to her than is Quilp. Quilp is a horror to Nell, but in his monstrosity he is easily recognized and always predictable, because he always behaves "in character." Indeed, part of the horror of Quilp is that he is as if standardized; his cruelty is not excess but norm. Even when Nell is far from London in a strange town at night, she has no doubts about Quilp's identity: "The instant he appeared, she recognized him — Who could have failed to recognize, in that instant, the ugly misshapen Quilp!" (276). But the figure who sneaks into Nell's room and steals her money is unrecognizable:

> A figure was there. Yes, . . . there, between the foot of the bed and the dark casement, it crouched and slunk along, groping its way with noiseless hands, and stealing round the bed. She had no voice to cry for help, no power to move, but lay still, watching it.
>
> On it came — on, silently and stealthily, to the bed's head. . . . Back again it stole to the window — then turned its head towards her.
>
> . . . At length, still keeping the face towards her, it busied its hands in something, and she heard the chink of money.
>
> Then, on it came again, silent and stealthy as before, and . . . dropped upon its hands and knees, and crawled away. (301)

The sensational character of this event is due to its physicality, the unrecognizability of the "figure," and the watching of each figure by the other.

After the figure has left, "The first impulse of the child was to fly from the terror of being by herself in that room — to have somebody by —

not to be alone—and then her power of speech would be restored"
(301). But when Nell hurries into her grandfather's room, she sees an
equally frightening scene that keeps her silent:

> What sight was that which met her view!
>   The bed had not been lain on, but was smooth and empty. And at a
> table sat the old man himself, the only living creature there, his white face
> pinched and sharpened by the greediness which made his eyes unnaturally
> bright, counting the money of which his hands had robbed her. (302)

This terrifying figure should be Quilp, if all of Dickens's characters
behaved in character. Dickens suggests even that it might be a wax figure, because the grandfather, turned sneak and thief, demonstrates the
convertibility of Mrs. Jarley's collection.

In the face of such changeability, Nell is terrified and helpless. The
reality here is even beyond fancy, so that she can represent this experience in neither speech nor imagination:

> The feeling which beset the child was one of dim uncertain horror. She had
> no fear of the dear old grandfather, in whose love for her this disease of the
> brain had been engendered; but the man she had seen that night, . . . lurking
> in her room, . . . seemed like another creature in his shape, a monstrous distor-
> tion of his image. . . . She could scarcely connect her own affectionate com-
> panion, save by his loss, with this old man, so like yet so unlike him. (303)

To see the monstrous as a likeness of the innocent is to see a connection Nell cannot make except as the loss of one in the other. Unable
to put the two together, she finds "relief" (303) not in representation
but in returning to look at her grandfather asleep; then he appears an
empty image, with "no passion in the face, no avarice, no anxiety, no
wild desire; all gentle, tranquil, and at peace" (304). Ruling out both
his and her own internal conflicts by identifying him as a body without consciousness, Nell needs to reproduce him as pure surface. To
maintain this peaceful surface, the illusion of innocence in both him
and herself, Nell produces a show the next morning: "The old man
was ready, and in a few seconds they were on their road. The child
thought he rather avoided her eye, and appeared to expect that she
would tell him of her loss [of the money he has stolen]. She felt she
must do that, or he might suspect the truth" (304). In the dynamics of
a theatrical or market relationship, Nell's grandfather reads her accep-

tance of him as dependent on her ignorance of him. Nell reproduces for him an appearance of innocence that masks her knowledge of his actions; this is the only representation of which she is capable.

In a sense, this marks Nell as a knowing person. Yet her knowledge here is still innocent of responsibility. Nell has simply watched as her grandfather has deteriorated into a madness in which he cannot be said to be responsible for his actions either. As the grandfather becomes monstrous, then, he also becomes innocent. Monstrosity and innocence have in common a lack of any integration of differences. The monstrous Quilp or the monstrous grandfather has many parts that do not fit together; the innocent Nell is unable to connect good and evil, present and past. The theatrical relation of Nell and her grandfather at this point in the novel is a logical reproduction of monster and innocent, neither of whom can negotiate the differences they have seen in the grandfather's behavior.

Mary Shelley polarizes the psyche into conflicting parts of monstrosity and innocence that are recognized in Frankenstein's monstrous production. For Dickens, the polarities of monstrosity and innocence are themselves produced, not recognized, by knowledge. Conventions of public knowledge in *The Old Curiosity Shop* both reproduce and assume monstrosity and innocence in persons. As a reproduction of recognizable experience, knowledge aims at repetition, recovery, returns. When Nell identifies her grandfather as an innocent in the preceding passages, she pares down experience to terms of consistency to recover "her own affectionate companion." This return occurs only at the cost of many other things "dwindling away"; most important, the return consumes resources of time and space required to change Nell's situation.

Reproducing Oppression

The repetitive aim of productivity in this process of knowledge is evident in a wide range of characters in *The Old Curiosity Shop* for whom a return of some sort, rather than change or development, is desirable. Quilp wants to recover the money he has loaned the grandfather; the grandfather wants to recover, by gambling, the money he has lost; many characters yearn and search for the recovery of some lost object or past life. Kit wants Nell back because he loves her; Nell wants to return to the happy life she once lived with her grandfather; the grandfather's brother returns from abroad to find his long-lost brother. Every one of these returns is thwarted. Each object desired is used up or exhausted so that it cannot be recovered. Insistent on the historical character of things and on their uses rather than their appearances, Dickens identifies a realm of change beneath and beyond the reproductive capacities of public knowledge.

If only objects are knowable, with no relations between them, objects begin to pile up, close in on, collapse into each other in both space and time. The scene in the manufacturing town through which Nell and her grandfather walk provides an example:

> On every side, and far as the eye could see into the heavy distance, tall chimneys, crowding on each other, and presenting that endless repetition of the same dull, ugly form, which is the horror of oppressive dreams, poured out their plague of smoke, obscured the light, and made foul the melancholy air. On mounds of ashes by the wayside, ... strange engines spun and writhed like tortured creatures.... Dismantled houses here and there appeared, tottering to the earth, propped up by fragments of others that had fallen down, unroofed, ... but yet inhabited. Men, women, children, wan in their looks and ragged in attire, tended the engines, fed their tributary fires, begged upon the road.... Then came more of the wrathful monsters...; and still, before, behind, and to the right and left, was the same interminable perspective of brick towers, never ceasing in their black vomit, blasting all things living or inanimate, shutting out the face of day, and closing in on all these horrors with a dense dark cloud. (423–24)

Filling in space and taking up time in apparently endless repetitions, the imagery here evidences a monstrous quality as it proliferates in endless, horrifying details. The sense of things closing in is increased by the collapsing of spaces between things: smoke fills the air, and "the same interminable perspective of brick towers" appears in every direction. Moreover, differences between things are collapsed by identifying machines as animate, and both machines and persons as monstrous.

Trapped spatially by a repetitive vista that indicates few differences, the scene is trapped temporally not only by repetitive sounds and sights but also by the fact that nothing is allowed to pass away: the rotting houses are still propped up and lived in. Exhausting for Nell, this environment also uses up her time and energy. This is not only because of her physical surroundings but also because of her own innocence, which prevents her from seeing anything but what is present and leaves her subject to being overwhelmed by what is present.

Yet, in addition to the physical and monstrous dimensions of this scene, there is another dimension that cannot be represented by physical imagery but instead is indicated by subjective descriptive terms: "mournful," "dismal," "agonies," and so on. This relation of emotions and objects is made not only in the author's descriptions but also, implicitly, in the minds of the observers of the scene, who are emotionally as well as physically exhausted by their environment. Moreover, the subjective dimension of vision may be responsible for the limits put on both the spatial and temporal dimensions of the scene. Just as, throughout her journey, it is not clear whether Nell is imagining Quilp pursuing her or is actually managing to stay only one step ahead of him, here the oppression of the scene may be a projection of Nell's fears. But she has no means of recognizing this, because she has no awareness of how her subjectivity produces her reality.

Subjective Productivity

Yet Dickens offers alternatives in *The Old Curiosity Shop* to nonproductive surfaces of knowledge, in both public exhibitions and subjectivity. These alternatives rely on subjective investments of imagination and curiosity in what is seen by those who observe it. The last of the public exhibits in the novel is the only public institution in which knowledge depends on imagination: it is the church that Nell is hired to show to visitors. Dickens skirts the religious character of the church and addresses instead its historical character, both its past history and its capacity to cause change.

There is very little in the church building. As an almost empty space, its interior does, however, contain depths below, in the crypt, and heights above, in the galleries. The recognizability of things in this interior is lessened by these spatial dimensions and by the objects' age and deterioration — as is the case with the "rotting scraps of armour up above" — as well as by the dependence of recognition on historical information — as is the case with the "small galleries" "high up in the old walls, . . . where the nuns had been wont to glide along" (498). Punch is always recognizable, even slung over a gravestone, and Mrs. Jarley's waxworks are recognizable when their stories are told; but recognizing the nuns' galleries depends on seeing them other than they appear, in representations provided by the guide and by the imagination:

> [H]e took her down into the old crypt, now a mere dull vault, and showed her how it had been lighted up in the time of the monks, and how, amid lamps depending from the roof, and swinging censers exhaling scented odours, and habits glittering with gold and silver, and pictures, and precious stuffs, and jewels, all flashing and glistening through the low arches, the chaunt of aged voices had been many a time heard there, at midnight in old days, while hooded figures knelt and prayed around, and told their rosaries of beads. (498)

Knowledge of this church is available only as knowledge of change and depends for realization not on the senses but on the imagination.

Recovery here occurs as a spiritual and imaginative projection into the past. The recovering subjectivity, aware of the difference between what is imaginatively recovered and what is present to the senses, is aware of itself making the difference between times and places, and between what is and what is not. For this reason, the bachelor identifies memory of church legend with reform. Whereas Mr. Codlin eyes his audience to see if his show will produce his dinner, the bachelor tells his story about the reformed crusader in the hope of producing reform within his audience.

If subjectivity enters into such spaces as the empty church, subjectivity also has the capacity to open up spaces that appear physically confined. Such capacity depends, however, on a lack of innocence; it is exercised only by characters neither innocent nor monstrous. Both Dick Swiveller and "the Marchioness" (the nickname Dick gives the otherwise nameless girl who works as the Brasses' servant) initiate action to change their circumstances. Both seem able to do so because they are morally dubious; that is, because they have a sense of internal variations and moral options, they seem to be able to project difference into the world around them. These two characters produce change by realizing depths of experience that lie below surfaces of knowledge and render experience inconsistent in time and space.

As Dick's surname indicates, he can go either way. His moral am-
bivalence is also realized as physical mobility, and his moral quandary
in the novel is depicted in spatial terms. He begins irresponsibly, running up debts and doing nothing about them. Because of this, Dick
sees himself as limited by his circumstances and identifies his environment as one of shrinking dimensions. Like Nell, he feels increasingly
closed in. And further like Nell, who reproduces the limitations on
her life in the show she puts on for her grandfather, Dick reproduces
the limits of his confinement. Every time he purchases something, on
credit, that he cannot pay for, he makes a note:

> "I enter in this little book the names of the streets that I can't go down
> while the shops are open. This dinner to-day closes Long Acre. I bought a
> pair of boots in Great Queen Street last week, and made that no thorough-
> fare too. There's only one avenue to the Strand left open now, and I shall
> have to stop up that to-night with a pair of gloves. The roads are closing so
> fast in every direction, that in about a month's time, unless my aunt sends
> me a remittance, I shall have to go three or four miles out of town to get
> over the way." (109)

Writing a book in which he accumulates "no thoroughfares," Dick
contributes to the body of knowledge growing in the novel, a body
that increases only as increasing confinement and limitation. As a monstrous incursion, the reproduction of knowledge fills in space, fills up
books, and takes up time, using them up and reducing them to narrow, surface dimensions. Dick represents his knowledge in his book as a
kind of map, a surface image that, because it is always two-dimensional,
further confines the directions open to him.

Even as he maps his experience, however, and so provides a mea-
sured knowledge of time and space, Dick's perspective is clearly skewed.
Roads are blocked by dinners, boots, and gloves. Here are evident some
of the changes in objects that Leiss and Agnew identify with modern
consumerism. Detached from their identity as useful objects, the food
and clothing assume an absurd exchangeability and are converted into
roadblocks in Dick's representation. Although Dick, like Nell, feels
closed in, this passage makes clear that his confinement is a matter of
representation. The gap indicated here between objects and their representation marks a space in which change can occur.

It is this potential Dick acts on when he decides to earn some money to pay his debts; he takes a job as the Brasses' clerk. But before he can begin work, he confronts another monstrous phenomenon that threatens to deprive him of power and mobility. This is the monstrous Sally Brass, a tall woman "of a gaunt and bony figure" with various masculine characteristics, such as hair on her face and a deep voice (320–21). Collapsing differences between genders, Sally's appearance immobilizes Dick. He stands "gazing upon Miss Sally Brass, seeing or thinking of nothing else, and rooted to the spot" (327). Likened by Dickens to "the fabled vampire" (321), Sally threatens, as a form of the "living dead," to leave Dick even less room than his creditors leave him in the streets of London, because she, like Frankenstein's monster, collapses differences between life and death as well as between genders.

Looking at Sally, Dick conducts a sort of survey of her parts, as the first narrator does when gazing at Quilp. But Dick is unable to convert his survey into knowledge; he cannot separate Sally's parts into discrete characteristics. Rather than dividing her into parts, he is overwhelmed by her, becoming stupid rather than knowledgeable:

> There stood Dick, gazing now at the green gown, now at the brown head-dress, now at the face, and now at the rapid pen, in a state of stupid perplexity, wondering how he got into the company of that strange monster, and whether it was a dream and he would ever wake. (328)

Unable to know, Dick is also unable to write, because when he looks up to dip his pen in ink, he sees Sally again, "and more tremendous than ever" (328). Eventually, however, Dick finds relief when he finds a ruler on the desk:

> From rubbing his nose with the ruler, to poising it in his hand and giving it an occasional flourish after the tomahawk manner, the transition was easy and natural. In some of these flourishes it went close to Miss Sally's head. . . .
> Well, this was a great relief. It was a good thing to write doggedly and obstinately until he was desperate, and then snatch up the ruler and whirl it about the brown head-dress with the consciousness that he could have it off if he liked. . . . By these means Mr. Swiveller calmed the agitation of his feelings, until his applications to the ruler became less fierce and frequent, and he could even write as many as half-a-dozen consecutive lines without having recourse to it, — which was a great victory. (328–29)

Dick's use of a ruler here identifies his action with his earlier mapping. But in this case Dick is able to do more than measure distance and record the collapse of space. His "victory" here consists of realizing his own power to break up space and things, by cutting through the air and, possibly at least, cutting up Sally's body. He can now open up spaces — between her parts and between himself and her — so as to set limits to her monstrous incursions. Not only does he break up space, Dick also breaks up the routine of work that allows Sally, who works "like a steam-engine" (328), no time for anything else.

Now able to make all these breaks and to limit Sally's incursions on time and space, Dick is also able to write. Later in the novel, he goes further. Driven by curiosity, he makes incursions on Sally's territory, invading the depths of the Brasses' house to learn about "the Marchioness":

> One circumstance troubled Mr. Swiveller's mind very much, and that was that the small servant always remained somewhere in the bowels of the earth under Bevis Marks, and never came to the surface unless the single gentleman rang his bell. (349)
> "Now," said Dick, . . . "I'd give something — if I had it — to know how they use that child, and where they keep her. My mother must have been a very inquisitive woman. . . . I should like to know how they use her!" (350)

Having inherited his mother's curiosity, Dick may "swivel" between genders as he does between moral categories. It is his feminine curiosity that drives him to follow Sally downstairs and become a spy himself. To most observers of life in the Brasses' house, the Marchioness is unknown and as if invisible. She is seldom above stairs when other people are present; moreover, as a servant, she is in a sense "not there" for people of Dick Swiveller's class even when they are present. Yet, given the spirit of the times, an investigator — one of Edwin Chadwick's men, for example, sent out to observe working conditions in England — might nevertheless seek her out.

For such an inquirer, Miss Brass is prepared and has prepared the girl, with whom she rehearses a routine as Dick Swiveller secretly watches. Sally gives the child a small piece of meat:

> "Then don't you ever go and say . . . that you hadn't meat here. There, eat it up."

This was soon done. "Now, do you want any more?" said Miss Sally.
The hungry creature answered with a faint "No." They were evidently
going through an established form.

"You've been helped once to meat," said Miss Brass, summing up the
facts; "you have had as much as you can eat, you're asked if you want any
more, and you answer, 'no!' Then don't you ever go and say you were al-
lowanced, mind that." (351)

This routine reproduces the public version of the child's life, producible
on demand for an audience seeking to discover the truth about her.
But Dick does not aim at knowledge. Rather than bringing the Marchioness to light, even when he suspects her of the theft that is blamed
on Kit, Swiveller joins her in the cellar. This is where he brings her
food and where they spend evenings playing cribbage.

Dick Swiveller is something of a hero in these actions, though he is
aggressive, violent in his imagination, and a violator of others' privacy
and property in deed. What sets him apart from other characters whose
knowledge violates peoples' lives, such as Sally Brass and Quilp, is that
Dick opens up possibilities of change. He produces changes in things
and people rather than simply regulating and reproducing knowledge.
And he acts beneath surfaces. Because of this, perhaps, Dick's androg-
yny does not carry the threat to others that Sally's display of male and
female parts poses. Whereas she collapses those parts together in time
and space so as to indicate no difference between them, Dick exercises
feminine curiosity behind the scenes and uses his curiosity, moreover,
to make differences. Thus, his curiosity about the Marchioness leads
her to tell him about her own curiosity. Curiosity is part of a production of change that reaches beneath surfaces into hidden depths of experience and frees experience from constraints.

The Marchioness herself is a spy. Sneaking at night out of the cellar
where Sally Brass has kept her locked up, she watches and listens at
keyholes to find out where Sally has hidden the key to the food cup-
board. In this way she has heard the Brasses conspiring against Kit,
whom they have framed for theft (587–88). Unlike Nell, the Marchioness
is adept at breaking out of restrictive limits. She finds a key that lets
her out of the kitchen, and this gives her access to other keyholes in
the house, through which she hears the information that will release

Kit from jail. Seeing through limitations placed on surfaces of knowledge, she learns what Dick later learns from her when he also sees through Sally's representations. She passes her information to him, he passes it to others, and Kip is freed from jail.

Gendering Knowledge

Most characters in *The Old Curiosity Shop* assume roles as voyeurs. Watching and reproducing the world as a series of images, they practice a detachment from objects similar to that practiced in *The Castle of Otranto* and one that similarly limits their exchanges — their desires, their satisfactions, their knowledge — to representations. In *The Old Curiosity Shop*, certain characters are able, like Austen's Emma, to bring depths to knowledge. Surface images and likenesses are seen through, to expose hidden depths. This capacity is evident in both male and female characters in Dickens's novel, as is the more widespread refusal to recognize depths of experience.

But if knowledge in this novel is not distinctly gendered, Dickens nevertheless indicates a gender gap that widens in later novels, one that postmodern feminist theories of voyeurism elucidate in their readings of movie spectators. The consumption of images by moviegoers has been identified with voyeurism as well as fetishism, because of the detachments apparent in both watching subjects and watched objects. As Mary Ann Doane has argued, positions of both fetishism and voyeurism are less accessible to women than to men:

> A distance from the image is less negotiable for the female spectator than for the male because the woman is so forcefully linked with the iconic and spectacle or, in [Laura] Mulvey's terms, "to-be-looked-at-ness." Voyeurism, the desire most fully exploited by the classical cinema, is the property of the masculine spectator. Fetishism — the ability to balance knowledge and belief and hence to maintain a distance from the lure of the image — is also inaccessible to the woman, who has no need of the fetish as a defense against a castration which has always already taken place. Female spectatorship, because it is conceived of temporally as immediacy (in the reading of the image — the result of the very absence of fetishism) and spatially as proximity (the distance between subject and object, spectator and image is collapsed), can only be understood as the confounding of desire.[23]

According to this analysis, women have difficulty achieving the distance from objects that characterizes the gaze of a male spectator and male desire. Whereas men maintain an internal distance from "the lure" of objects and identify objects at a distance from self, women experience little difference between their own identities as subject and as object. The means of distance, time and space, are collapsed for the female self, and because of this indifference of subject and object, desire is "confounded."

In *The Old Curiosity Shop*, time and space are collapsed by the re-production of knowledge. Images of public knowledge preclude change over time and difference in space because such representations delimit time and space to regulate experience. Dick Swiveller and the Marchioness produce knowledge more open to change. As spies, both these characters appear as voyeurs. But unlike voyeurs, their "object" is not to watch something from which they can detach themselves, it is to see through deceptive surfaces, and this leads both to an attachment of the spectator to what is seen and a use by the spectator of what is discovered. This information is taken out of the spaces in which it has been confined and is applied to other persons, at other times, in other situations.

What nevertheless indicates a gendering of knowledge in the novel is the importance attached to innocence and monstrosity in the heroic and villainous female characters. What disables Nell from escaping constraints on knowledge is her innocence rather than her gender per se. If Dickens recognizes that the social reproduction of images is what empties subjectivity of the power to change circumstances, he nevertheless reproduces in Nell an image of an innocent child/woman that is clearly ideal even as it is the cause of her death. No depths of feeling come to the surface in the depiction of Nell. Although it is tempting to identify depths at work — particularly, to think that Nell dies to punish her grandfather for his refusal to care for her — she remains a surface to be looked at, capable of understanding only surface impressions.

Like Nell's innocence, Sally Brass's monstrosity means that she conforms to the gendering of voyeurism that Doane discusses. There is no clear reason why Dick Swiveller is motivated to break through constraints on knowledge only when confronted with a "monstrous" woman. But the scene in which Dick is first rendered powerless and then learns to produce distance between subject and object distinctly resembles the experience of Doane's male spectators. Dick learns that he can cut himself off from Sally, and that he could cut her up, too; he thereby protects himself from violation while imagining that he can practice it on her.

In *The Old Curiosity Shop,* the limitation of spaces open to women is indicated by their restriction to conditions of monstrosity and innocence. This opposition is eventually collapsed by Dickens, as it is by Mary Shelley; it is finally difficult to differentiate Nell from Sally Brass. But this recognition does not alter the constraints on the two characters. Sally Brass is one of only a few women in the novel who exercise any sort of domination. Yet when she has been identified as a monster, her body is confined and the secret recesses of her house are penetrated. The innocent Nell experiences similar incursions and confinements. Driven out of her room in her grandfather's house by Quilp, who likes to sit in her bed, then driven out of the house altogether, Nell feels pursued, even when wandering around the open countryside. This ends only with her death. Yet when Nell lies dead on her bed, with four men — her grandfather, the bachelor, the schoolmaster, and Kit — crowding into the room to look at her, her situation in some ways shows little change.[24]

Unlike the monstrous figures who threaten to leave no room for others, Nell is herself crowded out of subjectivity. Whereas the monstrous body is excessive in its parts, she is reduced to only part of herself, an emaciated body that consumes nothing. Yet like the monstrous Sally, Nell is one of the living dead as she lies there. Still spoken of and spoken to by her grandfather as if she were alive, her corpse is displayed like Mrs. Jarley's wax figures: "so like life, that if wax-work only spoke and walked about, you'd hardly know the difference" (272). Like the monstrous waxworks, Nell looks the same alive and dead because she is innocent of any subjective capacity to know and change her experience.

4
Public Knowledge, Common Knowledge,
and Classifications of Will:
Barchester Towers and Little Dorrit

In two novels published in 1857, Trollope's *Barchester Towers* and Dickens's *Little Dorrit*, the bureaucratic behavior of public institutions stymies action and thwarts progress. In *Barchester Towers*, bureaucratic patterns of production, characterized by displacement and indirection, develop with the dissolution of a hierarchical chain of command in the Barchester chapter of the church. Displacement is evident first in the sidestepping of patriarchal lines of inheritance: Bishop Grantly's son, Dr. Grantly, is not given the bishopric on the death of his father. Dr. Proudie is appointed in what Dr. Grantly has thought of as his place. But then in place of Dr. Proudie appear two "coadjutor bishops" who have even less right to be there than he does. These are Mrs. Proudie, who "is not satisfied with . . . home dominion, and stretches her power over all [Dr. Proudie's] movements, and will not even abstain from things spiritual"; and Mr. Slope, the bishop's chaplain, who is also determined to have power over Dr. Proudie and "flattered himself that he could out-manoeuvre" Mrs. Proudie to get it.[1] Much of the novel concerns the "war" between Grantly and Slope. The actions of the war, however, are very much confused by the confused chains of command on either "side." Mr. Slope must fight Mrs. Proudie as well as Dr. Grantly. Dr. Grantly must contend not only with his enemies but also with persons of his own "party" who challenge his authority, particularly his sister-in-law, Eleanor Bold, who for part of the novel seems in danger of going over to the enemy and marrying Mr. Slope.

Rather than a clear and direct confrontation of opposing sides, then, the war in *Barchester Towers* proceeds circuitously, both because power is dispersed among various persons and because, due in part to this dispersion, confrontations are never completed. Self-productive and self-sustaining, bureaucratic displacements cause the war to proceed as routine and normative institutional behavior, as D. A. Miller explains in his analysis of the novel:

> [I]n Trollope's vision of the institution-as-"schism," resistance follows the usual bureaucratic instructions to apply elsewhere, in another department. Mediated by numerous overlapping and realigning divisions of power, so-cial warfare is kept from lapsing into a single and sustained binary opposi-tion, or from aggregating the intensities that drive it forward into mass movements. Not only are there always more than two sides in this war; they are reapportioned in every skirmish as well.[2]

This organization follows the pattern of Bentham's systematic exercise of various self-interests that check and balance one another. Momen-tum is dispersed among various interests and among procedures that check, as well as procedures that serve, interests.

The mediations and dispersions of energy that moderate while fuel-ing warfare in *Barchester Towers* are evident in the opening maneuvers, which initiate action as a series of checks on action. Slope makes his first move by getting the bishop to ask the dean to allow him to preach in the cathedral. This move is successfully offensive but is checked, because the dean is Dr. Grantly's ally and has the authority to prevent Slope from preaching again. Similarly, because Slope is the bishop's chaplain, he is in a position to check Dr. Grantly's attempts to confront the bishop:

> It will . . . be remembered that the archdeacon had indignantly declined see-ing Mr Slope, and had, instead, written a strong letter to the bishop, in which he all but demanded the situation of warden for Mr Harding. To this letter the archdeacon received an immediate formal reply from Mr Slope, in which it was stated, that the bishop had received and would give his best consideration to the archdeacon's letter.
> The archdeacon felt himself somewhat checked by this reply. (213)

Individual "checks" balance each other, so that equilibrium prevails. War, no longer a means to an end, becomes a continuing process of experience.

The formal character of action is crucial to the success of these bureaucratic procedures. In depictions of both public institutions and personal experience in the early nineteenth century, an emphasis on form contributes to their systematic and reproducible character. For Dickens, formal procedures limit productivity to repetitive reproduction, because they use up time and space needed to make changes and because they limit human action to systematic process. This is evident in *Little Dorrit* as Arthur Clennam attempts to find out, at the Circumlocution Office, the circumstances of William Dorrit's imprisonment for debt. The way Arthur is to go about his business at the Circumlocution Office involves both forms to be filled out and forms to be observed. The young Barnacle instructs him:

> "Then you'll memorialise that Department (according to regular forms which you'll find out) for leave to memorialise this Department. If you get it (which you may after a time), that memorial must be entered in that Department, sent to be registered in this Department, sent back to be signed by that Department, sent back to be countersigned by this Department. . . .
> . . . "When the business is regularly before that Department, whatever it is, . . . then you can watch it from time to time through that Department. When it comes regularly before this Department, then you must watch it from time to time through this Department."[3]

The role of watching enforces the passivity of the individual going through, or "observing," the forms. Forms and procedures are observed and produce more forms and procedures, in an excess of activity that has no object but to go repeatedly through the motions that characterize it. As in *The Old Curiosity Shop*, both objects and subjects lose currency in a reproductive process directed by and toward no apparent ends.

But in *Little Dorrit* the reproductive character of public administration has been institutionalized to the extent that the inability of the system to accomplish anything has become a governing principle. The Circumlocution Office is the home of "the one sublime principle involving the difficult art of governing a country":

Whatever was required to be done, the Circumlocution Office was before-hand with all the public departments in the art of perceiving—HOW NOT TO DO IT.

...It is true that How not to do it was the great study and object of all public departments and professional politicians all round the Circumlocution Office. It is true that every new premier and every new government, coming in because they had upheld a certain thing as necessary to be done, were no sooner come in than they applied their utmost faculties to discovering How not to do it....All this is true, but the Circumlocution Office went beyond it.

Because the Circumlocution Office went on mechanically, every day, keeping this wonderful, all-sufficient wheel of statesmanship, How not to do it, in motion. (145–46)

It is the development of doing nothing, from a simple absence of action into a positive, active process, that makes Dickens's bureaucracy so difficult to deal with, change, or get rid of. "How not to do it" is a way of doing business, even a productive occupation. It accomplishes nothing, having no ends and interested only in perpetuating itself, but it is a full-time occupation, of many people, much time, and much space, that keeps busy by reproducing its business. As in *Barchester Towers,* the bureaucratic process is endless activity in which constant displacement checks decisive action: "It's like a limited game of cricket. A field of outsiders are always going in to bowl at the Public Service, and we block the balls" (804).

Social Class

For both Trollope and Dickens in 1857, bureaucratic process disperses power and action in the public sphere so that it is virtually impossible either to assign responsibility to individuals, or to identify purposes in or make changes in administrative behavior. The confusion and obscurity that characterize the activity of public institutions are offset, however, by another public order that, although hidden beneath the forms of bureaucratic reproduction, is clear in its distinctions and definite in its purposes. This order is social class, which both Trollope and Dickens identify as an order dominating social life beneath its surfaces. Trollope is sympathetic to class order. He identifies class as a set of both personal and public values, of both subjective depths and objective surfaces of life. Once recognized, these values allow for both personal satisfaction and public order and thereby resist the fragmentations caused by bureaucratic practices. Dickens, on the other hand, identifies class domination as the hidden aim of bureaucratic administration; the upper class profits by the obscurity of purpose and action within the public sphere. Allying the upper class with bureaucracy, he resists the effects of both by turning, as in *The Old Curiosity Shop*, to human will and its capacity to change society. For Trollope, the exercise of will occurs within institutions and social class; for Dickens, it is repressed by both. Whereas Trollope identifies the integrity of social class with personal integrity, for Dickens integrity seems possible only in the private life of individuals.

In *Barchester Towers* and *Little Dorrit*, persons most successful in the public sphere appear to be emptied of character. Persons become figures, forms without content, meaning, or action that is self-determined. The public figure who assumes the bishopric of Barchester is identified as "a puppet to be played by others; a mere wax doll, done up in an apron and a shovel hat, to be stuck on a throne or elsewhere, and pulled about by wires as others chose" (37). Like Punch or Mrs. Jarley's waxworks in *The Old Curiosity Shop*, the bishop, in his lack of personal and bodily agency, can be said to represent bureaucratic agency: he is impersonal, pulled in different directions by various forces, with a left hand that doesn't know what the right hand is doing. In *Little Dorrit*, the dispersion of agency evident in Trollope's public figure has spread further, to empty of thought and direction not only public figures but also public opinion altogether.

As the Dorrits travel in Italy with Mrs. General, who has been hired to "form the minds" of Amy and Fanny (500), Amy finds that

> Everybody was walking about St. Peter's and the Vatican on somebody else's cork legs, and straining every visible object through somebody else's sieve. Nobody said what anything was, but everybody said what the Mrs Generals, or Mr Eustace, or somebody else said it was. . . . Through the rugged remains of temples and tombs and palaces and senate-halls and theatres and amphitheatres of ancient days, hosts of tongue-tied and blindfolded moderns were carefully feeling their way, incessantly repeating Prunes and Prism in the endeavour to set their lips according to the received form. Mrs General was in her pure element. Nobody had an opinion. There was a forma-

tion of surface going on around her on an amazing scale, and it had not a
flaw of courage or honest free speech in it. (566)

Here the exchangeability of forms applies to bodies, whose natural
parts have been displaced by somebody else's. With passages into and
out of their minds cut off by blindfolds and tied tongues, these people
become mere surfaces, blanks to be filled in. Receiving and reproducing forms, persons become like Trollope's puppet bishop, doing or saying what someone else does and says. Doing what "everybody" does
and says, with "nobody" thinking, renders "everybody," "somebody else,"
and "nobody" indifferent, exchangeable terms with no representative
significance. Forms have taken over here, as in the Circumlocution
Office, to constitute a "pure element" of nothing but surfaces and signs.

For both Trollope and Dickens, the public opinion expressed and
represented by empty figures has no capacity to govern society except
by repression. Both writers concur with the demotion of public opinion that disqualified it as a determinant of public policy in the mid-
nineteenth century. Habermas identifies this change in the value
assigned to public opinion as a result of the increasing size of "the public." As I have discussed earlier, reason no longer seemed to characterize public opinion when "the public" was enlarged to include persons
with more disparate interests. Rather than being expressed as debate,
public opinion was identified as the interest of the majority, a coercive
force:

> [T]he unreconciled interests which, with the broadening of the public,
> flooded the public sphere were represented in a divided public opinion and
> turned public opinion (in the form of the currently dominant opinion)
> into a coercive force, whereas it had once been supposed to dissolve any
> kind of coercion into the compulsion of reason. Thus [J. S.] Mill even de-
> plored the "yoke of public opinion" or "moral means of coercion in the
> form of public opinion."[4]

With public opinion determined no longer through rational debate
but through an unthinking tyranny of the majority, individual differences, according to liberal thinkers, became threatened by its power.
Whereas the eighteenth-century private person, understood to be an
economically and rationally autonomous male, could enter the public

sphere by virtue of his autonomy, public opinion in the nineteenth century is seen to wipe out individual autonomy.

Thus, even as it increased in size, the public sphere lost, Habermas says, "its political *function,* namely: that of subjecting the affairs that it had made public to the control of a critical public."[5] Becoming more and more an administrative apparatus, government by bureaucracy expanded the dimensions of public experience; but this expansion seemed uncontrolled by theory or rational planning. On the one hand, Marx and other socialists insisted on the need to dismantle bureaucracy. Liberals such as John Stuart Mill, on the other hand, proposed a new hierarchy in which an elite group of representative persons would determine public policy by public debate. With "the public" represented by persons who then represented ideas in debate, debate could still determine policy in "a public sphere literally declassed and structured into layers of representation."[6]

Both Trollope and Dickens attack bureaucratic organizations and administrations of power, and both deride the "reasoning" of public opinion. Newspapers, for example, an important eighteenth-century vehicle of political criticism, are published in *Barchester Towers* in the form of reasonable political criticism and debate, but they are an expression of special interests, which can be bought. Dickens's tourists indicate that public opinion is a wholly mindless phenomenon. But both writers insist that neither representation nor education can alter the practices of such institutions, because representation and education have themselves become institutionalized reproductions of mere forms of behavior. There are no "layers of representation" to be found, for example, among the tourists in *Little Dorrit* who repeat received forms. Emptied of representative function, signs and symbols are reproduced for the sake of their surfaces, like the images of commodities.

But if, for Trollope and Dickens, there are no layers of representation in public life, there are nevertheless various levels — surfaces and depths — of experience. Social class is a hierarchical structure, for example, with some persons set above others. Human character also has different levels, with emotional depths beneath the surface. For Trollope, depths of character are identifiable with class, although for Dickens they are not. In *Barchester Towers,* therefore, Trollope is able to identify a public order responsive to depths of personal feeling, and private persons capable of producing public order. In *Little Dorrit,* depths of personal experience have been emptied of public power.

Generic and Singular Identities

According to Trollope's depiction, bureaucratic dispersions and divisions of power serve self-interest and produce increasing individuality among persons. In his alliance of bureaucratic administrative practices with individual interests, institutional behavior can be attributed to individual behavior. In Barchester, the dispersion of power among the bishop, his wife, and his chaplain divides up the common ground on which Dr. Grantly might meet Dr. Proudie and settle differences. At their first meeting,

> There were four persons there, each of whom considered himself the most important personage in the diocese; himself, indeed, or herself, as Mrs Proudie was one of them; and with such a difference of opinion it was not probable that they would get on pleasantly together. The bishop himself actually wore the visible apron, and trusted mainly to that — to that and his title, both being facts which could not be overlooked. The archdeacon knew his subject, and really understood the business of bishoping, which the others did not; and this was his strong ground. Mrs Proudie had her sex to back her, and her habit of command, and was nothing daunted by the high tone of Dr Grantly's face and figure. Mr Slope had only himself and his own courage and tact to depend on, but he nevertheless was perfectly self-assured, and did not doubt but that he should soon get the better of weak men who trusted so much to externals, as both bishop and archdeacon appeared to do. (31)

With the bishop's "visible apron" and title representing nothing, the others in the room are free to think themselves Dr. Proudie's equal. Trollope identifies these characters according to their individual distinctions. What they may have in common is ignored, as indeed is any sense of the character of each person as a whole. Individual identity is a matter of one part of the self, chosen for the sake of distinction from others.

Nineteenth-century novels suggest that such identifications of persons in parts increased over time. For one thing, knowledge became increasingly productive of discriminations of parts of persons and things. In addition, the increase in economic consumption depended on a recognition of multiple parts and attributes of persons to identify them in exchangeable terms. But for Trollope, it is for reasons of self-interest that persons are seen, and see themselves, in parts, and this is nothing new. The force of Trollope's critique of contemporary political behavior depends on being able to demonstrate that nothing new is happening.[7] He undermines forms of progress not only by resisting the changes they cause but also by exposing those changes as false claims of change. Thus he stages the political struggle in Barchester as a replay of the same old Christian struggle between the individual will and the greater good. Whereas Dickens, as in *The Old Curiosity Shop*, sees persons divided into parts by a repressive reproduction of public order that increasingly works to deny individual will, Trollope sees individual will choosing to see the self in parts.

Institutions, then, are not necessarily alienating in their effects. Self-interest accounts for self-division and divisions among some persons in Barchester politics. But there is also a community of persons who have individual integrity and who are unified as a whole. Among these persons, who make up Dr. Grantly's party, institutional dispersions of power do not conflict with individual integrity. On the contrary, Dr. Grantly uses institutional power to protect personal integrity, and he uses personal integrity to consolidate his institutional power.

When Dr. Grantly first declares war, he is willing to do whatever it takes to defeat the opposition:

> Dr Proudie and his crew were of the lowest possible order of Church of England clergymen, and therefore it behoved him, Dr Grantly, to be of the very highest. Dr Proudie would abolish all forms and ceremonies, and therefore Dr Grantly felt the sudden necessity of multiplying them. (40)

Yet there are limits to what he can do:

> It was true that he could not himself intone the service, but he could procure the co-operation of any number of gentleman-like curates well-trained in the mystery of doing so. He would not willingly alter his own fashion of dress, but he could people Barchester with young clergymen dressed in the longest frocks. (40)

Dr. Grantly can remain just as he has always been, and not assume a false or externally determined identity, if he brings in others to do the actual opposing. Moreover, these clergymen will "really" oppose Slope, for Grantly can hire men who wear long coats and intone services for reasons of personal belief. Personal integrity is served by an institutional evasion of direct action, and vice versa. Here the division of labor seems ideally suited to individual freedom. There is a place for everyone to exercise his particular beliefs within a system requiring that diverse work be done.

It is on the other "side," among the bishop's people, that institutional and individual integrity are corrupted. Bishop Proudie, or Mrs. Proudie, has allowed Mr. Slope to take the bishop's place:

> Could [Dr. Grantly] have ignored the chaplain, and have fought the bishop, there would have been, at any rate, nothing degrading in such a contest. Let the Queen make whom she would Bishop of Barchester; a man, or even an ape, when once a bishop, would be a respectable adversary, if he would but fight, himself. But what was such a person as Dr Grantly to do, when such another person as Mr Slope was put forward as his antagonist?
>
> If he, our archdeacon, refused the combat, Mr Slope would walk triumphant over the field. . . .
>
> If, on the other hand, the archdeacon accepted as his enemy the man whom the new puppet bishop put before him as such, he would have to . . . in all matters treat with Mr Slope, as a being standing, in some degree, on ground similar to his own. He would have to meet Mr Slope; to — Bah! the idea was sickening. He could not bring himself to have to do with Mr Slope. (38)

Though there is a clear hierarchy of power in the structure of church positions, there is nothing to prevent a bishop from becoming a puppet or figurehead and letting others take his place. Proudie and his party identify persons in external, exchangeable terms. Dr. Grantly identifies persons according to "deeper" characteristics; his own men he identifies according to their beliefs, and Mr. Slope he identifies according to character rather than position.

If Dr. Grantly fights Mr. Slope in place of the bishop, he will participate in the indiscrimination that the bishop practices. But if the institutional structure of the church can be leveled by this kind of displacement, the class structure — in which people theoretically hold

positions by virtue of internal qualities rather than external appoint-
ments — can be held secure. Very early in the novel, Dr. Grantly "swore
deeply in the bottom of his heart, that no earthly consideration should
ever again induce him to touch the paw of that impure and filthy animal [Slope]" (36). And although he is wrong about a lot of things, Dr.
Grantly never does meet Mr. Slope again.

If positions are negotiable within the church structure, the position
of a gentleman is not. In the church, whether a clergyman is self-made
or made by descent "in a direct line from one of the apostles" is a matter of debate (113). But what makes a gentleman a gentleman is not
debatable. When Dr. Stanhope is expected home, for example, it is
thought that he might join either side in the "war." On the one hand,
he has Whig relatives allied to the bishop, and this is "sufficient to give
Mr. Slope high hope" (72). On the other hand, Dr. Stanhope was at
Oxford with Dr. Grantly. But Dr. Stanhope's choice is not made on
these bases. He has only to take one look at Mr. Slope to know they
have nothing in common:

> Mr Slope was presented, and was delighted to make the acquaintance of
> one of whom he had heard so much. The doctor bowed very low, and then
> looked as if he could not return the compliment as regarded Mr Slope, of
> whom, indeed, he had heard nothing. The doctor, in spite of his long ab-
> sence, knew an English gentleman when he saw him. (79–80)

The grounds on which Dr. Stanhope takes sides here, without thinking and also without speaking, are not debatable or divisible. They are
not even recognizable to Mr. Slope; Mr. Slope is no gentleman, and it
takes one to know one.

What Trollope identifies as the class of gentlemen in *Barchester Towers* is bound together by shared qualities of experience both internal and
external. What exactly it takes to be a gentleman is not delineated; one
is supposed to know without being told. And this is much of the power
and security of the class: that it transcends representation and inheres
in depths of character and experience that do not require representation to be recognized.[8] Recognition is subliminal and as automatic as
physical sensation. Intuitive rather than rational, this recognition suggests the comprehensive quality of gentility in its integration of emotional, sensual, and social experience.

Class Divisions

Pierre Bourdieu, in his analysis of twentieth-century consumption as a class phenomenon, has identified how "taste" governs consumption from both public and private directions. "Taste" acts as a denominator of social class and also as a mark of personal, subjective, even apparently natural preferences. The tasteful consumption of the upper classes, following the Kantian aesthetic, identifies persons at a distance from objects consumed. The "aesthetic aristocracy" in modern French society is detached from any need of objects as well as from their use and function; objects have aesthetic value only in form or style, not in substance.[9] As Daniel Miller explains, "The Kantian aesthetic is one of refusal, a forgoing of the immediate pleasure of the sensual and the evident in favour of a cultivated and abstracted appropriation through an achieved understanding." These various detachments of subject from object differentiate upper from lower classes as they differentiate high from popular culture. Consumption is more governed by need and use in lower classes, and, according to the aesthetic of lower-class taste, it is not form but "the substance and the signified which are of importance."[10]

Moreover, because these distinctions are understood as tastes, they are identified not with social order but with personal preference. It is because social class is experienced as essential to personal identity, through subjective, familial, and natural inclinations, that its reproduction is assured. As Arthur W. Frank emphasizes, "what Bourdieu calls 'habitus,' is the member's internalization, as natural, of the tastes of his or her class. . . . The member [of a class] is disposed to like that which she or he has grown up having, and by displaying these tastes, continues to mark her or himself as a member of that class." Moreover, the higher the class habitus, the more natural it appears: "In the contemporary class system, even 'breeding' may be effaced. Excellence should be carried as a natural inclination."[11]

Dickens dismantles assumptions of "habitus" in *Little Dorrit*. Critical of upper-class taste along the same lines that Bourdieu follows, Dickens insists that the identification of good taste with form and with disinterestedness obscures interest, effort, will, and history at work beneath the surfaces of form. But Trollope's depiction of class follows Bourdieu's analysis less closely. For Trollope, it is not the upper class but the lower classes that are identified with formal and superficial value. The "habitus" that Trollope cultivates within the upper class is characterized primarily by its inclusiveness, openness, and tolerance, whereas other people are exclusive, repressive, and judgmental. Part of the tolerant "nature" of gentlemen in *Barchester Towers* is that they do not judge much; they accept human faults, they enjoy worldly pleasures, they are moved by passions and interests as well as principles. In their "judgment," gentlemen do not rely on reason or representation, both of which processes are seen instead to characterize a "lower" middle-class form of thinking. Consulting depths of feeling in their judgment, as Dr. Stanhope does when he meets Mr. Slope, gentlemen seem to know intuitively the value of persons and things.

Moreover, gentlemen make use of the inherent, substantial qualities of persons and things. Dr. Grantly uses the beliefs of the "high" church-men who are his allies when he needs men to oppose Proudie, whereas the positions that persons take in Proudie's party are matters of form. The most important mark of inclusiveness among gentlemen is their loyalty to their class; gentlemen identify their interests in interests they share with others rather than in individual interests. In this, Trollope's gentlemen partake in a disinterestedness comparable to that of the Kantian aesthetic in its denial of need. However, as a class, gentlemen in the novel do experience and exercise an interest in institutional power and in political success.

Gendering Consensus

It is the gentleman's integration of parts of experience divided up by others that marks his superiority in *Barchester Towers*. Dr. Grantly is liberal in the comprehensiveness of his worldly and spiritual outlook (27). He holds power insofar as he respects the common experience of those he rules:

> He cordially despised any brother rector who thought harm of dinner-par-
> ties, or dreaded the dangers of a moderate claret-jug; consequently dinner-
> parties and claret-jugs were common in the diocese. He liked to give laws
> and to be obeyed in them implicity, but he endeavoured that his ordinances

should be within the compass of the man, and not unpalatable to the gentleman. He had ruled among his clerical neighbours now for sundry years, and as he had maintained his power without becoming unpopular, it may be presumed that he had exercised some wisdom. (27)

The implicit consensus among gentlemen here marks the inclusiveness of Dr. Grantly's politics, which extend to body as well as mind, appetite as well as rules, taste as well as judgment—sensual, consensual, and conscientious experience.

This consensus, of course, does not include everyone. But those who are not part of it are excluded, Trollope suggests, by virtue of their own exclusiveness, intolerance, and selfishness. The men who oppose Dr. Grantly's interest are narrow-minded, hypocritical, self-serving; they are inherently of a "lower" class. The power of the community and consensus of gentlemen in Barchester is most threatened, however, not by men of "low" character but by women, who do not clearly have any character at all. Men in the novel are divisible into lower and upper classes. Women are instead déclassée, disqualified from the class of gentlemen not exactly by depths of character but by a shallowness that excludes the deep feelings and affiliations that make gentlemen what they are. Even Mr. Slope has depths of passion—as when he falls in love with Madeline Neroni—that cause him to act, involuntarily, against both his interests and his principles. But women, as in many other Victorian novels, seem void of subjective depths. However, Trollope departs from most depictions of empty women by assigning them agency in their own emptiness. Women in *Barchester Towers* actively repress depths of feeling; they repress both themselves and others as they rule out-of-bounds behavior they disapprove. Identifying social class with depths of feeling, Trollope empties class of women and empties women of feeling to confirm that identification.

It is not by distinguishing between classes of men, then, but by distinguishing gentlemen from women that Trollope most clearly defines his superior characters. Gentlemen are united, and women are united with men who are not gentlemen: women and Mr. Slope become the dangerous alliance in Barchester. Whereas gentlemen value diverse elements of experience (and, by including disparate elements, moderate extremes of behavior), women, along with men who are not gentle-

men, are both exclusive and immoderate. Gentlemen take part in bureaucracy as a kind of game in which "wars" are not really won or lost,
competition is neither aggressive nor destructive, and opponents merely
go through the motions of opposition. In this they practice a disinterestedness, as they follow the rules rather than serve themselves. But
women, and Mr. Slope, are not good sports. They play to win, and they
mean to hurt people.

When Eleanor Bold slugs Mr. Slope for making "advances," she becomes the only character in the novel to engage in hand-to-hand com-
bat (213). Women in the novel tend to fight to the finish, like Charlotte Stanhope, who "knew well enough how to play the game, and
played it without mercy" (307). When the signora has had enough of
Mr. Slope, she, like Eleanor, does whatever she has to do to get rid of
him, even though by doing so she compromises herself (448). Women,
in fact, seem to accomplish much more in the novel, because they act
according to desired ends, whereas gentlemen act according to the rules.
The clarity of women's selfish ends focuses the fights in which they
take part.

This singleness of purpose is further reflected in singleness of other
kinds. Charlotte Stanhope and Miss Thorne are unmarried; Eleanor
Bold is a widow; the signora is separated from her husband. Mrs.
Proudie is, in a sense, equally independent, because she is absolutely
unwilling to defer to her husband or even to share power with him:
"she rules supreme over her titular lord, and rules with a rod of iron"
(19). Apparently related to the single-mindedness of their self-interest
is a way of thinking among women that simplifies—indeed, clearly
oversimplifies—their views of the world.

Miss Thorne is the most adamant idealist in the novel, primarily a
nostalgic idealist:

> She imagined that a purity had existed which was now gone.... She was ac-
> customed to speak of Cranmer as though he had been the firmest and most
> simple-minded of martyrs, and of Elizabeth as though the pure Protestant
> faith of her people had been the one anxiety of her life. It would have been...
> impossible to make her believe that the one was a time-serving priest, will-
> ing to go any length to keep his place, and that the other was in heart a pa-
> pist, with this sole proviso, that she should be her own pope. (196)

Such purity is also desired by Eleanor Bold, who repeatedly rebukes her relatives, especially Dr. Grantly, for unchristian conduct (fighting, prejudice, etc.). These women want people to live up to their names and to conform themselves to representations. Such single-mindedness, Trollope insists, is not only narrow-minded but also ignorant. With deeper understanding, more knowledge, and greater generosity, gentlemen see that the world is never what it ought to be and allow for differences between what things are called and what things actually are.

Identified with form, women are short on substance. Gentlemen are sensitive to immediate physical as well as mediate and symbolic meaning; they intuit as well as rationalize, have good taste as well as judgment. Women's superficiality accounts for their alliance with Mr. Slope:

> And so a party absolutely formed itself in Barchester on Mr Slope's side of the question! This consisted, among the upper classes, chiefly of ladies. No man — that is, no gentleman — could possibly be attracted by Mr Slope.... Ladies are sometimes less nice in their appreciation of physical disqualification; and, provided that a man speak to them well, they will listen, though he speak from a mouth never so deformed and hideous. (49)

Here and elsewhere practicing "the wiles of the serpent," Mr. Slope appeals to women by flattery and "a soft word in the proper place" (55). This is an old story. Willful, hungry for power, and insensitive, women are identified as shallow, having only part of the understanding that gentlemen have.

Women's dependence on words means that significance for them is external. If Mrs. Proudie, like Dr. Grantly, is unwilling to degrade herself within a social hierarchy, it is a different kind of sensibility that tells her what behavior is proper to one in her position:

> It would be a calumny on Mrs Proudie to suggest that she was sitting in her bedroom with her ear at the keyhole during this interview [between the bishop and Mr. Slope]. She had within her a spirit of decorum which prevented her from descending to such baseness. To put her ear to a keyhole, or to listen at a chink, was a trick for a housemaid. Mrs Proudie knew this, and therefore she did not do it; but she stationed herself as near to the door as she well could, that she might, if possible, get the advantage which the housemaid would have had, without descending to the housemaid's artifice. (147)

Here judgment is wholly externalized, a matter of external position—both social position and the position of the body listening—rather than of intuition or integrity. It is the form rather than the substance of the housemaid's behavior from which Mrs. Proudie wants to distinguish herself. Such attempts to identify value in externals locate value so that anyone can have it. As arbitrary as any symbolic code, Mrs. Proudie's sense of her own and others' positions makes any position available to anyone by denying positions' attachment to anything outside the code.

To an extent, female understanding in the novel promotes a "leveling" of experience. Many women, including Mrs. Proudie, Mrs. Quiverful, Eleanor, and the signora, refuse to subordinate themselves to men; thus they resist the patriarchal hierarchy of power. But female idealism is linked to a merely symbolic understanding of experience that represses things as they are, to impose an identity on things as they ought to be. Women institute repression. Mrs. Proudie, who "rules with a rod of iron," is far more repressive and authoritarian in her treatment of others than is any man in the novel. And Eleanor must repress her personal feelings to be fair to Mr. Slope:

> She thought of this man . . . exactly as her father did, exactly as the Grantlys did. At least she esteemed him personally as they did. But she believed him to be in the main an honest man, and one truly inclined to assist her father. . . . It was nauseous to her to have a man like Mr Slope commenting on her personal attractions; and she did not think it necessary to dilate with her father upon what was nauseous. She never supposed they could disagree on such a subject. . . . In encountering such a man she had encountered what was disagreeable, as she might do in walking the streets. But in such encounters she never thought it necessary to dwell on what disgusted her. (265–66)

Here it is evident that Eleanor shares the physical revulsion gentlemen feel around Mr. Slope, but she buries it beneath the fairness she wishes to practice. The power of the "habitus" that makes her tastes the same as her father's is something she excludes from her knowledge. Eleanor thus divides herself into unspoken and spoken, public and personal parts, and refuses to deal with the conflicting elements of her own character.

The Tolerance of Commonness

It is an alliance of personal and common experience that Trollope wishes to put into public play in place of the symbolic values of women in *Barchester Towers*. According to his representation, common values are denied public play by self-interest. It is eventually clear, for example, that Eleanor represses much of what she has in common with Dr. Grantly not on any principle of fairness but to stake out her fair share of power, to distinguish herself and claim her independence from her family.

Trollope counters such desires with commonness. In the things Eleanor claims as distinctions—the things she insists she does differently from Dr. Grantly—she is little different from him. She claims fairness but judges him unfairly. Thus she remains blind to the dangers of Mr. Slope, deciding that Dr. Grantly has warned her against him only to make her do what Dr. Grantly wants (272). Assigning prejudice to Dr. Grantly in her own prejudice against him, Eleanor is exposed as the archdeacon's double.

Distinguishing the self is identified as a negative process depending on a repression of likeness, rather than as an assertion of any positive character. Trollope attempts to create a common identity capable of including rather than repressing differences. Crucial to this project is the narrative resolution of communal disturbance by means of common knowledge. Like Dickens, Trollope is concerned to identify a kind of knowledge that is not objective, to be located within persons rather than around objects. In *The Old Curiosity Shop* such knowledge must be subjective because it must be imaginative. But Trollope identifies a body of knowledge that is more consensual than individual.

This knowledge consists of a lot of maxims, clichés, and truisms: " 'Better the d—— you know than the d—— you don't know,' is an old saying, and perhaps a true one; but the bishop had not yet realized the truth of it" (231); and

> There is an old song which gives us some very good advice about courting:
>
> > It's gude to be off with the auld luve
> > Before ye be on wi' the new.
>
> Of the wisdom of this maxim Mr. Slope was ignorant. (240–41)

Such sayings always turn out to be right in *Barchester Towers,* and those who don't know their wisdom are self-interested individuals, such as the bishop and his chaplain.

To such dependable common knowledge is added a consensus that Trollope develops with his readers. Thus, he can say of Mr. Harding,

> it must be remembered that such a marriage as that which the archdeacon contemplated with disgust, which we who know Mr Slope so well would regard with equal disgust, did not appear so monstrous to Mr Harding, because in his charity he did not hate the chaplain as the archdeacon did, and as we do. (151)

The cultivation of such consensus does not pretend to be fair; this common "judgment" is distinctly partisan, short on rationality, and prejudiced. Trollope cultivates partiality: "My readers will guess from what I have written that I myself do not like Mr Slope" (55). And he does so by cultivating taste—specifically, in the case of Mr. Slope, disgust—as a virtually physical, natural, unconscious set of reactions to experience: "I never could endure to shake hands with Mr Slope. A cold, clammy perspiration always exudes from him, the small drops are ever to be seen standing on his brow, and his friendly grasp is unpleasant" (25). It is not judgment that is invited here. Explaining nothing, Trollope identifies a distaste that assumes certain class distinctions, especially in that what arouses disgust is effort and an excess of interest. But this distaste is experienced by sensation and so seems neither voluntary nor learned.

Trollope thereby implies a "habitus" that seems natural. It is crucial to the value of class as an order of experience that its origins be obscured, so that they seem to lie beneath the forms that Trollope identifies with the newcomers to Barchester and with women. With its unconscious depths, class identifies persons and groups as unities rather than parts. Inasmuch as women are depicted as incapable of the gentility that distinguishes gentlemen, they therefore fill an important place in the community. Doing the work—getting rid of Slope—that gentlemen cannot bear to touch, women are necessary to gentlemen, not because they are forced into use but because they freely choose to do the dirty work.

It is not that gentlemen do nothing; gentlemen struggle in this novel. Indeed, the consensus that binds them together requires the active exercise of struggle, within the church and within the individual conscience. The class in which these struggles occur is marked by the fact that the struggles are not physical. Nevertheless, Mr. Arabin defends squabbling:

> "More scandal would fall on the Church if there were no such contentions. We have but one way to avoid them — that of acknowledging a common head of our Church, whose word on all points of doctrine shall be authoritative..."
> ... He paused and stood silent for a while, thinking of the time when he had so nearly sacrificed all he had, his powers of mind, his free agency, ... his very inner self, for an easy path in which no fighting would be needed [a reference to his near conversion to Roman Catholicism]...."There is nothing god-like about us: we differ from each other with the acerbity common to man — we triumph over each other with human frailty." (184)

Here the human nature "common to man" is the justification for fighting. Within the self and in relations with others, multiple sides are natural. The conflict in which gentlemen participate, therefore, is both an extension of human nature and a practice inclusive of the whole character of man.

Mr. Arabin has in fact made the mistake of taking an "easy path," because, although he did not go over to Rome, he has led a one-sided life. At the beginning of the novel, he is in the sad situation, at the age of forty, of having "fallen between two stools" (178). Having spent his life concentrating on spiritual and scholarly matters, he now finds himself interested in worldly pleasures such as a wife and family and material comforts. Having been too narrow in his interests, he is now unable to find happiness in either the spiritual or the worldly sphere. Had Mr. Arabin kept both parts of himself in play, in open struggle, he would now be whole. Struggle constitutes the terms in which wholeness is realized.

Given these terms, there is really no one who does not or cannot belong in this community, willingly or not. The community's inclusiveness can be identified with the exercise of "free agency," but community nevertheless seems an imposition, something nobody can get out of. Community thereby resembles the discipline that Foucault identifies in modern punitive and disciplinary systems that developed from reductive impositions of law to expansive and productive exercises of discipline. Modern discipline covers much more ground. It emphasizes not the extraordinary breaking of laws but the ordinary practice and observation of them, becoming more inclusive than exclusive.

Under discipline, for example, people are punished not only for what they do but also for what they do not do. Discipline includes not only deprivations but also rewards. And discipline is exercised as a constant means of actively controlling daily life. "Disciplinary punishment has the function of reducing gaps" and does so, in part, by opening up the whole range of behavior to scrutiny and quantification: "[I]nstead of the simple division of the prohibition, as practised in penal justice, we have a distribution between a positive pole and a negative pole; all behaviour falls in the field between good and bad marks, good and bad points."[12] Law identifies certain things one can't do; discipline identifies the relative value of everything one does.

Foucault's analysis of the inclusiveness of discipline suggests the disciplinary character of Trollope's consensus and even his freedom of choice. To choose to differ, as do Mr. Arabin and Eleanor Bold, seems on the one hand to move a person outside the norm of the group; both characters are rebels against norms. On the other hand, Trollope locates their behavior not in extremes or margins, but instead "between two stools" (178). Arabin is divided between worldly and spiritual interests, and Eleanor Bold is divided between her desire to be fair and her repulsion for Mr. Slope. The two characters fall between two stools because they have repressed part of what they are. To be exceptional in this novel is to be lacking. To be normal is to be a "full" character, a struggling combination of different parts. Normality emphasizes not sameness but inclusive difference, ranging widely and relatively over the possibilities that lie between opposite alternatives, bridging gaps and suspending choices with a constant juggling of the various parts of self and of community.

Dickens's Upper Class

In *Little Dorrit,* the upper class of gentlemen exists as a dominant social class whose power is obscured by bureaucratic institutions such as the Circumlocution Office but that profits from this obscurity. It is clear to the gentlemen inside the government administration that its apparent functions are not its real purposes. The "airy young Barnacle" at the Circumlocution Office, for example,

> had "got up" the Department in a private secretaryship, that he might be ready for any little bit of fat that came to hand; and he fully understood the Department to be a politico-diplomatic hocus pocus piece of machinery for the assistance of the nobs in keeping off the snobs. (157–58)

This governing class serves its interests by producing class distinctions rather than any substantial product. To maintain distances between two similar groups, nobs and snobs, gentlemen in *Little Dorrit* present themselves in accordance with a kind of Kantian aesthetic. Their value is marked by their uselessness, their lack of substance, their devotion to form. Most of all, gentlemen appear careless and indifferent, like the "airy young Barnacle," as if unconcerned in the production of differences on which their power depends. This indifference, more than anything else, marks gentility.

For Dickens, the upper class is a fraud. Beneath surfaces of disinterestedness, he identifies powerful interests in the bureaucratic reproduction of "nothing but forms" (804). The obscurity of gentility is evident in the places it occupies. Though gentlemen locate gentility in positions they assume, in the novel Dickens puts the most dedicated gentlemen in jail. For the debtor William Dorrit, as for the criminal Rigaud, to be a gentleman is to do nothing but go through the forms and routines that distinguish gentlemen from others. As Rigaud brags to his cellmate in the Marseilles prison,

> "Have I ever done anything here? Ever touched the broom, or spread the mats, or rolled them up...?"
> "Never!"
> "Have you ever thought of looking to me to do any kind of work?"
> John Baptist answered with... the most expressive negative in the Italian language.
> "No! You knew from the first moment when you saw me here, that I was a gentleman?" (47)

Mr. Dorrit also assumes his position as "Father of the Marshalsea" by never working and by establishing certain forms of behavior:

All newcomers were presented to him. He was punctilious in the exaction of this ceremony. . . . He received them in his poor room (he disliked an introduction in the mere yard, as informal — a thing that might happen to anybody), with a kind of bowed-down beneficence. . . .

It became a not unusual circumstance for letters to be put under his door at night, enclosing half-a-crown, two half-crowns. . . . He received the gifts as tributes, from admirers, to a public character. (105–6)

Mr. Dorrit and Rigaud are able to reproduce their gentility in and from unlikely circumstances, because they deal exclusively in forms. The most successful gentlemen in the novel are those able to present themselves as if they are images, especially aesthetic objects that confirm their distance and indifference. Arthur Clennam calls on Mr. Tite Barnacle, who "seemed to have been sitting for his portrait to Sir Thomas Lawrence all the days of his life" (152). Mr. Casby also sits at home most of the time, in front of a portrait of himself as a child, "which anybody seeing him would have identified as Master Christopher Casby, aged ten," because he has "changed very little in his progress through life" (186). The absolute image of a patriarch, Mr. Casby has "been accosted in the streets, and respectfully solicited to become a Patriarch for painters and for sculptors" (187).

Representation as an image is desirable not for knowledge but for obscurity. In *The Old Curiosity Shop,* public character is stabilized through representations of persons as fixed images; the images comprise knowledge. In *Little Dorrit,* the practice of referring identity to an image seems desirable because it produces doubt. William Dorrit imagines himself as a portrait, wishing that he had been painted. It is when Amy sees that her father wants her to give sexual encouragement to men so that they will do him favors, that he first introduces the idea of this picture:

"If I had but a picture of myself in those days, though it was ever so ill done, you would be proud of it. . . . Now, let me be a warning! Let no man . . . fail to preserve at least that little of the times of his prosperity and respect. Let his children have that clue to what he was. Unless my face, when I am dead, subsides into that long departed look . . . my children will have never seen me." (272)

It is not exactly a substitution of image for reality that is attempted here. To refer to the picture is to produce, more than anything else, a difference: a difference between what William Dorrit is and what others know, a difference that always stands in place of knowledge as a barrier to it. For this purpose—the production of unknowability—it is preferable that there be no actual picture.

This is to deny what characters in *The Old Curiosity Shop* assert: that the evidence of the senses constitutes a determinate body of knowledge. Here the image functions as a commodity valued for its indefinition, according to which its qualities are variable and exchangeable. To pose as the subject of a portrait by Lawrence is to present oneself as a kind of image that is not realized as an object at all. Barnacle looks like, but isn't, a Lawrence portrait. Thus, others attribute to Barnacle characteristics of Lawrence's subjects and pictures, but with no certainty that these attributes belong to Barnacle himself.

As in the mirroring process that has been theorized as part of commodity consumption in the twentieth century, such images of the self reflect potential, temporary, experimental, or "tried-on" selves characterized most of all by convertibility. The capacity of images to provisionally attribute rather than represent character is particularly marked in Mr. Meagles's art collection, which he likes to show to visitors:

> There were views, like and unlike, of a multitude of places; and there was one little picture-room devoted to a few of the regular sticky old Saints, with sinews like whipcord . . . and such coats of varnish that every holy personage served for a fly-trap, and became what is now called in the vulgar tongue a Catch-em-alive O. Of these pictorial acquisitions Mr Meagles spoke in the usual manner. He was no judge, he said, except of what pleased himself; he had picked them up, dirt-cheap, and people *had* considered them rather fine. One man, who at any rate ought to know something of the subject, had declared that "Sage, Reading" . . . to be a fine Guercino. As for Sebastian del Piombo there, you would judge for yourself; if it were not his later manner, the question was, Who was it? Titian, that might or might not be—perhaps he had only touched it. Daniel Doyce said perhaps he hadn't touched it, but Mr Meagles rather declined to overhear the remark. (237)

Claiming little knowledge of his pictures, Mr. Meagles is able to suggest that they might be anything. As he attributes indefinite value to them, he displays his own indifference and carelessness about them. The distance Mr. Meagles creates between himself and his works of art is not exactly that of the Kantian aesthetic. But he reproduces characteristics of the upper class that he wishes to inhabit. His paintings allow him to put on a display for visitors as if he were the aristocratic owner of a country house. For Dickens, the "habitus" that Trollope identifies with history, nature, and inherent value is itself exchangeable, an image reproduced as a new self-image.

Yet the attributes Mr. Meagles assumes here are not, for the most part, positive attributes but rather lacks, or the appearance of lacks: distances, uncertainties, indifference. These attributes, like his aristocratic pose, are reflected by the paintings. The indifference of Mr. Meagles implies the undifferentiated values of the paintings. His apparent lack of need implies their uselessness, and vice versa. The paintings become equivalent and exchangeable as they are disconnected from history, from their own production, and from productive use (except, in the eyes of the narrator, as fly catchers). No longer attributable to the persons who painted them, they become attributable to potentially anyone, even Titian. But Mr. Meagles doesn't claim to have a Titian. He seems to use the name Titian to render attribution uncertain, and he himself becomes correspondingly difficult to know.

The unknowability of the painting provides it with more distinction than knowledge could produce. The object of such an evaluative process is to keep the indefinition going. Like Trollope's women, these men — Dorrit, Barnacle, Meagles — are responsible for limiting value to signs. They become the prototype of the modern consumer. Dickens does not gender consumerism so much as he classes it. The upper class and those who would belong to it in *Little Dorrit* promote consumerism in their demand for exchangeable and useless things. The apparent disinterestedness of upper-class consumption not only functions as economic demand, it also demands useless commodities and is responsible for the distance between use and value that allows for an increasing market of useless objects.

The Production of Unknowability

In Dickens's depiction of increasing obscurity in both public and private life, multiple social and psychological realms experience the same kind of runaround that Arthur Clennam is given at the Circumlocution Office. This does not just happen; Dickens identifies human productivity in conditions others accept as natural or inevitable. What appear as limits to knowledge, therefore, are identified as set by, and in the interests of, individuals.

The way the buck is passed in the bureaucracy is reproduced, for example, in the mind of Mrs. General, who "had a little circular set of mental grooves or rails on which she started little trains of other people's opinions, which never overtook one another, and never got anywhere" (503). In Mrs. General, as in other models of propriety and good taste, mobility and displacement provide identity that once depended on secure placement. Just as Mr. Meagles attributes to his belongings not security but uncertainty, other characters are interested in appearing to belong nowhere. Displacement has become the most desirable "status," for example, among the upper-class inhabitants of Hampton Court:

> The venerable inhabitants of that venerable pile seemed, in those times, to be encamped there like a sort of civilised gipsies. There was a temporary air about their establishments, as if they were going away the moment they could get anything better. . . . Genteel blinds and makeshifts were more or less observable as soon as their doors were opened; screens not half high enough, which made dining rooms out of arched passages, . . . curtains which called upon you to believe that they didn't hide anything; panes of glass which requested you not to see them; many objects of various forms, feigning to have no connection with their guilty secret, a bed. . . . Mental reservations and artful mysteries grew out of these things. Callers looking into the eyes of their receivers, pretended not to smell cooking three feet off; people, confronting closets accidentally left open, pretended not to see bottles. . . . There was no end to the small social accommodation-bills of this nature which the gipsies of gentility were constantly drawing upon, and accepting for, one another. (359)

Here Dickens depicts a kind of "habitus" in the intricate connections of living spaces, habits, manners, and mental life that seem to grow out of one another in this upper-class life. He places these people, whereas they displace themselves. Not only do they use their places and objects to create an appearance of displacement, they also cultivate a reflective uncertainty in subjects. The tasteful interior decoration in these rooms makes objects into mere surfaces; then these forms reform the mental experience of their observers. Knowledge is obstructed in

part by the screens and blinds in the room. More crucial to the cultivation of obscurity, however, is the process of rendering persons unable
to trust their senses. Not only sensible material but even sensation itself is obscured.

As in the passage quoted earlier describing tourists being blindfolded
and tongue-tied, here passages are blocked. One arched passage has
become closed off as a dining room. Other passages are blocked when
people cannot see through obstructions. The obstructive process checks
vision not by hiding things but by making apparent both things and
the screens that hide them. Both the supposedly hidden and the supposedly hiding things are on the surface of sensible reality, which presents on one level what are supposed to be two different levels of phenomena: the apparent and the hidden. This surfacing of apparent and
hidden forms is exacerbated by the insistence that neither is supposed
to be seen. Some things—functional things, such as beds and bottles—
are supposed to be hidden. Other things function to hide them. The
curtains and closets that cover up things are themselves only "more or
less observable," however; their function is altogether obscured, because
people are not supposed to see that there is a screening process going
on. At least, people assume they are not supposed to see this. Useful
and material things, and the sensation of useful and material things,
are by this process rendered useless and immaterial. In addition, subjective assumptions and suppositions about these things are rendered
dubious. The process of attribution is forced into immaterial and doubt-
ful identifications.

The "genteel blinds and makeshifts" in this situation, from which
grow "mental reservations and artful mysteries," suggest the cultivations
of obscurity that have become a standard process of creating a social
identity in Dickens's society. This process develops along the lines of
Frank Churchill's behavior in Austen's *Emma*. Social relations are treated
as series of blinds to mislead others about what one is and what one is
doing. Such a desire to blind society, as Austen suggests, may stem less
from a wish to hide a particular secret, such as Frank's engagement to
Jane Fairfax, than from an insecurity about one's identity, such as Frank
experiences as both the son of his father and the adopted son of the
Churchills. Given such insecurity, unknowability becomes the most

desirable identity. It is desirable both because it renders the self unknowable and because it transfers responsibility for the limits of knowledge to the mind of the observer. Others may recognize the process, but they cannot know Frank Churchill. Or, in the case of Dickens's gypsies, others can identify the mystification that is occurring without being able to identify, except as displaced persons, the people who cause the mystification. What occurs is a displacement of knowledge itself, from substance to form, from cause and effect to continuous process.

Bureaucratic versus Human Agency

For Dickens, the only way to know what is going on is to identify human agents responsible for these displacements. Such knowledge is more difficult to acquire in *Little Dorrit* than in *Emma,* however, because people no longer identify themselves as responsible agents. The public and institutional character of what in *Little Dorrit* Dickens treats as a cultivation of obscurity can be indicated by a brief consideration of influential scientific knowledge at midcentury. If political theorists such as Marx and Mill resisted the disconnection of activity from human agency, physical theorists did not. Theories of the conservation of energy, which came into prominence in the 1840s and were increasingly influential in the following decades, were concerned less with causality, accepting that an essential cause is unknowable, than with dynamic transformations of energy in all matter.

For Herbert Spencer, who was most influential in the spread of the idea of conservation of energy, will is inseparable from processes of change and differentiation in the world at large. For Spencer, will, like body, is a "condition" of experience, as Bruce Haley says, "in which one form of energy changed into another kind."[13] As mind and body became increasingly difficult to differentiate according to the conservation of energy, internal experience became increasingly subject to quantification. Jonathan Crary points out the importance of thermodynamics to the quantification of sensual experience in the work of the psychophysicist Gustav Fechner, among others, at midcentury. As in the law of conservation of energy, "Fechner's formalization of perception renders the specific contents of vision irrelevant."[14]

However, there is, according to the conservation of energy, a non-quantifiable energy that passes through all forms and renders them only relatively knowable. In Spencer's *First Principles* (1862), "the key concept, uniting mind, matter and motion, was Force,... which 'can be regarded only as a conditioned effect of the Unconditioned Cause—as the relative reality indicating to us an Absolute Reality by which it is immediately produced.' "[15] Only the relative reality is knowable. Knowledge shifts to focus on effects rather than causes.[16]

Like the bureaucratic dispersion or "leveling" of power into positions with relative but never absolute responsibility, the theory of conservation of energy effectively equates all phenomena as relatively similar forms of a common, constantly transferred energy. According to this theory, the inseparability of particular phenomena from the "closed circuit" of transforming energy means that particular phenomena have no causal power and little qualitative difference from one another. As in Adam Smith's theory of the self-regulating economy, individual elements of the system should not interfere in its workings, which will be beneficial as they develop "naturally." Following the assumptions of Smith's division of labor, Spencer advocates inactivity and noninterference in relation to the system as a whole.[17]

Whereas Emma can learn to discriminate between "blinds" and what people hide beneath them, then, it is no longer common knowledge in 1857 that the obscurity of cause and agency is either the result of human action or reparable by human action. In bureaucratic agencies and in personal relations, persons may become mere means through which forces pass. Dickens resists this form of knowledge by identifying it, too, as a belief cultivated by powerful persons in the interest of obscuring power. The most powerful characters in *Little Dorrit* appear self-denying and disinterested and identify themselves as mere means, rather than ends, of action. This is true of the men in the Circumlocution Office, of those such as Mrs. General who influence public opinion, and even of the self-made millionaire "man of prodigious enterprise," Mr. Merdle: "He was the most disinterested of men,—did everything for Society, and got as little for himself out of all his gain and care, as a man might" (292–93). In private life, those who exercise dominant and repressive will also deny it; Mrs. Clennam, for example, always identifies herself as carrying out the will of God.

If these characters are frauds, there are nevertheless other characters who are unable to exercise will and who believe themselves powerless. Arthur Clennam, the hero of the novel, claims at the beginning, "I have no will" (59). In the private lives of Little Dorrit and of Arthur, Dickens represents the apparently impersonal and systematic agency of social institutions as the personal responsibility of powerful individuals, a father and a mother, who use other people to obscure their responsibility and who cultivate insecurity of will in their children.

Mr. Dorrit and Mrs. Clennam cultivate distance between themselves and their children as it is cultivated in the interior decoration of Hampton Court. The screening process evident in those rooms is evident in these parents' repeated use of things and persons to come between parent and child. Mr. Dorrit's imaginary portrait mediates others' knowledge of him; when he puts it between himself and others, he can assert that his children do not know him. Later, when touring Italy, Mr. Dorrit finds Mrs. General convenient to place between himself and Amy, because Amy knows too much about his past:

> "Amy," said Mr Dorrit, "you have just now been the subject of some conversation between myself and Mrs General. We agree that you scarcely seem at home here. Ha—how is this?"
>
> A pause.
>
> "I think, father, I require a little time."
>
> "Papa is a preferable mode of address," observed Mrs General. "Father is rather vulgar, my dear. The word Papa, besides, gives a pretty form to the lips. Papa, potatoes, poultry, prunes, and prism are all very good words for the lips. . . ."
>
> "Pray, my child," said Mr Dorrit, "attend to the—hum—precepts of Mrs General." (528–29)

After Mrs. General is deferred to, she distances Amy from her father not only by getting between them but also by formalizing their relation. She provides forms of relation that displace relations made up of past associations, feelings, and time. These forms do not screen anything; that is, they do not function to cover up the past and feelings. They work simply to effect "the formation of a surface" (530).

This creates a relation neither of knowledge nor of ignorance but of sheer, permanent, and abstract difference. After her father is converted into "Papa" in this code, Little Dorrit cannot distinguish him from the other words that produce a nice form of the mouth; when she next speaks to him, she "very nearly addressed [him] as poultry" (529). This very confusion, like the confusion of Titians and Sebastian del Piombos by Mr. Meagles, secures Mr. Dorrit from recognition by maintaining difference as mere form. "I have come to be at a distance from him," Little Dorrit says of her father (523).

Arthur Clennam's mother also cultivates such distance. She uses Flint-winch in much the same manner that Mr. Dorrit uses Mrs. General, to keep a distance between herself and other people, especially her son. But at the Clennam house, internal as well as external distances are cultivated. Distances are reproduced internally as an extraordinary lack of confidence that has developed in both Arthur, the son of the house, and Affery, a longtime servant. Arthur has apparently been transformed into a "nobody" by the treatment he receives from his mother, even now in his middle age.[18] But her story is one of her own repression or displacement: of a husband who loved another woman in place of her, and of the reaction to his adultery that she claims was the Lord's, not hers: "Not unto me the strength be ascribed; not unto me the wringing of the expiation," she insists (845). Nor is Arthur hers, though she has "devoted" herself "to bring him up in fear and trembling, and in a life of practical contrition" (846). In the pattern of Mrs. Clennam's experience, people do not occupy places that belong to them, and this interchangeability places "nobodies" in positions of responsibility.

Like Trollope, Dickens suggests that evangelical deferrals of happiness to the afterlife and of individual will to God's will function to cover up self-interest. But unlike Trollope, Dickens suggests that those who practice repression of will in name only may nevertheless effectively repress will in others. Whether phony in Mrs. Clennam or not, her repressiveness creates a deep sense of emptiness in Arthur, as she herself says: "With an empty place in his heart that he has never known the meaning of, he has turned away from me" (860). Little Dorrit, on the other hand, does not experience a lack of will, despite her father's

treatment of her. But Mr. Dorrit varies in his behavior, at times reject-
ing Amy and at times feeling such insecurity himself that he acknowledges his dependence on her. Mr. Dorrit's dependence on Amy while
he lives in prison is difficult to obscure, moreover, because Amy brings
home the money and food he lives on.

A different kind of internal gap has been caused in Affery's mind by
life in the Clennam house. It is not her emotions but, as is the case
with visitors to Hampton Court, her senses that are dubious. Affery
sees Flintwinch with his brother at night, for example, but she is not
sure she has actually seen them and refers to the incident as a dream.
This idea is planted in her mind first by Flintwinch, who finds her on
the stairs and, wishing to deny her knowledge, insists that she has
been sleepwalking (83–84). But Affery's inability to trust her senses is
also due to her physical environment:

> The debilitated old house in the city, wrapped in its mantle of soot, and
> leaning heavily on the crutches that had partaken of its decay and worn out
> with it, never knew a healthy or a cheerful interval, let what would betide.
> If the sun ever touched it, it was but with a ray, and that was gone in half
> an hour.... You should alike find rain, hail, frost, and thaw lingering in
> that dismal enclosure when they had vanished from other places; and as to
> snow, you should see it there for weeks, long after it had changed from yel-
> low to black.... As to street noises, the rumbling of wheels in the lane merely
> rushed in at the gateway in going past, and rushed out again: making the
> listening Mistress Affery feel as if she were deaf, and recovered the sense of
> hearing by instantaneous flashes. So with whistling, singing, talking, laugh-
> ing, and all pleasant human sounds. They leaped the gap in a moment, and
> went upon their way. (220–21)

There are no significant intervals here: no "healthy or cheerful inter-
val" in the dismal surroundings of the house, for example, to provide
a break in the constant, walled-in environment. The only gap left open
is the one in the wall, a blank space through which come bits of sound,
which is all there is space or time for. These bits of sound produce in
Affery "mental reservations" similar to those produced by the blinds
and screens of the "genteel gipsies." Breaking apart impressions of experience that last more than a moment, the wall makes Affery think
she can only partially hear.

Emptying out Experience

One characteristic of Dickens's writing is a proliferation of things. Gillian Beer and George Levine have both identified this with Darwin's interest in heterogeneous forms of life.[19] A proliferation of various forms is also evident in Herbert Spencer's emphasis on the increasing differentiation of forms in both the natural and social worlds. In *Little Dorrit*, however, something different is evident. Dickens seems less interested in the production of things and forms than in the production of gaps or holes in the fabric of material reality. There is still an excess of things, as in the long passage describing the Hampton Court apartments, but there is a more emphatic proliferation of breaks between things. The various mediations I have discussed are one mark of this attention to what lies between things, though mediators such as the screens at Hampton Court or Mrs. General are, of course, also things or forms that come between things; they produce blanks, in that they are things that break things apart in the understanding and also break apart the understanding itself.

As the senses become unreliable, the parts of perception become inadequate to comprehension. Foucault suggests that routines of discipline fill up experience, leaving few gaps. Dickens insists that routine and sameness can appropriate differences in time, space, and subjectivity only by means of processes that delimit and regulate differences. Differences are opened up into gaps between persons and things in order to create blanks to be filled in with forms, which also have blanks to be filled in with forms. The process is not inclusive except of the differences it produces in the first place. It produces no opening in the symbolic dimension, no passage through to any other means of comprehension. According to this process, people become more aware of what they do not know than of what they know, more aware of lacks of knowledge than of knowledge. In part, what is being recorded here is an increasingly relative reality. But Dickens makes a distinction between kinds of relations. He sees that new forms of relativism tend to identify some emptiness between things; what comes between, therefore, in effect denies or at least interferes with the causal relatedness of things.

This change in Dickens's representation of things can be identified in the opening description of Marseilles in *Little Dorrit*:

Thirty years ago, Marseilles lay burning in the sun, one day. A blazing sun upon a fierce August day was no greater rarity in southern France then, than at any other time, before or since. Everything in Marseilles, and about Marseilles, had stared at the fervid sky, and been stared at in return, until a staring habit had become universal there. Strangers were stared out of countenance by staring white houses, staring white walls, staring white streets, staring tracts of arid road....

...Hindoos, Russians, Chinese, Spaniards, Portuguese, Englishmen, Frenchmen, Genoese, Neapolitans, Venetians, Greeks, Turks... sought the shade alike—taking refuge in any hiding-place from a sea too intensely blue to be looked at, and a sky of purple, set with one great flaming jewel of fire.

The universal stare made the eyes ache....

Blinds, shutters, curtains, awnings, were all closed and drawn to keep out the stare. Grant it but a chink or keyhole, and it shot in like a white-hot arrow. The churches were the freest from it. To come out of the twilight of pillars and arches... was to plunge into a fiery river, and swim for life to the nearest strip of shade....

In Marseilles that day there was a villainous prison. In one of its chambers, so repulsive a place that even the obtrusive stare blinked at it, and left it to such refuse of reflected light as it could find for itself, were two men....

...A prison taint was on everything there. The imprisoned air, the imprisoned light, the imprisoned damps, the imprisoned men, were all deteriorated by confinement.... Like a well, like a vault, like a tomb, the prison had no knowledge of the brightness outside, and would have kept its polluted atmosphere intact in one of the spice islands of the Indian ocean. (39–41)

Here the bleakness of the landscape seems natural.[20] Apparently not the product of human action, it also does not produce action or movement, except of an extremely limited kind. The energy of the sun has the effect not of energizing but of deadening action. Thus, though there is a multiplicity of things, there is a monotony of action.

The blankness of the scene is due mostly to the blankness of the stare that is repeated all over the place: an inactive relation of mutual staring evokes a mood of indifference and exhaustion that is passively developed. Even the human action that occurs is helplessly repetitive: the rushing from one shade to another, seeking relief from the stare.

The "blankness" of the scene is also evident in the language used to describe it. *Stare* is repeated again and again. In addition, the list of persons affected by the stare is a series of unindividuated names, providing distinctions by place rather than, for example, by actions. Another list — "blinds, shutters, curtains, awnings" — also consists of different forms of the same thing, as far as action or function is concerned. Dickens participates here in the formalization of difference that abstracts difference from action, producing a static, monotonous, and peculiarly abstract description. The stare itself, of course, can be considered an indication of abstraction, though one within persons, because this staring is not clearly intentional but seems merely due to an absence of thought, motive, or interest.

The action of this scene is confined to one set of variations, in the move from sun to shade, from discomfort to relief, and back again. "Sun and Shadow," which is the title of the first chapter, constitute an opposition that is utterly relative and self-sustaining. The opposition sustains itself in the sense that shadow exists only as a lack of sun, but as long as there is shadow there is sun. Though the opening scene may seem to be a natural situation, it is not so, I argue, but is instead about a process of human differentiation in which people create shadows, first, to create clear and distinct positions in relation to one another and, second, to make themselves unknowable. This occurs in the kind of binary opposition that provides difference in a symbolic code.

In *Little Dorrit*, then, the production of difference is equated with indifference because of the purely formal character of differentiation. When emotional dimensions of experience have been rendered indifferent, indifference itself becomes the chief subjective response to experience: people don't care. Other subjective experience is also emptied out. Dickens's sense of human creativity leads him to see that those in power who resist change by denying their capacity to make changes are in fact emptying humanity of that capacity.

Filling in the Blanks Otherwise

Dickens's identification of a cultivation of obscurity in society means that knowledge is not simply repressed, like a hidden secret. Instead of true facts hidden behind false fronts, truth is obscured, as in the houses of the genteel gypsies, by a complete system of production that produces both the hidden and the apparent. Repression surfaces, in a sense, as relativism. What is obscured by relativism is not beneath but already on the surface, with no identity except as a differential and so no possibility of positive realization.

As a closed circuit, such a system of references never indicates anything missing. The work of bureaucracy has the same effect. The problem is not that the Circumlocution Office does nothing but that it does so much, is such a full-time occupation that it becomes difficult to recognize the absence of action. The work of symbolic codes that contain difference within oppositions of positives and negatives has the same effect. Seemingly complete in its relative differences, such a code leaves no place for substantial shades of meaning that it has obscured by emptying shadows of any but relative meaning.[21]

Dickens breaks these circuits of meaning by realizing what is emptied of substance within them. This means that he sees things in the shadows whose meaning is not merely relative to what is in the light; shadows have consistency. Little Dorrit herself is the most important of the characters who materialize out of shades and shadows. She appears first in the shadows of Mrs. Clennam's room, "almost hidden in the dark corner" (80). And Arthur's relation to her begins when he shadows her through London to find out where she lives. With Amy Dorrit, Dickens returns to a female heroine like Nell in *The Old Curiosity Shop*: diminutive, "selfless," with a corrupt father whom she supports without complaint. But Little Dorrit is less innocent than Nell. She exercises agency and experiences desire; and when she appears without desire, that apparent void is due to her own repression. Amy hides her love for Arthur from others, believing it unreturned, and represents her desire, in the story she tells to Maggy of the princess and the little woman, as "a shadow" kept in "a very secret place" (341). Unlike Trollope's repressive women, Little Dorrit lives in the shadow of her desire and acts in consistency with it.

In the bureaucratic cultivation of obscurity, forms are filled out and blanks filled in for purposes of moving on to new forms and new blanks.

Dickens counters such productivity with productions of feeling and action, in both of which Little Dorrit is an agent. When Mr. Dorrit is rich and the family is touring Europe, Amy's life becomes a series of empty spaces and her existence becomes groundless:

> To have no work to do was strange, but not half so strange as having glided into a corner where she had no one to think for, nothing to plan and contrive, no cares of others to load herself with. Strange as that was, it was far stranger yet to find a space between herself and her father, where others occupied themselves in taking care of him, and where she was never expected to be. . . . [S]he now sat in her corner of the luxurious carriage with her little patient hands folded before her, quite displaced even from the last point of the old standing ground in life on which her feet had lingered.
>
> It was from this position that all she saw appeared unreal; the more surprising the scenes, the more they resembled the unreality of her own inner life as she went through its vacant places all day long. (516–17)

For Dickens, it is doing, as a relation of self and other, that realizes the world. Here Little Dorrit is emptied out and converted into a practitioner of "How not to do it," with a position but no positive sense of place, no sense of the actuality of her self or her surroundings.

Still, by remembering, Little Dorrit is able to fill in some of the gaps in her life. Memory of the past works as a relation linking otherwise disconnected elements of experience as it passes through moments of time. It is this kind of relation over time that Mr. Dorrit is most terrified of when he is out of prison. Never having accepted the reality of the prison, he now attempts to repress the past altogether. For Little Dorrit, however, memory is a means of realizing her connections in time and space. She writes to Arthur from Italy that she is unable to enjoy sightseeing in these "new countries":

> I am not collected enough — not familiar enough with myself, if you can quite understand what I mean — to have all the pleasure in them that I might have. What I knew before them, blends with them, too, so curiously. For instance, when we were among the mountains, I often felt . . . as if the Marshalsea must be behind that great rock; or as if Mrs Clennam's room where I have worked so many days, and where I first saw you, must be just beyond that snow. Do you remember one night when I came with Maggy to your lodging in Covent Garden? That room I have often and often fan-

cied I have seen before me, travelling along for miles by the side of our car-
riage, when I have looked out of the carriage-window after dark. (522–23)

Projecting occupants into the shadows and darkness outside the car-
riage, Little Dorrit comes into relation with her new surroundings only
by "blending" them with the old. Rather than being "collected" herself, she sees dimensions of space that extend into the past and effectively disperse her consciousness, both in time and space, beyond the
bounds of the present.

This blending, of past and present and of substance and shadow, is
a kind of shading different from the shadows of the opening scene of
the novel. For one thing, it is an active process, something Amy does.
Moreover, it is a relation of things that joins them together, not with
anything between them but through a sharing in common of parts of
themselves. This kind of mixing makes heterogeneous what systematic
relativism renders homogeneous. Different elements are mixed into
one another rather than being sorted out and differentiated by something between them. The past and present are not mediated by something separable from them but themselves become inseparable as each
merges with the other.

That Little Dorrit's sense of space is more substantial than that of
most characters in the novel is also evident in her perception of buildings. What she "sees" are not the walls and barriers that separate space
into "collected" parts, but the spaces — the buildings, the rooms — that
people occupy and in which people are occupied by work. Both spaces
and people are identified in terms of function and use, and it is these
occupations that fill what others identify as voids. Although Little Dorrit tends to spatialize history as she identifies the past with shadows
lurking behind present objects, her shadows do not effect distinctions,
because they are not void. Instead, they effect a blurring of differences,
even of differences between time and space; time is one means of changing spaces and so is not differentiable from spatial phenomena.

Little Dorrit's is not an empty subjectivity. But she is not a distinguished subject either. She appears to other characters as a void — void
of meaning, interest, value — because within the representative system

that produces value in the public world of *Little Dorrit,* she has no distinction. Amy's capacity to produce temporal and spatial confusions requires a subjectivity that is incongruent with orderly productions of either public knowledge or private subjects. Hers is a shady character, capable of breaking through boundaries of distinction that constrain experience, but confused in its dimensions and uncollected in its parts.

5

Gender as Order in Public and Private:
East Lynne

East Lynne, written by Mrs. Henry Wood and published in 1861, is a melodramatic "sensation novel" that provides a private perspective on both public and private life. The narrative demonstrates a knowledge of domestic experience that purports to be otherwise unavailable to most people in public life because it is knowledge of female emotions, of which gentlemen are ignorant. To a greater extent than in *Barchester Towers* or *Little Dorrit,* characters in *East Lynne* are strictly divided, by social class and, even more emphatically, by gender.

A century earlier, in Walpole's *The Castle of Otranto,* women and men inhabited different spheres within the castle; women spent time together dealing with emotional crises, men with political crises. In the nineteenth-century novels I have discussed, women and men spend more time together in domestic settings and share, to some degree, interests in both private and public life. But in *East Lynne,* in which there is again a strict separation of female from male concerns, both emotional and domestic life become the province of women, who live to a great extent in a world of their own.

From within this world, spheres of public life are identified primarily as space beyond the bounds of female experience. This is evident at the beginning of the novel, for example, when Barbara Hare, at home with her mother one evening, suddenly leaves the house:

She strolled down the straight, formal path, and stood at the iron gate, looking over it into the public road. Not very public in that spot, and at that hour, but as lonely as one could wish. . . .

"When will he come home?" she murmured, as she leaned her head upon the gate. "Oh, what would life be without him? How miserable these few days have been! I wonder what took him there! I wonder what is detaining him! Cornelia said he had only gone for a day."

The faint echo of footsteps in the distance stole upon her ear, and Barbara drew back a little, and hid herself under the shelter of the trees, not choosing to be seen by any stray passer-by. But, as they neared, a sudden change came over her; . . . for she knew those footsteps, and loved them, only too well.

Cautiously peeping over the gate again, she looked down the road. A tall form . . . was advancing rapidly towards her from the direction of West Lynne. Again she shrank away: true love is ever timid: and whatever may have been Barbara Hare's other qualities, her love at least was true and deep. But, . . . the footsteps seemed to pass onwards. . . .

Yes, surely enough, he was striding on, not thinking of her, not coming to her.[1]

Here the public road is open but empty, lonely rather than populous; emptied of action, public space is merely a mark of the limits on Barbara's action. She, like other women in this novel, spends much of her time waiting for something to happen, at the edge of action as she stands at the edge of public space.

Barbara's action seems limited, moreover, to an observation of forms. She observes the limits of proper female movement, and she watches a form appear on the road. Unlike those who observe forms in Dickens's *Little Dorrit,* however, Barbara's senses are active, as are her deep feelings. And whereas Nell, watching and waiting at the window in *The Old Curiosity Shop,* remains in an isolated emotional state, Barbara's emotions seem to connect her personally to the objects she observes. Moreover, her senses quickly recognize the object of her desire, coming to her out of the distance.

Yet Barbara has eyes and ears *only,* it would appear, for this one object. She sees and hears nothing else as she stands at the gate. Her senses do not, therefore, provide much connection to the world around her. Nor does she have other means of connecting to the world. If Barbara feels deeply, she knows nothing but what her senses tell her. Her ignorance about the man she desires is due not only to the fact that he has told her nothing about his actions, but also to the fact that the information she has received from a woman is unreliable. Even after her senses recognize shape and sound, Barbara is in a state of uncertainty: moving forward, pulling back, she alternately asserts and hides herself. Like characters in *Little Dorrit* who observe forms, she has difficulty exercising will or acquiring knowledge and instead reproduces obscurity.

Those characters in *Little Dorrit* reproduce distances between subjects and objects that obscure both. Individual interest is one thing obscured, so that persons appear disinterested. The apparently indifferent individual confronts, moreover, apparently equivalent and exchangeable objects; and, for Dickens, both kinds of indifference are fraudulent. In contrast, in the preceding scene in *East Lynne,* Barbara Hare displays and feels no lack of interest. But in this novel, depths of emotion have no capacity to differentiate the self. In fact, it is in her love for Archibald Carlyle that Barbara Hare is rendered both an indifferent subject and an indifferent object. Because of that love, she is like the other women who desire him; yet she is also identifiable as an object of comparatively little interest to him. As the passage suggests, Archibald neither knows anything of Barbara's feelings nor has any interest in knowing them.

In *East Lynne,* the private realm of women's emotional, domestic experience is the location of the confusion and obscurity that Dickens and Trollope identify in bureaucratic processes of government administration. Internalized both within the home and within the female psyche, experience that for those writers is superficial and artificial moves into depths that make it seem natural. Women become, not through the repression but through the activation of feeling, exchangeable objects, the image of one another.[2] Through women's emotional interests, Mrs. Henry Wood identifies consumption as not only a private but also a "naturally" feminine concern.

This leaves the public sphere of law, courts, and parliamentary elections a sphere in which gentlemen, backed by public opinion, are able to represent the interests of the public and to accomplish the productive aims of knowledge and justice. It is because they do not know, and are apparently incapable of knowing, what goes on in the world of women, any more than they are capable of knowing what goes on among criminal men, that gentlemen such as Archibald Carlyle can govern well. The "habitus" of middle-class women — both the places they inhabit and the habits that characterize their behavior — is shared with criminals; they exist together as an underclass in a kind of underworld that, as in *Barchester Towers,* is "naturally" inaccessible to gentlemen. On the one hand, the separateness of women's experience in *East Lynne* guarantees stability and integrity to masculine public spheres. On the other hand, the stability and integrity of gentlemen's lives and gentlemen's government depend on an enormous ignorance of depths of experience they can neither change nor control.

Plotting Sexual Difference

In *East Lynne* there is a double register of action, according to which the experience of men and women is gradually but consistently divided. To suggest that men and women double each other is somewhat misleading, because the capacity of one person to take the place of another is primarily a female capacity in the novel. But Mrs. Henry Wood employs a double plot of mistaken identities: in one a man and in the other a woman is confused with someone else. This doubling is temporary, and it works to clarify that if the exchangeability that characterizes women's experience applies to men, it applies only to those who are not "manly."

One case of mistaken identity involves Richard Hare, Barbara's brother. Some years earlier, in West Lynne, Richard ran away from a murder scene because he was afraid of being thought guilty. He was indeed accused of murder, and he is hunted as a criminal until, eventually, the real murderer is identified, tried, and imprisoned. At the end of the novel, Richard, who has lived for years as a laborer, returns to testify against the real murderer, to be reunited with his family, and to resume his place as a gentleman. In this plotline, men are mistakenly confused with and then distinguished from one another. Repetition yields to development of plot as confusion yields to distinctions of individuals. Initially put in the place of another, Richard later becomes his own man. "I was young and green once: you don't suppose I have remained so," he says at the end of the novel to Afy Hallijohn, the woman he once loved but whom he has learned to see as a selfish, undeserving jilt (618). In this plot, a number of mistakes of identity are corrected.

In another, female plot, a series of women become increasingly confused with one another. In this case the confusion does not seem mistaken and does not yield to distinctions. At the beginning of the novel, Barbara is in love with Archibald Carlyle, whom she has known since they were children. Archibald, oblivious to Barbara's love for him, falls in love with Lady Isabel Vane, who marries him because she is penniless and unwanted by the relatives with whom she must otherwise live. Lady Isabel's married life at East Lynne is shadowed by depression, jealousy, and feelings of humiliation. One reason for this is the way she is treated by Cornelia Carlyle, Archibald's older sister, who has strongly disapproved of the marriage but lives with the couple at East Lynne as its "real mistress" (169).

Another source of humiliation and depression is Isabel's fear that her husband loves Barbara Hare, who thereby appears as another kind of mistress taking Isabel's place. Barbara in turn is jealous of Isabel. Eventually, after having three children, Isabel in her jealousy runs away with another man, Francis Levison. Archibald divorces her and, when he hears she has been killed in a train crash, marries Barbara. Isabel, not dead but badly disfigured in the accident, abandoned by Levison and desirous of seeing her children again, returns unrecognized to East Lynne as governess. Unlike Richard Hare, she is only physically reunited with her family; until just before her death, she remains unrecognized, a servant, unable to resume her place as lady, wife, mother, or mistress. She spends the rest of the novel watching Archibald with Barbara as Barbara once watched Archibald with her.

Among these women, which one belongs in the position of Archibald's wife is unclear. Both Cornelia and Barbara see themselves in Isabel's place when they watch her with her husband. "I'll tell you what I saw last night," Cornelia says to Barbara shortly after Isabel's marriage.

"There was my lady's cambric handkerchief, soaked in eau-de-Cologne, lying on his forehead; and there was my lady herself, kneeling down and looking at him, he with his arm thrown round her to hold her there.... If ever he had a headache before he was married, I used to mix him up a good dose of salts and senna, and tell him to go to bed early and sleep the pain off." (162)

After being told this, Barbara goes into the house, overhears Isabel playing the piano in the next room, and then does "as Miss Carlyle confessed to have done, pushed open the door between the two rooms, and looked in" to watch a scene of affection between Isabel and Archibald (162–63). Much later in the novel, after Isabel returns as Madame Vine, she watches Barbara play and sing to Archibald: "So, once had stolen, so, once had peeped the unhappy Barbara, to hear this self-same song. *She* had been his wife then; she had received his kisses when it was over. Their positions were reversed" (441). Such reversed images, like those in a mirror, suggest that each woman sees herself reflected in the behavior of the woman presently closest to Archibald. These "mirroring bodies" see themselves as images of one another and as reproductions of others' desires. As is true for Jane Austen's *Emma*, women become exchangeable and replaceable, both as objects of men's desires and as subjects of desire. This is, in part, what fits them for consumerism.

Yet this reversibility of women's positions is not stabilized at the end of *East Lynne*. After hearing that the dead Madame Vine was Isabel, Barbara needs to be reassured of Archibald's love:

He took both her hands in one of his. . . .

"I had thought my wife possessed entire trust in me."

"Oh, I do, I do; you know I do. Forgive me, Archibald," she softly whispered.

"I deemed it better to impart this to you. Barbara. My darling, I have told it you in love."

. . . "It was a foolish feeling to cross my heart, Archibald. . . ."

"Never let it come back again, Barbara. Neither need her name be mentioned again between us. A barred name it has hitherto been: let it so continue." (639)

This, the final scene of the novel, bears a resemblance to a much earlier scene in which Archibald, having been married to Isabel a year, reassures his wife that he loves her and not Barbara:

"I had not thought that the past year was quite thrown away. What proof can a man give of true and earnest love, that I have not given to you?"

> She looked up, her eyelashes wet with contrition. . . .
> . . . "I am bound to you by fond ties as well as by legal ones, remember, Isabel; and it is out of Barbara Hare's power to step in between us." (184–85)

In both scenes of reassurance, Archibald claims his wife's trust even as he withholds some information about the other woman from her. The withheld information does not necessarily incriminate him, but in each case Archibald withholds the same fact: he has just received outpourings of love from the woman of whom his wife is jealous. Nevertheless, it is the wife who is contrite and apologetic in each case.

The replaceability and exchangeability of women that such likenesses indicate is the more emphatic because gentlemen are clearly not interchangeable. Various men are confused with and about one another in the novel: Richard Hare; Francis Levison, alias "Thorn" at the time he murdered Hallijohn; a real Major Thorn, who is a visitor in the town; and Bethel and Locksley, who were out poaching near the Hallijohn house on the night of the murder. Yet confusions among these men are cleared up so as to preclude their recurrence, by means unavailable to most women in the novel. One such means is the discovery of hidden truths. Discoveries that the mysterious Thorn was Francis Levison, that Bethel was poaching, and that Levison bribed Bethel to deny he saw him, make evident a reality about the murder that was hitherto undetected. These facts are learned by men who ask a lot of questions, both in private and in courts of law.

Internalizing Confusion

There is no such knowledge to preclude the interchangeability of jealous women in *East Lynne,* because it is their very jealousy that makes them seem replaceable. Because they are jealous, they see other women in what they identify as their own places. Thus women's emotions reproduce, internally, conditions of confusion that remain external to men. In jealousy, the narrator says, "the most fanciful surmises wear the aspect of truth, the greatest improbabilities appear as consistent realities" (185). Women are unable to know as men know because their emotions preclude the discrimination of surmises from truth, by means of which men clear up confusions among themselves.

This internalization renders the woman herself responsible for the kind of confusions that Richard Hare suffers only at the hands of others. Moreover, whereas women's emotions become the cause of their own equivalence, men are provided distinction not only by their reason but also by public and institutionalized tribunals. One is the court of law that declares Richard innocent and Levison guilty of murder. Another is the parliamentary election in which Levison suffers humiliating defeat and Archibald is declared the victor, a contest decided by the public between two men whose rivalry would otherwise be that of competitors for Isabel and would make them difficult to distinguish from the jealous women in the novel. Such a public arena of judgment is unavailable to women for both public and private reasons. Women are excluded from parliamentary elections by law, but they are also excluded from the clarity and decisiveness of such institutional behavior by the confusion that characterizes their judgment.

Women's very internalizations of conditions that for men are external mark their confusion of things that men keep straight. In male institutions of the public sphere, humiliation and loss, as well as triumph and gain, are attributed to men by others. Men are declared guilty or innocent by judges assigned the work of justice; they are given victory or defeat by voters assigned the responsibility of election. Understanding such characteristics as externally imposed attributions rather than internally acquired or natural attributes, men maintain a sense of character that is separable from others' judgment. Because he maintains his own innocence, Richard Hare is able to hold off the police, go into hiding, and work at finding the real murderer. Women are humiliated in their own eyes, however, by behavior and characteristics that seem to belong inherently to them.

Isabel's own "deep consciousness of humiliation" is due to a number of things: she is "timid and sensitive by nature," has been "reared in seclusion," and has no money (171). Because she feels humiliated, she is unable to withstand Cornelia's humiliating treatment of her. She is not even able to tell her husband about these humiliations:

> Oh, that she had had the courage to speak openly to her husband! that he might, by a single word of earnest love and assurance, have taken the weight

from her heart, and rejoiced it with the truth—that all these miserable complaints were but the phantoms of his narrow-minded sister. But Isabel never did so; when Miss Corny lapsed into her grumbling mood, she would bear in silence, or gently bend her aching forehead in her hands, never retorting. (171)

If she could speak to a man, he could tell her the truth. As in the courts of men, an exchange of words could clear things up. But Isabel cannot produce the words that would bring her case to justice; instead, her mind produces the same "phantoms" of humiliation that Miss Corny imagines. Unable to distinguish her own sense of humiliation from that imposed on her by Cornelia, Isabel has no way out of humiliation. The difference apparent to men between internal and external conditions is invisible to her.

As Isabel feels increasingly humiliated by her jealousy of Barbara Hare, she remains unable to appeal to Archibald. She has overheard two conversations among servants in the house who in the past worked at the Hares' house and who therefore know of Barbara's love for Archibald:

An impulse arose with her that she would tell him all; . . . but in that moment of renewed confidence it appeared to her that she must have been very foolish to attach importance to it—that a sort of humiliation, in listening to the converse of servants, was reflected on her; and she remained silent. (184–85)

Here again Isabel sees a reflection of herself in others' humiliation of her. The means by which men discover different facts in the novel and differentiate themselves—gathering evidence from other people's memories and words—becomes a means of reflection and repetition for women. Whereas men treat humiliation as an exchangeable object, women cannot acquire or get rid of humiliation by exchange. The very exchange of words about humiliation becomes humiliating.

Barbara Hare does speak out, most emphatically when, shortly after his marriage, she lets Archibald know how much she loves him. But this outburst is also a humiliating expression of female humiliation:

Her love, her jealousy, the never-dying pain always preying on her heartstrings since the marriage took place, her keen sense of the humiliation which had come home to her, were all rising fiercely, bubbling up with fiery heat. . . . [W]hat was her existence to him? A little self-control and Barbara

would not have uttered words that must remain on her mind hereafter as
an incubus, dyeing her cheeks red whenever she recalled them. (165)

Here self-expression is mistaken, as it seems to be when exercised by
Isabel too. Though the narrator insists that she should speak out, the
fact is that when Isabel does express a desire — to take the children
with her to France (204–5), to not invite Francis Levison to the house
(227–28) — her wishes are contradicted by her husband. This identifies
female expression with humiliation yet again. If at times these women
seem to seek humiliation, at other times they ask for other things and
are humiliated by refusals to grant them.

Being Indifferent

In *Little Dorrit*, this kind of process, in which productivity is limited
to exchanges that perpetually defer knowledge or satisfaction, can be
altered by depths of feeling. Repetitive and circular processes are identified with an assumption of emotional indifference, and the expression of desire can convert circularity into change. In *East Lynne*, however, women's emotions themselves reproduce and circulate images that
interfere with knowledge and satisfaction. Whereas men produce differences between self and other, women produce an indifference of
self and other. They exchange reflections among themselves that confirm their equivalence; even when they try to do something different by
entering into exchange with men, this makes no difference. For women,
indifference is not a matter of feeling, as it is for men, but of being.

Therefore, to be mistaken in this novel is a very different experience
for men and for women. For the most part, men are mistaken in others or by others, but women are mistaken in themselves. Whereas he
was once jealous because Afy Hallijohn preferred another man, Richard
Hare learns that she isn't worthy of him. But women jealous of Archibald's affection are not mistaken in their object; it is their subjectivity
that is prone to make mistakes. Richard is one man who makes mistakes. He runs away from home in fear, just as Isabel runs away from
home in jealousy. But Richard regains courage, comes back home, and
is proven innocent. Moreover, he becomes a man and identifies his mistakes with mistakes about his gender: "[M]y cursed cowardice. They
had better have made a woman of me, and brought me up in petticoats"

(51). For Isabel, mistaken judgment causes changes that are irreversible. Richard's mistakes are extraneous to the criminal case in which he is implicated; but when Isabel runs away, that itself is the crime. Moreover, Richard is right to fear that he will be thought guilty. But when Isabel's uncle visits her in France, he makes her see "that her own blind jealousy had been utterly mistaken and unfounded" (312); Archibald had been spending so much time with Barbara Hare only to save Richard. This pulls the ground out from under Isabel's actions, leaving her with no reason for being what she is but no way to return to what she was.

This sense that women are somehow groundless, indistinct, or shadowy in identity is repeated in a number of ways throughout the novel. It is evident because female characters repeat one another in small details as well as lay claim to the same positions. It is also evident because jealousy seems to be the ruling female passion. Jealousy confuses objects in that it assigns a lack of love to another in place of the self. It further confuses objects in that it is a term applied to, and a feeling felt for, both the rival and the loved object. Women's indistinction is thus internalized. Moreover, it is not cleared up by public institutions. Isabel's crime is one for which she is never tried or even heard; Archibald is granted a divorce without her testimony. Thus, whereas Richard Hare has a chance to correct his mistaken judgment and retrieve his public stature, and thereby to integrate his public and private identity, Isabel is left with a public identity at odds with her private experience, suspended between guilt and innocence.

It is fitting, then, that Isabel returns to East Lynne as a kind of ghost. Occupying a body so altered as to be unrecognizable, Isabel returns to the house in the position of governess. She also takes another position, that which Barbara held as the "other woman" during Isabel's own marriage to Archibald Carlyle. This means, for Isabel and for the reader, a haunting sense of precedent for Barbara's actions, a sense underscored repeatedly by the narrator: "Oh! can you imagine what it was for Lady Isabel? So had he tossed, so had he kissed her children, she standing by, the fond, proud, happy mother, as Barbara was standing now" (421–22); and, again: "Barbara was with him, hanging fondly on his arm, about to accompany him to the park gates. So had *she* fondly hung, so had *she* accompanied him, in the days gone by for ever" (427).

The shadows cast by such images are permanent. Richard Hare, who has been taken for the murderer that Levison really is, can clear himself by identifying the real criminal. He shadows Levison through London with a repressed truth insistent on recognition. Isabel shadows Barbara not with some hidden truth that will clear up the identity of Barbara or herself, but with their common exchangeability, their truly indistinct and insecure character. Whereas Richard and Levison in a sense compete for innocence and guilt, each of which is assigned to only one, there is no such distinction available to Barbara or Isabel. Each represents a perpetual possibility of displacement for the other.

Dickens's Little Dorrit lives in shadows cast by memory and history. She produces such shadows, which alter the dimensions of experience and are never exchangeable with present objects. Although they merge into such objects and render their identity indefinite over time, shadows of the past also differentiate present objects from one another, precluding likenesses of forms in space with substantial effects of time. Mrs. Henry Wood, however, enters shadows into a female economy in which the indefinite and inactive character of women renders them exchangeable as shadows of one another. Without substance in this economy, women have no means of resisting exchangeability.

Depths of Indifference

Indistinct, confused, unassertive, women's deep emotions condemn them to murkiness and lump them together. Undifferentiated, women in their depths of experience are identified with forms of life that are not usually apparent in novels written before this time. I have discussed depths of self in earlier novels, focusing on parts of the self identified beneath the surfaces of conscious knowledge. These buried parts are forms of will—both will as interest in or desire for objects, and will as creative energy that can accomplish objects in action. In *Emma* and *Frankenstein,* emotional depths are recognized as parts of the self only through reflections of the self in others; parts of Emma are reflected in Harriet, parts of Frankenstein are reflected in his monstrous creature. In *The Old Curiosity Shop,* emotional depths are repressed rather than recognized through social exchanges that limit value to visual, demonstrable experience. In *Barchester Towers* and *Little Dorrit*, too, deep emotions are obscured by social exchange. In these three Victorian novels, however, the repression of will is identified as an act of will. In the face of scientific theories of the indifference of natural and institutional processes to human will, Dickens and Trollope both insist on the power of will.

In *East Lynne,* the depths of emotion that Mrs. Henry Wood identifies in women are not depths of will but depths of indifference. It is as if scientific theory has caught up with the novel, but only with its female characters. The virtual underworld that women inhabit in *East Lynne* is not a world of repressed emotion. Women's emotions are consciously felt; if they are not usually expressed to men, they are expressed and exchanged among women. But these emotions, unlike will, have the effect of confusing women and rendering them like one another. Archaic in their undifferentiation, women's confusion may signal not only depths of emotion but also a prehistoric sphere of nature identified by evolutionary scientists in an unchanging and elemental past. As Gillian Beer explains,

> Lying behind diversity in Darwinian theory, slumbers the form of some remote progenitor, irrecoverable because precedent to history or anterior to consciousness. That idea of "the single form" becomes itself a new and powerful source of nostalgia. In this period we see the determination to liberate science and philosophy from the idea of origins, from the study of final causes. But . . . [history's] drive is always backwards. The activity of describing development may be history, but it seeks always to reach further back into the past, further and further towards the comforting limits of initiation. Freud's enterprise is the analytical form of this obsession, in relation to the individual, but we find it before him in the preoccupation with "roots" (of language or of species).[3]

Such late-nineteenth-century searches for past and archaic origins occurred not only among evolutionists; Nietzsche as well as Freud discovered reservoirs of elemental and unconscious experience both necessary to and repressed by modern culture. In England during the 1850s and 1860s, moreover, as Jonathan Loesberg has shown, there was a fearful sense of "lower depths" in which class differences would disappear.

This was voiced during the debate over parliamentary reform that preceded the Second Reform Bill (1868) and may, as Loesberg argues, be an important context in which to read the experience of Isabel Vane in *East Lynne*.[4]

Mrs. Henry Wood's identification of women with undifferentiated form allows her to set women at the edge of various progressive social practices in which men in the novel take part. Whereas Trollope identifies women with surfaces and forms of apparent social progress, Mrs. Henry Wood identifies women with formless depths that mark a limit of progress. Yet the women of *East Lynne* remain, like the women of *Barchester Towers,* identified with convertible and exchangeable value. In both novels women form an underclass lacking the integrity of gentlemen; but in *Barchester Towers* the underclass of women is identified as shallow and superficial, whereas in *East Lynne* women are deeply confused and emotionally insecure.

These females are effectively declassed both in their experience of undifferentiation and in their experience of representation. Engaged in processes of reflection that characterize the market, which expands by increasing "needless" production and consumption, women's interests are represented in likenesses and images that confuse identity and preclude distinction. Women in the novel are evidently an underclass, insofar as their experience of representation allows an open exchange in which any one can take the place of another, and insofar as only personal interests are represented. It is more accurate, perhaps, to say that representation is itself a male experience in the novel. Women only barely experience representation, because women have trouble telling the difference between a representation and what it represents. Representation is one more kind of experience that men use to put distance between themselves and others and that results for women in being jammed together. The only secure means of differentiation that women have is their bodies, which they can use to put distance between themselves and others, on the one hand, by bodily movement and, on the other hand, by bodily disfigurement.

Gentlemen, in contrast, practice orderly representation. Not only are they able to represent their thoughts and feelings in clear and rational expressions, they are also able to engage in political representation in which persons can keep distinct their own and others' interests. The parliamentary election at West Lynne, in which Archibald Carlyle defeats Francis Levison, allows Archibald to represent his (male) constituency in Parliament: "That he would have the interest of West Lynne at heart, was certain, and he knew that he should serve his constituents to the best of his power and ability. They knew it also" (446). Here Archibald's "heart" contains others' interests, in a transfer that resembles the confusion of women who all love the same man. But Archibald can keep his own interests distinct from the public interest. He rises to the level of Matthew Arnold's ideal, "impersonal" representative of the state.[5] His disinterestedness is repaid, moreover, by the public defeat and humiliation of Levison, the rival who has run away with Archibald's wife. Not only can Archibald represent the interests of West Lynne, but the men of West Lynne can represent his interests too. This satisfying exchange is orderly, voluntary, and just—necessary, not needless, according to the principles as well as interests of the men of West Lynne.

Psychological Depths

Particularly in the work of feminists, recent theory has suggested reasons for women's "backwardness" in Western cultures: their failure to develop along the lines Freud and others identified in the male ego as normal development. Notably, theories of spatial configurations of female selfhood clarify the nondevelopmental character of early female experience. Part of the "backwardness" of female experience in *East Lynne* is its spatial character: women, so similar in their internal experience, depend on place rather than character—on where they are rather than who they are—for their individuality.

It is possible, according to recent thinking, that the male child more easily sees himself *as* a self, an entity separate from his mother, because of physical differences and, later, gendered differences. This in turn may mean a difference in the ability of males and females to identify objects of desire. According to Mary Ann Doane's distinction between male and female relations to objects,

> The male gaze is fixed to the image of the castrated maternal body and obsessed with its implications for the coherence of male identity.... The visual pleasure that body gives to the male thus has its basis in ontological se-

curity. The woman, on the other hand, cannot *look* at that body (except in the mirror of her own narcissism) because she *is* it. Female scopophilia is a drive without an object, an undirected and free-floating drive which is conducive to the operation of the phobia.[6]

But it is not only in relations of subject and objects that the male acquires greater distinction and security than the female. Certain means of exchange crucial to the psychological development of male children may be unavailable to females.

The following summary by Anika Lemaire indicates the importance of various exchanges and substitutions to Jacques Lacan's theories of psychological development.

> By assuming the Law of his father the child passes from the register of being (being the all-powerful phallus) to the register of having (having a limited and legitimate desire which can be formulated in an utterance) and enters into a quest for objects which are further and further removed from the initial object of his desire. Parallel to this, he follows a dialectic of identifications in which his Ego constitutes itself and in which the ideal of the self takes shape. We can see that it is in the transition from being to having that the subject's Spaltung is situated, the division between his conscious being and his unconscious being. The desire to be the phallus which is lacking in the mother, the desire for union with the mother, is repressed and replaced by a substitute which names it and at the same time transforms it: the symbol. If the Name-of-the-Father fulfills this function of symbolizing desire, if being "a" father henceforth replaces the desire for fusion, it is because the father reveals himself as he who *has* the desired phallus and as he who is able to use it in a socially normalized relationship.[7]

The possession of a means of representation and expression moves the child from being to having, from identification with objects to possession of objects. The object possessed, however, is not quite an object but a means of exchange; it enters the child into language and culture.

East Lynne could be said to tell the story of a man in "quest for objects which are further and further removed from the initial object of his desire." But the novel tells this from the perspectives of the objects who are picked up and put down, to be replaced by others — not those who possess means of exchange but those who are themselves exchangeable. According to this perspective, females and males do not have the same options of being and having. Unable to enter into exchanges whereby she separates herself from others, the female perceives her self constantly subject to claims by others. This is to say not only that the female is an object rather than a subject, but also that in the symbolic register, because she is without means of exchange, she is always in debt. Rather than being or having, she owes.

Isabel's constant indebtedness is due to a lack of various means of exchange. The daughter of an earl who never paid his debts, she is without money of her own. Made to feel she is a "great expense" by Cornelia, Isabel has "nothing to repay [Archibald] with" (154), because she doesn't love him either. Emotional means of payment are put out of her reach as involuntary means: "Lady Isabel did not love Mr. Carlyle; but his tenderness . . . caused her to lift up her heart to him with gratitude, and to try earnestly to love him. But — to try to love! Vain effort: Love never yet came for *trying*" (202). Not only means of payment but also means of expression are put beyond Isabel. Unable to tell her husband things the narrator insists should be spoken — her jealousy, her suffering at the hands of Cornelia, her fear of Francis Levison — Isabel cannot express desires either.

But although the narrator repeatedly bewails Isabel's silence, the issue of her expression is not an issue of desire for objects. The expressions Isabel keeps to herself are fears, insecurities, humiliations that insist on her own status as object. Women in this novel don't clearly have objects, they have places, which are taken not as objects are taken into possession, but as locations of selfhood into which females move, to benefit from their spatial boundaries and from the spaces between one place and another. The female self may be said to take place rather than to take possession.

This follows from the hypothesis that females have much greater difficulty than males experiencing separation and distinction from the mother. Males may enter into symbolic exchange and shift from being to having. This means identifying themselves in terms of desires for objects at a remove from their initial object(s) of desire. But for females, the shift from being to having is less easily made, or is not made, because being itself is less easily experienced. The male entity confronts the undifferentiated mother first with physical difference and then with symbolic mediation; the symbolic register comes between the male self and undifferentiation. The female entity confronts the undifferentiated mother by making a space between them. The gap between difference and undifferentiation is experienced not as the gap between symbolic and real experience, but as distance imposed between two substantially similar entities.[8]

This distance is not mediated by symbolic exchange, but it may be mediated by the exchange of women. What it is that precludes females entering into mediation is difficult to specify at an early age. But it is evident in *East Lynne* that women as adults have much less access to means of exchange than men do. Insofar as women identify themselves as objects of others' desires, their identification with being rather than having is encouraged. Yet insofar as women identify themselves as replaceable by other women, with whom they exchange places in their imagination, they repeatedly go through the motions of displacement that may be both frightening and attractive. Loss of place is frightening, but mobility is attractive.

Lady Isabel Vane first appears in *East Lynne* as an object of desire in whom something seems to be missing. She thereby corresponds to the image of castration that has been theorized as the object of male desire:

> Who — what — was it? Mr. Carlyle looked, not quite sure whether it was a human being: he almost thought it more like an angel.
> ... [T]he extraordinary loveliness of the young girl before him almost took away his senses and his self-possession. It was not so much the perfect contour of the exquisite features that struck him, or the rich damask of the delicate cheek, or the luxuriant falling hair; no, it was the sweet expression of the soft dark eyes. Never in his life had he seen eyes so pleasing. He could not withhold his gaze from her, and he became conscious, as he grew more familiar with her face, that there was in its character a sad, sorrowful look. Only at times was it to be noticed, when the features were in repose, and it lay chiefly in the very eyes he was admiring. Never does this unconsciously mournful expression exist, but it is a sure index of sorrow and suffering; but Mr. Carlyle understood it not. (7–8)

What threatens Archibald's self-possession and holds his gaze is a certain absence. A Freudian perspective might identify this absence with castration; a female perspective may see something else. What it is that Isabel is seeing with her "sad, sorrowful look," what she misses, mourns, or regrets at this point, is never identified. Perhaps the female emotions apparent in this scene have no object. Or perhaps they have no object other than the self. Recognition of the self as an object of the man's gaze may move the woman into mourning for the self, lost once it is taken as the object of male desire. In the face of Archibald's attraction to her, Isabel's response is to project herself elsewhere.

Repeatedly Isabel is humiliated in the novel by her inability to use means of exchange to assert herself or her desires. But if she seems humiliated in her inability to identify her self as subject, she may court humiliation to avoid identifying herself as object. Perpetually regretting her own inadequacy, Isabel repeatedly imposes a difference between what she is and what a desirable object is. Thus, her mournful expression in the preceding scene projects her self beyond the reach of the gaze that, growing "familiar" with her body, threatens the distance between self and other. This may be a female version of quest, not for objects but for space between objects. It is possible to read this as the trajectory of Isabel's experience in the novel, in which "fulfillment" comes with her return to East Lynne as the shadow of her former self. After she returns, she exists in double registers of being and not-being that constitute the only secure separation she is able to achieve between her self and herself as the object of others' desires.

What Do Women Want?

According to this reading, Isabel and other women become the location and cause of practices that Dickens identifies with the fraudulent reproduction of unknowability in *Little Dorrit.* As Isabel opens up spaces, she produces gaps that Dickens identifies with attempts to empty out subjective and objective reality; she produces shadows such as Dickens identifies with a willful obscuring of reality. In addition, she assumes identity as a likeness, first as a portrait in men's eyes and later as only a partial likeness of her former self. But in *East Lynne,* this behavior is involuntary and uncontrollable.

If in Dickens's novels such behavior is primarily productive or reproductive, the women in *East Lynne* repeat this behavior as consumers. Women identify themselves in indistinct terms out of need. Unlike disinterested gentlemen, who assume distance between the self and the objects desired, women are in desperate need and so resemble consumers of the lower classes. Yet women do not desire objects, they desire space itself; they want the distance that men can assume between subject and object. Thus, in *East Lynne* women seem most aggressive in their incursions on spaces and places that belong to others. They often intrude on other people's spaces, walking into rooms without being asked or wanted, spying on people, trespassing where they don't belong. And women often defend themselves by running away rather than, like men in court, representing a rational defense.

If what women want is space, they desire also the distance that characterizes upper-class male disinterestedness. Yet women need less to cultivate distance from objects they desire than to cultivate distance from others who desire them as objects. They are unable to do this as disinterested men do it. For one thing, women in *East Lynne* have poor taste. Both Isabel and Barbara make mistakes in their dress that cause others to sneer at their appearance and their judgment. For another thing, women do not feel they can afford, either economically or emotionally, to be at any distance from men. Cornelia moves, unwanted, into East Lynne to live with her brother and his wife for reasons of economy, despite the fact that she has a house and an income of her own. Isabel follows Archibald around and waits at the gate for him to come home from work, like a devoted pet. The distance that women cultivate, therefore, is internal, in gaps within themselves.

This occurs in the initial meeting between Isabel and Archibald, when she projects her eyes and her attention away from her body. It also occurs, gradually, in Isabel's relation to East Lynne, the house in which she lived as a child and in which she lives again as Archibald's wife. In the first chapter of the novel, Archibald has bought the estate from Isabel's father. Never in the course of the novel does he doubt his right to the place. But Isabel, who has experienced the estate not as a belonging but as the place where she belongs, learns to feel insecure about her place there until, eventually, "home" is for her a place of displacement.

When she first appears at East Lynne, Isabel is already dispossessed of it, though she doesn't know that her father has sold the house to Archibald. Because the piano is old and out of tune, she mentions to Archibald that "Were we to be much at East Lynne, I should ask papa to exchange it for a new one." At this, "the earl coughed, and exchanged a smile and a glance with his guest," Archibald, both of them knowing what Isabel does not (67). Cut off from exchange, which already has occurred and continues to occur between men, Isabel does not experience the humiliation that such knowledge would bring. But this scene implies that to enter exchange would be for Isabel to enter into humiliation. Whereas males enter exchange to possess objects, females enter exchange to realize their dispossession. But dispossession and humiliation later become Isabel's means of exchange, whereby not only can she deny her value in Archibald's eyes but also, eventually, she can actively acquire what she wants.

On her second return to East Lynne, after she has married Archibald, Isabel begins to realize that she doesn't belong there, and she realizes it in the form of humiliation. She first feels it because of the presence of Cornelia, who even on Isabel's first day back contradicts and dismisses her wishes. Thus "it did not seem like coming home to East Lynne," and Isabel asks Archibald if she may stay in her own room "and not go down again tonight," only to be reprimanded: "*May* you not go down again! Have you forgotten that you are at last in your own home?" (143–44). At this point, Archibald insists on Isabel's knowledge that the house is hers. But it is as if Isabel's consciousness is only now feeling the dispossession that was kept from her knowledge earlier; she begins to assume the humble and dependent position that she didn't know enough to assume then.

The last time she returns to the house, as Madame Vine, Isabel has assumed a humble and dependent position completely. She has realized humiliation, in mind, in body, and in her social position as servant. Now, not even her bedroom is hers:

> The doors of her old bed and dressing-rooms stood open, and she glanced in with a yearning look. No, never more, never more could they be hers: she had put them from her by her own free act and deed. Not less comfortable did they look, than in former days: but they had passed into another's occupancy. (409)

In the course of this regressive progression, Isabel's experience moves from unconsciousness to consciousness of her condition and then to an active manipulation of it.

Actively dispossessing herself, Isabel has not gotten rid of East Lynne exactly. She instead both lives there and knows she doesn't belong there. She is like Dickens's "genteel gipsies" living at Hampton Court, who arrange their furniture "as if they were going away the moment they could get anything better," except that Isabel embodies what they use their furniture to represent: that she does not belong where she nevertheless lives, and that the things in a room dislocate persons from place. The disconnection that initially was external to her is internalized, and she has to remind herself of it again and again. Constantly reproducing the gap between herself and her place in feelings of loss, Isabel suffers separation as an emotional break. Moreover, in the broken body that she now inhabits, Isabel experiences a physical breakage of her self into pieces that screens her identity from others just as the "gipsies" screen visitors' knowledge of who they are. She can now be recognized as only a partial likeness of herself, because, even behind the veil and the glasses she wears, very little of her body remains as it was. Thus, Cornelia, when she sees Isabel without her glasses, does not recognize Isabel but sees "an extraordinary likeness" (474). This leads to doubt but no knowledge.

It is as if Isabel's progression is the acquisition of dubious value, which she gains by the active exercise of her own humiliation. Isabel first acquires earning power when she decides, after having run away, to pay for her sins with suffering: "What a cross was hers to take up! But she must do it; . . . she had fully earned all its weight and its sharp pain, and must not shrink from her burden" (305). Her plan to return to East Lynne is one in which her humiliation becomes a means of exchange and acquires an object: "Humiliation for me! no; I will not put that in comparison with seeing and being with my children" (406). In place of her repeated humiliation at the hands of others, she now actively humiliates herself to get what she wants. In return for identifying herself as a broken body and a broken spirit, she can be where she wants to be.

If, according to Bourdieu, the bodies of persons reproduce their habitus, then a certain degree of class "solidarity" might be identifiable in bodies' representations of the classes to which they belong. But in *East Lynne,* fracture is characteristic of, and embodied in, certain "classes" of persons, specifically women and male criminals. Gentlemen, and other classes of men too, appear whole, unified, of a piece; this is a crucial mark of the superiority of their class and gender. In their apparent wholeness, the distance gentlemen keep from objects allows them to distance consumption from need. But women, internalizing the distance between subject and object, are broken up by it. In addition, it seems that women *need* to be broken up; they *need* to act out the fragmentation that in earlier novels is identified with needless consumption. Needless consumption now becomes, for women, necessary and satisfying because the insecurity and convertibility it entails serve as means to escape being known and possessed as objects. Once again, women internalize what has seemed external to men, and they "naturalize" what has seemed man-made.

The Shadow of Her Self

Isabel experiences various separations in mind and body that are directly felt rather than feared. If males enter exchange to fend off castration, females seem to enter exchange after actually realizing bodily and spiritual splitting. Isabel is subject to "depressing illness" (304) after the birth of each of her children. Not identified as postpartum depression nor assigned any particular object, what Isabel experiences is nevertheless, again, a kind of mourning, "a feeling as if all whom she had loved in the world had died, leaving her living and alone. It was a painful depression, this vacuum in her heart which was making itself felt in its keen intensity" (223). It would be interesting to speculate on childbirth as an experience, like castration, of a loss of part of the body. Though it is neither symbolic loss nor an experience common to all women, it may be common as an imaginary experience of loss. In accord with the logic of the relation theorized between fear of castration and the symbolic register, at any rate, Isabel Vane experiences the strongest desire to be with her children after she is cut off from them. It is not merely her absence from them that increases her desire, it is also the knowledge that she is unrecognizable as their mother. Only when she has this knowledge do Isabel's desires acquire definite objects.

At a spa in Germany, Isabel meets a former neighbor and recognizes her own unrecognizability:

[M]eeting with Mrs. Ducie proved that she was altered beyond chance of recognition. She could go anywhere now.

But now, about the state of her mind? I do not know how to describe the vain yearning, the inward fever, the restless longing for what might not be. Longing for what? For her children. Let a mother, be she a duchess, or be she an apple-woman at a stall, be separated for a while from her little children: let *her* answer how she yearns for them.... What must it have been, then, for Lady Isabel, who had endured this longing for years? We hear of the *mal du pays,* which is said to attack the Swiss when exiled from their country; that is as nothing compared with the heartsickness which clung to Lady Isabel.... [N]ot the least that she had to endure now, was the thought that she had abandoned them to be trained by strangers.... Lady Isabel flung her hands before her eyes, and groaned in anguish. (397–98)

That Isabel's feelings may be about place is suggested by their comparison to the *mal du pays.* If she only now desires the place she has left, it may be because only now does she have the means of displacing herself even as she occupies that place. She needn't abandon her children to strangers any longer, because she is now available in estranged form.

Despite Mrs. Henry Wood's insistence that any mother would feel Isabel's longing, this is the first time it has been mentioned in the novel since Isabel left East Lynne, and its sudden appearance at this point seems due to Isabel's discovery that she is unrecognizable to those who knew her in the past. Her unrecognizability may be the bar necessary to the expression of female desire. Effectively barred from union with others by being unrecognizable as the object of their desire, Isabel is both placed and displaced as that object. After she arrives back at East Lynne, moreover, she is further displaced as the object of others' desire by the presence of Barbara in the place of the mother, the wife, the mistress of the house.

Thus Isabel makes her return, marking her progress in the novel as regression. She goes backward not exactly to reclaim a lost place or object, as does Richard Hare, but to realize herself *as* a lost place and a lost object. Having first appeared in the novel as a mourning object of desire, then, Isabel reappears at East Lynne to see herself mourned. Others now perform the detachment — of herself, as desirable object, from her own person — that she once imagined when Archibald looked at her. It is as witness to the space opened up by these detachments that Isabel returns home.

Isabel's daughter, Lucy, is the most vocal about her missing mother:

> "Lady Isabel was our very own mamma," pursued Lucy. "This mamma is not."
> "Do you love this one as you did the other?" breathed Lady Isabel.
> "Oh, I loved mamma! I loved mamma!" uttered Lucy, clasping her hands. "But it's all over. Wilson said we must not love her any longer. . . .
> . . . "[Wilson] said she need not have let that man kidnap her. I am afraid he beat her: for she died. I lie in my bed at night, and wonder whether he did beat her, and what made her die. It was after she died that our new mamma came home. Papa said she was come to be our mamma in place of Lady Isabel, and we were to love her dearly." (426–27)

Lucy's fantasies of her mother being beaten suggest that she reproduces for Isabel the identification-by-humiliation that Isabel herself practices. On the one hand, as Lucy says, the beating explains why her mother did not return to her. On the other hand, the beating punishes Isabel for not returning. Lucy seems to confuse loving and beating an object, both in herself and in her mother's lover. Humiliation is for Lucy a means of identifying the mother who no longer has any identity at East Lynne, where her name cannot be mentioned.[9]

In her children, Isabel sees herself mourned. In Archibald and Barbara, Isabel sees herself replaced. In each case, she witnesses her own displacement as object of desire. The distance between her self and the object of their desires, moreover, is a distance she buys into, having "earned" it as her punishment. Isabel thereby moves into an economic register, but along lines different from those by which a male is said to enter symbolic exchange. If males achieve subjective agency by repressing and displacing desires for certain objects, the female may repress subjective agency to displace herself as object of others' desires. It is not agency that can secure her as an entity separate from others, since her own desires would provide no defense against others' desires for her. Instead, Isabel experiences her self split between two places, and in neither location does she exercise agency. In one position she is the object of others' desires, and in the other position she watches her experience as the object of others' desires, barred from interfering or taking part in the exchange. As a passive spectator of her own humiliation, Isabel fills the conventional role of masochist, except that she takes on this role, as recent feminist revisions of masochism have suggested, as part of "a basic coping strategy to defend the ego."[10]

Because humiliation is the price of the distance she is unable to acquire by entering into other symbolic registers, Isabel can exercise agency only in ghost form, at one remove from her self. The trade-off, in short, is that she gives up self-control in order to get away from others' control. Her symbolic register is humiliation, which she uses to devalue herself as object. Thus, although it appears to Wilson and Cornelia that Isabel has a choice between agency and victimization — "she need not have let that man kidnap her" — it is evident to Lucy that Isabel's choices are between various kinds of victimization: even if she chose to go with Levison, she chose to subject herself to beating. The battered body, limping, scarred, and missing teeth, that returns to East Lynne as governess is another physical demonstration of the break between subject and object of others' desires that Isabel seeks, a splitting that is not repressed but is the active and repeated form — an expression of repression — that Isabel uses to displace others' desires for her.

A Woman's Place

If for much of the novel Richard and Isabel resemble each other, this reflection gradually dissolves until the two do not overlap at all. However, Barbara and Isabel come to resemble each other more as the novel goes on. Neither has any place that cannot be claimed by the other too. Women thus are crowded together, whereas men are separated in the course of the novel. Moreover, women's internal experience looks crowded. With the cause of their suffering always turned back into themselves, and with no way out of their limited mental perspectives, women are confined internally as well as externally. Processes of exchange, which move men out of themselves into different external spaces, merely reflect back to women the self with which they enter exchange and so keep them in the same place.

That women desire places more than objects may be due to the fact that desirable objects get crowded together in the limited space available to them. Even if objects are desirable to women, then, women nevertheless may not have room to experience such desires. Repeatedly in *East Lynne,* a lack of space seems to condemn women to confusions, overlappings, and conflicts of interests. Whereas men are able to distribute their desires in various directions and in various places, women experience various desires in the same place.

In the opening scene of the novel, Archibald meets with the earl of Mount Severn, Isabel's father, to negotiate the purchase of East Lynne. This is the first expansion on Archibald's part, by which he acquires options of desire. He now has a house that would justify a more ambitious marriage than the house in which he currently lives and which belonged to his father. Archibald does not give up the latter house, however. His law offices adjoin it, and even after he marries Isabel he returns every day to work there. To these two places Archibald will add, later in the novel, a place in Parliament:

> That he had long thought of sometime entering parliament was certain; though no definite period of the "when" had fixed itself in his mind. He did not see why he should confine his days entirely to toil, to the work of his calling. . . . That he would make a good and efficient public servant, he believed; his talents were great, his oratory was persuasive, and he had the gift of a true and honest spirit. That he would have the interest of West Lynne at heart, was certain, and he knew that he should serve his constituents to the best of his power and ability. (445–46)

Identified as an escape from confinement, entry into Parliament allows Archibald yet another place in which to live and work. This is a matter not merely of acquiring things or of increasing importance; it is suggested that Archibald himself will expand, with such opportunities to realize talents and increase powers he may not have used yet. Given the opportunity to add spatial dimensions to his daily life, Archibald has the opportunity to add dimension to his character.

In this masculine distribution of desire, multiple spaces are available for multiple objects. There is little overlap, little conflict of interest; indeed, new interests seem to come with new places. This makes possible clear distinctions that appear as moral integrity. When, late in the novel, Richard Hare needs a lawyer to make the case against Levison for the murder Richard is charged with, Archibald will not act, because Levison is also the man Isabel ran away with:

"I believe him to be guilty of the murder: but if lifting my finger would send him to his disgraceful death, I would cut off my hand, rather than lift it. For I could not, in my own mind, separate the man from my injury. Though I might ostensibly pursue him as the destroyer of Hallijohn, to me he would appear ever as the destroyer of another; and the world, always charitable, would congratulate Mr. Carlyle upon having gratified his revenge." (513)

Here a number of separations are insisted upon in order that there be no confusion about Archibald's motives. He is morally distinguished, in his own eyes and in those of others, by distinctions he makes. Archibald can satisfy this, his primary motive, yet also serve Richard's interests by finding, through his own professional contacts, another lawyer to help Richard.

The women of the novel, however, do not experience such distributions of desires. On the contrary, in women's experience various interests occur in the same place. This is true, for example, of Barbara Hare early in the novel as she experiences two desires analogous to Archibald's two desires: to help Richard, on the one hand, and to maintain her pride, on the other. Barbara needs advice about Richard's case; she is limited to personal rather than professional relations with lawyers and so chooses to go to Archibald. And even though he is a family friend, it is not proper for Barbara to appear in his offices; she tries it once but not again: "Is it quite sure that no stranger will come in? It would look so peculiar to see me here" (39). For this reason Barbara seeks out Archibald at his house, even after she has declared her love for him. Not only does this entail confusion and embarrassment for Barbara, it also results in confusion on Isabel's part. Because Isabel is told nothing about Richard, she assumes that Barbara and Archibald spend time together for reasons of personal desire.

Like Barbara, Isabel repeatedly finds that she does not have room for pride. When she agrees to marry Archibald, for example, her only apparent alternative is living with Lady Mount Severn, who insults her, even beats her. Although at this time Isabel is attracted to Francis Levison, Levison makes clear to her that he won't marry her. Humiliated by Levison as well as Lady Mount Severn, Isabel marries Archibald to have a place to live free of humiliation. Yet even this is potentially humiliating to her, because in time she becomes ashamed of not loving Archibald enough. There is no space for any distance between her sense of herself and her desire to please others. When Francis Levison comes to stay at East Lynne, despite Isabel's objections to his presence, she has even less room for her own perspective, confronted as she is by the conflicting demands of two men in the same house. Because of such crowding, Isabel's choices cannot consist of the separations that give Archibald his integrity.

Whereas for Archibald the willingness to cut off his hand rather than lose his disinterestedness is a representation of integrity, Isabel needs to be physically cut up before she can realize any separateness from the pressures of others. What is figure of speech for him is physical disfigurement for her, as she lacks even the field of representation in which to extend and reproduce her self. For Archibald, the desire to cut off his hand leads not to a loss of part of himself but to an addition to his integrity, dispersed and distributed in representation as well as action.

On the contrary, Isabel's options tend to overlap, and her interests conflict. One early example of this occurs before she is married, when she wants to help a local musician by giving her support to his concert. She dresses too richly for the event:

> The earl stared at her in amazement. "How could you dress yourself like that for a concert? . . ."
> " . . . But I did it on purpose, papa; I thought I would show those West Lynne people that *I* think the poor man's concert worth going to, and worth dressing for."
> "You will have the whole room staring at you."
> "I don't mind. . . . Let them stare."
> "You vain child! You have dressed yourself to please your vanity." (75)

In this case, Isabel oversteps the bounds of propriety, because her modesty conflicts with her desire to make a show on the musician's behalf. She cannot escape condemnation, because the generous motive produces the same result vanity would produce. She appears at the concert but appears out of place. Much later, when she returns to East Lynne as governess to her own children, Isabel experiences other conflicts of motives. She repeatedly has to stop herself from showing her love for her children to maintain her disguise. But whether she does or doesn't show her love, she is likely to feel "as if she had betrayed herself" (423). If she attempts to demonstrate her love in the role of the governess, she becomes, as she was at the concert, markedly out of place.

Other women in the novel also appear improper or morally dubious, difficult to clear of suspect behavior because of apparent conflicts of interest. Cornelia Carlyle remains, throughout the novel, a woman both dedicated to her brother and destructively jealous of his affection. She seems unable to make a clear distinction between her role as sister and other women's role as wife. Alice Challoner is another character who seems morally dubious even at her most generous. Knowing Francis Levison has seduced and ill-used another woman, Alice warns her sister Blanche not to marry him. Because she herself is that other woman, however, Alice cannot but appear self-interested (460–62). A certain crowding occurs in these instances. Not only are various emotions felt and displayed toward the same object, but also various women lay claim to the same object. Women overlap and appear replaceable one with another, not only as objects of desire but also in their own desires. It is this crowding and confusion, moreover, that seem to generate the most intense emotions of the novel, which are experienced among women rather than between men and women.

Masculine Privacy

Though it happens rarely, when Archibald is accused of a conflict of interest, it is quickly cleared up. On returning to England to find that Isabel has married Archibald, the earl of Mount Severn accuses Archibald of "taking advantage of my absence" to "clandestinely espouse" her (138). Archibald responds that he went to visit Isabel with no intention of proposing marriage and did so only because she was miserable living with Lady Mount Severn: "I learnt to love her at East Lynne; but I could have carried my love silently within me to the end of my life, and never betrayed it, but for that unexpected visit to Castle Marling" (141). Archibald's claim of integrity rests on his self-control, which prevents him from doing anything out of place. In this case, it is only because the earl has misunderstood Isabel's situation that Archibald's behavior appears out of place, and the earl ends the discussion by apologizing. Equally important to Archibald's appearance of integrity, however, is the fact that Mrs. Henry Wood has never described his love for Isabel. For the reader, therefore, Archibald's proposal of marriage seems a sudden response to the immediate situation rather than a long-standing emotion that would make his visit to Isabel seem dubious in the first place.

The emotional information withheld by the narrator constitutes a truly private realm of experience. The emotions of male characters in the novel are never elaborated, by themselves or by the narrator, in the way those of female characters are. One effect of this may be that males appear to have more integrity. Males also can appear more criminal than females, however; it seems that, whether good or evil, they are more definitely so than are the confusing female characters. At any rate, Archibald is able to keep his emotions to himself and thus able to keep separate from the confusing emotional sphere in which women, for the most part, live in this novel.

Archibald's emotions receive little attention and are assigned little complexity. "Oh, his was a true heart," the narrator says just after his marriage to Isabel; "he fervently intended to cherish this fair flower he had won: but, alas! it was just possible he might miss the way, unless he could emancipate himself from his sister's thraldom" (144). The only possible conflict here is external; that is, conflict, like other male emotional experience, is distributed across space to keep clear and distinct various male experiences. Archibald's maintenance of an emotional integrity is served also by his consistent ignorance of the emotions of the women around him. He remains oblivious to Isabel's jealousy, even after he has been told of it and even as he insists to her that he sees Barbara Hare so often because of "private business": "Mr. Carlyle on his part, never gave a thought to the supposition that she might be jealous: he had believed that nonsense at an end years ago" (263). Similarly, he is oblivious to Cornelia's jealousy: "[H]e was easy and unsuspicious; but had he only gained the faintest inkling of the truth, he would not have lost a moment in emancipating his wife from the thraldom of Miss Corny" (170). And he is ignorant of Barbara's love for him, even while behaving in ways she has interpreted as loving. After Barbara's outburst of love and jealousy, shortly after he has married Isabel, Archibald is "extremely annoyed and vexed":

"But, my dear Barbara, I never gave you cause to think that I — that I — cared for you more than I did care."

"Never gave me cause!" she gasped. "When you have been coming to our house constantly, almost as my shadow; . . . when you have been more intimate with me than a brother!"

"Stay, Barbara. There it is — a brother. I have been nothing else: it never occurred to me to be anything else," he added, in his straightforward truth. (167)

It is the repeated complaint of each of these women that she feels left out and excluded — as Barbara puts it, "as one isolated for ever, shut out from all that could make life dear" (165). Such exclusion, in keeping with the distribution of emotion among women, is blamed on another woman. Yet Archibald is the person for whom most of what matters to these women — most of their lives — simply doesn't exist.

Thus, Archibald is equally at a loss to understand all women and becomes, in relation to them, a kind of innocent. His innocence depends, however, on the absolute inaccessibility, in his experience, of the confusions women experience. Although Mrs. Henry Wood depicts no confusion whatever in Archibald's feelings, she seems to accomplish this only by providing very little depiction of his feelings at all. Innocence thereby becomes a matter of ignoring rather than lacking certain kinds of experience. On the one hand, Archibald zealously pursues the truth about Richard. On the other hand, he recognizes no clues to the truth about the lives of the women who surround him. A "practical, matter-of-fact man," Archibald is "honourable and true" (263), as he is when he claims innocence to Barbara "in his straightforward truth" (167). But these divergent truths — the truth of himself and the truths he doesn't know — are never reconciled.

Natural Superiorities

Archibald's practical repression of impractical truths marks the manliness with which he experiences and represses internal conflict. Mrs. Henry Wood labels Archibald "practical" because he is able to use representation to master conflict, without giving it a second thought or a second look. Strictly limited in his understanding, Archibald in fact knows much less than do the women of the novel, and this is his superiority. Women realize and practice the impractical, living out the conflict that superior men repress, and living it out in physical spaces rather than in representation. Here is evident a sorting out of conflicts. Women divide up their lives, their desires, their selves, their bodies, into parts. In parts, they experience conflicting elements of self and world that they neither contain nor repress. Unable to use representation to distance and differentiate parts of their experience, they have to practice, even incorporate, distance and differentiation.

Despite limited access to representation, which I have in earlier chapters identified as characteristic of needless consumption, women in *East Lynne* are consumers and identify consumption with the private domestic sphere. Representation is not necessary to their patterns of consumption, because for these women consumption is not needless. They desperately need, as I have argued, what once seemed needless consumption, for such consumption enables women to validate the fragmentation of self that gives them some security of existence. Women thereby naturalize patterns of consumption identified by Dickens, for example, as artificial. Women make necessary and inevitable patterns of experience that Dickens identified as both morally reprehensible and changeable. Cultivating unknowability and fragmentation, Mrs. Henry Wood's women characters remain "second-class"; moreover, their lack of moral stature is now known to be natural to them.

In such differences from superior men, women in *East Lynne* allow a sorting out of the "empirico-transcendental" tension that Michel Foucault identifies in Western culture beginning in the late eighteenth century. The tension that once characterized man, for example in Mary Shelley's *Frankenstein,* is relieved by the distribution of its conflicting elements. In *East Lynne,* if superior men experience these tensions, they don't know it. Their depths remain hidden, unknown and unexamined. Distributed among women, however, contradictory depths surface without being resolved. Socialized, the waste and frustration that Foucault locates in hidden depths of knowledge are acted out; uneconomical women "spend, wear out, and waste" resources in action that seems more evasive than progressive, while men alone progress.[11]

According to this transposition, kinds of experience that must be repressed if knowledge is to provide order, productivity, and progress, surface from depths. Even when recognized in the experience of women, waste and frustration and confusion are still contained by their location in women's private lives. This is not merely a geographical distinction. Women's emotions are shown to determine their identity in terms so incommensurable with male identity as to mark women as both a separate and, by nature, a "lower" species. This separation of genders, like that of Foucault's contradictory forms of male knowledge, remains one of height and depth, but these too are now socialized. Certain persons only — men — are capable of the reason, abstraction, and repressiveness necessary to public order. These persons naturally belong in positions of public power. Female persons belong beneath men in the social order because they experience kinds of confusion that belong in other kinds of depths: lower levels of morality, depths of emotion, and depths of nature that lie beneath civilized experience.

6

Naturalizing Class and Gender Distinctions:
The Return of the Native

The opening chapters of Thomas Hardy's *The Return of the Native*, published in 1878, provide an extraordinary representation of the state of knowledge in late Victorian England. I discussed in chapter 4 Dickens's depiction of knowledge in *Little Dorrit* as a production of unknowability. For Hardy, the production of the unknowable is in place as part of the production of knowledge, so that any discovery entails, in fact produces, a corresponding ignorance. The growth of knowledge increases both ignorance and knowledge, creating unknowns to be known, just as Dickens's bureaucracy creates blanks in forms to be filled in. For Hardy, however, the relativistic limits of knowledge are the necessary result of a conflict he stages between nature and culture. He in effect naturalizes the reproductive and self-referential character of Dickens's bureaucracy. Human consciousness is cut off from the surrounding world, as cut off as is Dickens's Circumlocution Office, to the extent that it cultivates knowledge. This is a "natural" effect of consciousness and knowledge, unavoidable given their structure and process.

The effects of cultivation are indicated in the scene in *The Return of the Native* in which the people on Egdon Heath, according to custom, build bonfires in early November:

> The cheerful blaze streaked the inner surface of the human circle ... with its own gold livery, and even overlaid the dark turf around with a lively lu-

minousness, which softened off into obscurity where the barrow rounded downwards out of sight. It showed the barrow to be the segment of a globe, as perfect as on the day when it was thrown up.... Not a plough had ever disturbed a grain of that stubborn soil. In the heath's barrenness to the farmer lay its fertility to the historian. There had been no obliteration, because there had been no tending.

It seemed as if the bonfire-makers were standing in some radiant upper storey of the world, detached from and independent of the dark stretches below. The heath down there was now a vast abyss, and no longer a continuation of what they stood on; for their eyes, adapted to the blaze, could see nothing of the deep beyond its influence.[1]

To build a fire on the barrow is to put the surrounding heath into darkness: the limited enlightenment produces unlimited darkness, "a vast abyss" beneath the barrow. To cultivate the fire is, like cultivating soil, to produce losses on the heath where "there had been no obliteration because there had been no tending."

In addition to the cultivation of the fire, Hardy is interested in another kind of culture. As the barrow is cut off from the heath by the tending of the fire, so the impression of the scene, in the cultivated mind of the observer, is disconnected from the objects actually seen:

Occasionally, it is true, a more vigorous flare than usual from their faggots sent darting lights like aides-de-camp down the inclines to some distant bush, pool, or patch of white sand, kindling these to replies of the same colour, till all was lost in darkness again. Then the whole black phenomenon beneath represented Limbo as viewed from the brink by the sublime Florentine in his vision, and the muttered articulations of the wind in the hollows were as complaints and petitions from the "souls of mighty worth" suspended therein.

... The brilliant lights and sooty shades which struggled upon the skin and clothes of the persons standing round caused their lineaments and general contours to be drawn with Düreresque vigour and dash.... Those whom Nature had depicted as merely quaint became grotesque, the grotesque became preternatural; for all was in extremity.

Hence it may be that the face of an old man, who had like others been called to the heights by the rising flames, was not really the mere nose and chin that it appeared to be, but an appreciable quantity of human countenance. (66–67)

Culture here produces in the mind of the observer various reflections on the scene before him, references to Dante and Dürer, for example.

This cultivation is also accompanied by certain losses. Culture works here against "Nature," which has depicted in one way what cultivation represents differently. Culture not only produces its own vision of things, it also produces a scheme of likeness and difference that is wholly relative. The sparks that fly "like aides-de-camp" into surrounding bushes, "kindling these to replies of the same colour," produce likenesses whose only cause is the fire. Similarly, likenesses produced by the cultivated mind "kindle" what is seen "to replies of the same colour" as Dante and Dürer. When the surrounding heath is made into a "vast abyss" by the fire, moreover, it evokes the *Inferno,* and this in turn produces still more resemblances, as between the wind on the heath and the sighs of the damned, between the scene in England and the *Divine Comedy.*

Such an extension of metaphor or likeness is itself cultivated in this passage. Not only in references to Dante but also in comparisons of sparks to aides-de-camp, of light to gold livery, and of moving shadows to leaves, Hardy practices and produces in his readers a tendency to see things in terms of other things quite distinct from Egdon Heath. Thus, by the time the reader reaches the old man, "who had like others been called to the heights," this figure has accumulated value because of the earlier conversions of the barrow into "heights" on which Dante might have stood. A kind of inflation is in process here. As various likenesses gain currency and "kindle replies" of their own, the scene accumulates value with no basis in what is actually there. There is a natural reality, Hardy insists, as in the old man's face, that is obscured by the light of the fire and that must be obscured to produce the likenesses detailed and implied in the passage. Once this obscurity occurs, value accrues in the production of symbolic relations that develop as part of a closed circuit of reference.

The new circuit of reference is created by fragmentation. Transferred onto a cultural grid of references to literature and art, the bits of the scene are given value in shades of light and darkness that provide a relative meaning only by blocking out most of what is present. The light changes images by breaking wholes into parts: only the nose and chin of a face show, only a few distant bushes are lit up. Then parts are represented as parts of something else: the bits of the face become the aesthetically pleasing brush strokes in a Dürer painting. The fragmentations make possible recombinations productive of more representations. This distortion of nature is necessary to art and to the symbolic order of difference. As in Dickens's "Sun and Shadow," the beginning chapter of *Little Dorrit*, light and shadow in Hardy's description here are purely relative — their meaning is supplied in relation to each other — and they distort reality by polarizing and relativizing it. For Dickens such distortions are avoidable, because they are caused by a desire to produce unknowability; but for Hardy such distortions are necessary to knowledge itself.

With this perspective, Hardy brings to the surface the "empirico-transcendental" tension that Michel Foucault identifies with modern Western knowledge. The human being both produces knowledge and recognizes that knowledge is limited because it is a human production. Thus, knowledge always produces control only with the sense of something eluding control. Hardy insists, in keeping with evolutionary theory, that human will and human knowledge have little extent and little power in the natural scheme of things. But he never simply recognizes these limits; he recognizes them in conflict with human knowledge and human will. That conflict comprises human experience yet perpetually splits it apart.

Nevertheless, in *The Return of the Native* as in *East Lynne,* this conflict is experienced to different degrees by different characters. Hardy, like Mrs. Henry Wood, effectively sorts out the tension, with only some characters fully experiencing it and other characters able to limit it. As in *East Lynne,* the intensity of empirico-transcendental tension is much greater for women, whereas middle-class men are able not only to ignore or repress the tension but also, like Hardy, to sort it out, to distribute it so that its effects are dispersed and their impact lessened. The lower-class "natives" of the heath, however, remain oblivious to such tensions. Hardy, then, offsets tension and confusion with a social order in which different groups experience different grades of tension and different capacities to sort out confusion.

Consuming Culture

According to Habermas, the late nineteenth century saw a transformation of public and private spheres as the two became "blurred" by disintegrations within each realm. In the twentieth century, "the public" in its consumption of culture is separated into classes of consumers who constitute a variety of audiences: "[T]he public is split apart into minorities of specialists who put their reason to use nonpublicly and the great mass of consumers whose receptiveness is public but uncritical." As the public becomes an audience, it changes from "a public critically reflecting on its culture to one that merely consumes it."[2] In another once-public sphere, that of government policy, public debate gave way in the nineteenth century to an administration of policy, which has now given way to a negotiation of policy not wholly public: "The process of the politically relevant exercise and equilibration of power now takes place directly between the private bureaucracies, special-interest associations, parties, and public administration."[3] Both public administration and public opinion are now influenced by private enterprise. Individuals who contribute their thoughts to the formation of public opinion are under pressure from political and economic agencies that advertise to shape public opinion. The individual who participates in public opinion is more consumer than rational, autonomous debater.

The identity of the individual in private has also increasingly become the identity of a consumer, due to a "surreptitious hollowing out of the family's intimate sphere"[4] that corresponds to the hollowing out of public opinion by advertising. The family has lost power as it has become less central to private enterprise, for one thing. In addition,

> [A]long with its functions in capital formation the family increasingly lost also the functions of upbringing and education, protection, care, and guidance. . . . Thus, in a certain fashion even the family, this private vestige, was deprivatized. . . . On the other hand, the family now evolved even more into a consumer of income and leisure time, into the recipient of publicly guaranteed compensations and support services. . . . As a result there arose the illusion of an intensified privacy in an interior domain whose scope had shrunk to comprise the conjugal family only insofar as it constituted a community of consumers.[5]

Thus consumption becomes the central experience of private life and of the individual in public life.

Such transformations of both public and private life by patterns of consumption blur distinctions between them but make possible other kinds of distinction. The fact that patterns of consumption indicate classes of consumers, the lower of which is the "mass audience," suggests a "refeudalized public sphere." Habermas emphasizes another resemblance to feudal behavior, as publicity and prestige, rather than public debate, give authority to public figures.[6] For Hardy, too, society is reclassed at the end of the nineteenth century in response to newly recognized realms of indistinction that threaten social order. The capacity of certain characters on Egdon Heath to represent cultural values publicly has become an unthinking process of display. Moreover, for Hardy as for Habermas, patterns of economic consumption account for this "refeudalization."

Hardy's Public Sphere

There is in *The Return of the Native* little evidence of government or public administration. Isolated as a rural community where little money is earned or spent, Egdon Heath is not connected to other parts of the country by a centralized government or economy. Indeed, the characters seem even more dispersed because of the local character of government agencies. This is suggested by the confusion that occurs over Thomasin and Wildeve's marriage. People can go to any of several nearby towns to obtain a license, and Wildeve has gotten a license at Budmouth. But he and Thomasin go to Anglebury to marry, only to find, as Wildeve says, "The license was useless at Anglebury. It was made out for Budmouth, but as I didn't read it I wasn't aware of that" (94). There seems to be no public institution or public arena that unites these people. They do not come together in church, even on Christmas morning: "In name they were parishioners, but virtually they belonged to no parish at all." People spend Christmas at friends' houses and "did not care to trudge two or three miles" to church (177).

Such dispersals of community leave as the only common ground the heath itself. But this natural common ground is also experienced dispersively. For one thing, characters are often on the heath simply to get somewhere; it is transitional space crossed by various paths and upon which are dispersed the few houses of its inhabitants. Moreover, characters often go out on the heath to be alone, or to be alone with one other person. If other people are seen, these meetings tend to be inadvertent, unwanted, or even unrecognized; characters follow people in secret, spy on one another, and eavesdrop, under cover of the trees, bushes, and darkness of the heath. For these characters, the heath is a public space into which they carry their privacy. It is experienced as a place divided into various private spaces, in which persons experience other people as threats to privacy rather than as parts of any common social identity.

Characters who meet on the heath to form a group tend to be characters of the lower class rather than the primary, middle-class characters of the novel. The lower-class natives of the heath meet according to tradition to take part in customary, often ritualistic events. This public sphere of action bears little resemblance to any sphere of government. Rather than exercising any conscious ordering mechanism, those who participate in the building of bonfires in early November, the mumming in late December, or maypole dancing in the spring repeat, often unconsciously, a natural order of events according to seasonal change. But it seems only as part of a natural order that characters regularly come together in the novel, and it is only the undistinguished characters of the lower class who regularly do so.

Hardy thus identifies two kinds of public order: nature and social class. Social classes, moreover, are primarily distinguished by their understanding of a particular relation between nature and culture. The only characters who share common, public experience are themselves "common," the undistinguished persons of the lower class who order their lives in repetitions that reflect rather than attempt to alter nature. These characters are undistinguished in part because they seem to have no private lives. They seldom appear alone in the novel, only one family of this class appears at home, and their internal lives are never represented. They speak a lot, but their thoughts and feelings appear only as they are publicly expressed. Moreover, much of what for the middle class is private and individual experience is experienced by the lower class in groups. Christian Cantle confesses to a group of people his fear that he is a man whom no woman will marry, and as a group they counsel him about his masculinity (74–78). Their conclusion, moreover, is that his failure is not a personal matter: "No moon, no man"; "The boy never comes to anything that's born at new moon" (76). As a group, too, the men have their hair cut and bathe on Sunday mornings: "[T]he local barbering was always done at this hour on this day; to be followed by the great Sunday wash of the inhabitants at noon, which in its turn was followed by the great Sunday dressing an hour later" (227).

Middle-class characters, on the other hand, are individually distinguished by their houses, their behavior in private, and their thoughts. Hardy identifies social class with a fragmentation of society that is not only economic but profoundly cultural. The middle-class characters of the novel actively cultivate themselves, whereas lower-class characters seem virtually unconscious of culture. The middle class is most distinguished as a group by its attempts to cultivate nature and thereby change experience that lower-class characters accept as naturally repetitive. The degree to which middle-class characters are invested in change, moreover, renders them subject to vastly increased fragmentation.

Nature, Culture, Gender, and Class

In *The Return of the Native,* characters who cultivate knowledge are thwarted by nature, which is identified as a confusing and obscure realm. But in Hardy's novel this natural conflict, as in *East Lynne,* is distributed unevenly among genders and social classes. Mrs. Henry Wood naturalizes obscurity and confusion in the emotional depths of women's experience that men cannot fathom. In *The Return of the Native,* depths of unknown feelings that conflict with conscious knowledge are present in men as well as women. But if it is human nature to be partly obscure and partly known, men are still able to remain ignorant of their own confusion. As in *East Lynne,* this distinction is available only to men who are "real men": Clym Yeobright, who has left behind an "effeminate" career in Paris (233), remains ignorant of much internal conflict, whereas Damon Wildeve, with "a lady-killing career" (93) in which women are the measure of his success, is a confused and ineffective character. Only the manly middle-class characters, Clym and Diggory Venn, are able to produce order and repress confusion both internal and external.

Yet for Hardy there is another dimension to confused "depths" of ignorance: the lower class of persons native to Egdon Heath. The characters of this class seem to experience obscurity as a wholly natural condition. They are identified, as I have suggested, with a culture that accepts as much as cultivates nature. And this means lower-class characters are repeatedly indifferent, whereas middle-class characters seek change and distinction. In their indifference and lack of distinction, lower-class characters are identified with the heath itself, which is indifferent to human cultivation and which is always the same:

> The untameable, Ishmaelitish thing that Egdon now was it always had been. Civilization was its enemy; and ever since the beginning of vegetation its soul had worn the same antique brown dress, the natural and invariable garment of the particular formation. . . .
>
> To recline on a stump of thorn in the central valley of Egdon . . . and to know that everything around and underneath had been from prehistoric times as unaltered as the stars over-head, gave ballast to the mind adrift on change, and harassed by the irrepressible New. The great inviolate place had an ancient permanence which the sea cannot claim. . . . The sea changed, the fields changed, the rivers, the villages, and the people changed, yet Egdon remained. . . . [E]ven the trifling irregularities were not caused by pickaxe, plough, or spade, but remained as the very finger-touches of the last geological change. (56)

This inviolate and unchanging place indicates a realm of prehistoric existence that, like the lower-class persons who inhabit it, resists cultivation and, indeed, any difference made by people.

In this place, then, Hardy situates his characters, at least his male characters, in classes, according to the level of conflict between nature and culture that they experience. The "highest" class of characters is made up of middle-class men who cultivate knowledge and order and are able to repress internal depths of confusion. These men adapt their desires to their environment, which is for them the location of conflict and confusion. Lower-class men avoid the antagonism of nature and culture by remaining internally indifferent to, even unconscious of, the conflict. Women, however, being internally divided between a desire for cultivation and emotions that conflict with cultivation, are déclassé. An internal conflict of nature and culture structures all their experience, so that they cannot bring any order to their lives. As in *East Lynne*, women cannot be classed because they have no capacity for order. If there are only two social classes in the novel, there are three levels of self-consciousness: men who are unconscious of their conflicting feelings, women and effeminate men who are conscious of their conflicting feelings, and a lower class of people who seem to live in a state bordering on unconsciousness.

In *The Return of the Native,* Hardy differentiates social classes in terms of their experience of production and consumption. What most characterizes these processes for Hardy is that they are difficult to distinguish. Any production also consumes something. Moreover, for Hardy there is an equally important third economic process, which is waste. Any production not only consumes but also wastes something. As in the transcendent depths underlying experience in Foucault's doubling of man, time and other resources are wasted in efforts to evade inevitable ends. Hardy thereby insists that productivity and consumption cannot be identified as a coherent or satisfying economic cycle in which one answers the other in an orderly exchange. Rather, production is identified as an artificial construct that merely represses the waste it causes.

Both men and women participate in the production and consumption of customs, of objects, of knowledge. But only men produce order. And only men are distinguished by order. Women in the novel may be distinguished from men, but they are distinguished by confusion, which they are depicted as both producing and consuming.

Masculine Economies

The counterproductive character of productivity in *The Return of the Native* is most sensationally evident in Clym Yeobright's efforts to become a schoolteacher. After he is married, and particularly after his wife and mother have quarreled, Clym "felt one thing to be indispensable — that he should speedily make some sign of progress in his scholastic plan." He begins to study "far into the small hours during many nights" (308), until he strains his eyes to the extent that "all thought of pursuing his work, or of reading print of any description, would have to be given up for a long time to come" (309). Almost using up his eyes, which in fact never recover, Clym's work produces learning at the cost of his body. His body has been wasted, Hardy indicates, not only because he cannot become a teacher but also because the beauty of his face is being ruined by the seriousness of his thinking: "The face was well-shaped, even excellently. But the mind within was beginning to use it as a mere waste tablet whereon to trace its idiosyncracies" (194).

Diggory Venn is another character for whom the overlap of production and consumption has sensational effects. Diggory sells reddle, used to mark sheep. The red dye that he distributes, however, he also absorbs, "and, like his van, he was completely red. One dye of that tincture covered his clothes, the cap upon his head, his boots, his face, and his hands. He was not temporarily overlaid with the colour; it permeated him" (58). Otherwise handsome, Diggory, like Clym, is "an instance of the pleasing being wasted to form the ground-work of the singular, when an ugly foundation would have done just as well for that purpose" (132).

The lower-class inhabitants of the heath tend not to use up their resources, and this seems so because they do not try to produce progress. Rather than attempting to change their own or others' lives, these characters engage in repetitive reproduction. The men work mostly producing fuel, cutting furze and turf; the production and consumption of fuel use up resources so gradually as to be unnoticed, and these resources eventually grow back. In other labor, the men repair things, such as the bucket that falls into Captain Vye's well. They also build bonfires and put up the maypole for community celebrations. Unlike Clym or Diggory, these men expect to consume what they produce, and they do not mind that they consume as much energy and resources as they produce. Nor do they mind waste. As natives of "the Egdon waste" (53), they are accustomed to uselessness.

For all these characters, production aims backward as well as forward. Hardy renders stages of economic growth indifferent as he identifies production with consumption and waste, and distribution with absorption. Yet the lower class, who work more at repairs and at production whose supplies are naturally replaced, are accustomed to the indifference of economic stages. Their "habitus," according to Pierre Bourdieu's classification of social classes according to taste, reproduces waste: they inhabit a waste, they waste a lot of time, and their patterns of consumption are wasteful.

Their indifference to use seems, however, to identify Hardy's lower class in terms Bourdieu uses to distinguish upper classes. For Bourdieu, twentieth-century consumption that is unrelated to need or use, but instead occurs on the basis of disinterested tastes, enables upper classes to distinguish themselves and their "good taste" from lower classes of poor people with poor taste.[7] Hardy's distinction of classes of consumers can be clarified by looking at his discussion of the mumming, a customary performance of the St. George play that is rehearsed at Captain Vye's house and performed at Mrs. Yeobright's house by lower-class men and boys:

> A traditional pastime is to be distinguished from a mere revival in no more striking feature than in this, that while in the revival all is excitement and fervour, the survival is carried on with a stolidity and absence of stir which sets one wondering why a thing that is done so perfunctorily should be kept up at all. Like Balaam and other unwilling prophets, the agents seem moved by an inner compulsion to say and do their allotted parts whether they will or no. This unweeting manner of performance is the true ring by which, in this refurbishing age, a fossilized survival may be known from a spurious reproduction. (178)

Here the persons for whom a custom survives have no apparent interest in its performance. Yet the fact that they are unconscious of the value of what they do gives their mumming "a true ring." Hardy distinguishes his lower class by its failure to cultivate its culture actively; the lower class reproduces, without desiring to change, even customs that have no apparent use.

The middle class, which would preserve customs like mumming as revivals or copies, has no use for them either, Bourdieu argues. Like antique objects, local customs are revived and preserved, though for Hardy this is a reproductive process: such customs are not original but instead are produced like commodities and kept like antiques to mark middle-class taste. Whereas the lower class doesn't care, the middle class cares but conceals its care; one practices "genuine" indifference, and the other only assumes indifference. The lower class maintains its customary way of life and so keeps things the same. The middle class keeps things the same in order to use them to represent its own distinction. For the middle class such things mark status, and that is why there is a demand for their reproduction. The close resemblance Hardy draws between middle and lower classes, whereby the middle class would seem to copy the lower for its own sense of status, is not merely ironic. It is part of Hardy's insistence on a fundamental indifference of progress and regress, so that to climb "higher," in social class or social progress, is also to return to "lower" forms of behavior. I will come back to this conflation in the last section of this chapter.

Diggory Venn and Clym Yeobright practice a middle-class form of indifference that links them to both middle- and lower-class men. They are identified with use but not with need, for what they desire is to be useful. In public service, Clym wants to start a school on the heath: "He wished to raise the class at the expense of individuals rather than individuals at the expense of the class. What was more, he was ready at once to be the first unit sacrificed" (230). Diggory is also disinterested, but he spends his time and energy "watching over Thomasin's interests" (134), sacrificing himself to an individual rather than a class. Neither of these men is actually useful to those they wish to serve. Clym goes blind and gives up teaching, and Diggory, with the best intentions, tends to make things worse instead of better for Thomasin and others. That their self-sacrifices seem wasted may be due to the fact that these men never consult those whose interests they claim to follow. They seem to create the needs they wish to fulfill.

Yet although they do not produce anything that is needed by anybody and thereby seem to reproduce only waste, both Diggory and Clym produce their own distinction. They mark themselves—as clearly as Diggory's reddle marks sheep—as disinterested, superior men. The men in the novel produce systematic distinctions by which they order their experience. Thus, despite their apparent nonproductivity, they reproduce the order that is the crucial need of their culture.

Uneconomical Women

The persons who are incapable of producing anything useful, either things or signs of distinction, are women. The indifference of the lower-class men who perform the mumming to preserving the custom of mumming allows changes to occur in its production. In *The Return of the Native*, it is women who are responsible for these changes; the wives and girlfriends of the performers have a use for the play that is merely decorative:

The girls could never be brought to respect tradition in designing and decorating the armour; they insisted on attaching loops and bows of silk and velvet in any situation pleasing to their taste. . . .

. . . During the making of the costumes it would come to the knowledge of Joe's sweetheart that Jim's was putting brilliant silk scallops at the bottom of her lover's surcoat. . . . Joe's sweetheart straightway placed brilliant silk on the scallops of the hem in question, and, going a little further, added ribbon tufts to the shoulder pieces. Jim's, not to be outdone, would affix bows and rosettes everywhere. The result was that in the end . . . Saint George himself might be mistaken for his deadly enemy, the Saracen. (178–79)

What seems at first production and consumption according to individual taste is then identified as driven by competition among women for decorative brilliance. The women's competition wipes out the marks of distinction otherwise present in the costumes of male rivals. Although they waste masculine distinctions, women seem unable to produce other forms of distinction; their men are feminized and rendered undistinguished by their competitive taste.

The other source of corruption of "original" custom in this performance is Eustacia Vye, who also has a use for the mumming. Though only men are mummers, Eustacia takes the place of Charley as the Turkish Knight to be at the Yeobrights' house and see Clym, who has just arrived from Paris. As when she builds a bonfire on the fifth of November to signal Wildeve, Eustacia participates in traditional rituals to get something out of them. Reproducing customs, Eustacia does not assume a middle- or a lower-class indifference to use. Like the lower-class women, she is identified with desire, corruption, competition, and waste.

Eustacia is so driven by desire that she seldom finds satisfaction in anything, even when she seems to get what she wants. Her uses of ritual are recognized as useless fairly soon after they are attempted. At the Yeobrights', disguised as the Turkish Knight, she sees not only Clym but also his cousin, Thomasin:

Eustacia felt a wild jealousy of Thomasin on the instant. . . . There was no knowing what affection might not soon break out between the two, so constantly in each other's society. . . .

. . . What a sheer waste of herself to be dressed thus while another was shining to advantage! . . . The power of her face all lost, the charm of her emotions all disguised. (200)

Each time Eustacia identifies an object of desire and attempts to gain it, she is frustrated. Use becomes useless, resources become waste.

Like the women who decorate the mummers' costumes, Eustacia drives production with competition. But Eustacia's taste is not for ribbons and scallops. An "epicure" of emotion (149), Eustacia is more interested in her feelings than in objects of feeling; "she seemed to long for the abstraction called passionate love more than for any particular lover" (121). Thus, at the Yeobrights', she apparently imagines that Thomasin frustrates her to produce emotional intensity: "To court their own discomfiture by love is a common instinct with certain perfervid women. Conflicting sensations of love, fear, and shame reduced Eustacia to a state of the utmost uneasiness" (201). Eustacia produces a conflict of sensation that, like the decorations on the mummers' costumes, erases certain distinctions to produce others. When a conflict between women replaces a conflict between men, there are no marks capable of maintaining distinctions between them. Masculine competition, reproduced in the mumming, profits from traditional distinctions. Female competition cannot keep straight the two sides. In fact, Eustacia's pleasure lies in a confusion of emotion. Both internally and externally, she courts confusion in her production and consumption of desire.

Relativism and Social Order

For Hardy, all persons who desire to change their experience are frustrated by the distance between their ability to change things and the apparently natural process of change that occurs in the world. In this natural process, human effort is only one of many factors contributing to change, which therefore is likely not to occur in accord with human aims. Human effort and human desire are parts of the way things happen but are not central or determinant. This is a form of fragmentation in the late nineteenth century that, unlike the social fragmentations that Habermas discusses, occurs in the field of knowledge, which is becoming increasingly relativistic across the disciplines, in philosophy and science alike.

In Hardy's fiction, relativism, which prevails in a natural order, causes fragmentations of experience that are identifiable both with patterns of consumption and with divisions of social class. On the one hand, all of his characters who experience desire are faced with the tragic recognition of the merely relative character of not only human desire but also all human understanding. Habermas discusses a "blurring" of public and private spheres of life toward the end of the nineteenth century. Hardy, from a relativistic perspective, identifies all human experience as in a blur, because he identifies the very cultivation of distinction as a production of difference and indifference at the same time. Differentiation only occurs relative to confusion. Yet on the other hand, even as Hardy enters his characters into a confused natural order in which relations obscure distinctions and classifications, he nevertheless classifies characters and so produces a social order.

The relativism of experience in *The Return of the Native* is evident in the tendency of subjects and objects alike to dissolve into relations between subjects and objects. Such relations have far more force in the lives of the characters than do subjects or objects themselves. This results in an indirectness of development in the novel. The love affair and subsequent marriage of Eustacia Vye and Clym Yeobright, for example, develop from an initial attraction on the basis of overheard, secondhand information. Eustacia eavesdrops on the gossip of men working outside her grandfather's house, hears that Clym is returning from Paris, and becomes infatuated with him. Clym hears of Eustacia, too, through a story, told by a local workman to Clym's mother, of Eustacia being stabbed with a needle in church by Susan Nonesuch, who thinks Eustacia is a witch (236–37). The indirection of information received in such ways allows imagination a lot of latitude. Building on bits of information that reflect only part of the person represented, Eustacia and Clym each identify the other in terms of her or his own desire for something else. She wants to leave the heath, and he wants to start a school; she believes he will take her to Paris, and he believes she will make a good schoolteacher. When she goes to look at his house and overhears him speaking to his mother, the abstraction of Eustacia's interest in Clym is indicated by the fact that it is not his words but his voice that appeals to her: "Was there anything in the voice of Mrs. Yeobright's son — for Clym it was — startling as a sound? No: it was simply comprehensive. All emotional things were possible to the speaker of that 'good night'. Eustacia's imagination supplied the rest" (172). Clym's voice is comprehensive in its possibilities because, as a form, it is open to endless interpretation. But Eustacia's imagination actually produces the comprehensiveness, which fits him into her dreams, plans, and emotions. This can be said of Clym too, but the two characters nevertheless experience very different degrees of isolation in their relativism.

Feminine Conflicts

Eustacia's desire for desire means that she cultivates intense emotions. This depends on being able to feel conflicting feelings, which intensify in relation to one another. On the evening she first sees Clym, "She glowed; remembering the mendacity of the imagination, she flagged; then she freshened; then she fired; then she cooled again. It was a cycle of aspects, produced by a cycle of visions" (172). Here the intensity and conflict of feeling are due to the lack of any direct knowledge of Clym; because she can only speculate, Eustacia is uncertain and changeable in her feelings about him. In her emotional life, then, is evident a closed circuit of reference that allows for a cultivation of emotional value. As in the depiction of knowledge in the scene of the bonfire building, in which light and shadow are relative differences that locate meaning in and limit value to symbolic relations, Eustacia's conflicting feelings constitute a realm of their own. Without reference to objects but intensified by their relation to one another, her emotions are valued in relation to one another rather than in relation to any object.

For Eustacia, value lies in difference rather than in material qualities. Her mind perceives relations rather than things and persons. And she identifies herself in relation to others, insisting on her difference more than anything else:

> In the matter of holidays, her mood was that of horses who, when turned out to grass, enjoy looking upon their kind at work on the highway. She only valued rest to herself when it came in the midst of other people's labour. Hence she hated Sundays when all was at rest, and often said they would be the death of her. To see the heathmen in their Sunday condition . . . walking leisurely among the turves and furze-faggots they had cut during the week . . . was a fearful heaviness to her. To relieve the tedium of this untimely day she would overhaul the cupboards containing her grandfather's old charts and other rubbish, humming Saturday-night ballads of the country people the while. But on Saturday nights she would frequently sing a psalm. (122–23)

Eustacia's need to be different means that she reacts to tedium by doing whatever others do not do. But it also causes her to feel tedium.
She keeps her distance from the world around her, spending a lot of
time looking through a telescope, always wishing to be in a sophisti-
cated town, always looking forward to a future different from the present. Absorbed mentally in imagined possibilities that have no resemblance to her immediate world, Eustacia in effect empties out her daily
life. When she has heard the heathmen talking of Clym,

> That five minutes of overhearing furnished Eustacia with visions enough to
> fill the whole blank afternoon.... She could never have believed in the morn-
> ing that her colourless inner world would before night become as animated
> as water under a microscope, and that without the arrival of a single visitor.
> (164)

Like an institution that creates forms with blanks to be filled in, functioning in wholly artificial and self-referential terms that invent demands
as well as supply answers to them, Eustacia's imaginative life both empties and fills up her time.

Absorbed in a symbolic system of meaning in which values are wholly
relative and constituted by conflicts of differences, Eustacia nevertheless focuses her desires on attaining certain objectives. This is yet another conflict within her experience, one between actual relations and
imagined objects. Escape from her unhappy life on the heath is the
goal of Eustacia's existence. It is because Clym is from Paris that he
first attracts her, and Eustacia remains resolute, even after marriage, in
hoping to go there with him. Yet if her conscious hopes are focused
on going someplace else, Eustacia's unconscious desires seem committed
less to another place than to constant displacement. It seems that, at this
deeper level, Eustacia is attracted to Clym because of his contrariness.

This is suggested in the dream she dreams on the night she first sees
him, of a knight with his visor closed, who dances with her:

> [S]he felt like a woman in Paradise. Suddenly these two wheeled out from
> the mass of dancers, dived into one of the pools of the heath, and came out
> somewhere beneath into an iridescent hollow, arched with rainbows. "It
> must be here," said the voice by her side, and blushingly looking up she
> saw him removing his casque to kiss her. At that moment there was a crack-
> ing noise, and his figure fell into fragments like a pack of cards. (174)

In part this dream seems premonition: Eustacia will die in a pool on the heath, and Clym's glory will fall apart when it is clear he is unable to take her away from Egdon. But seen as wish fulfillment, the dream seems to work not to achieve Eustacia's expressed desires but instead to maintain a conflict of desires, a conflation of the man who is to take her away with the man who says, "It must be here," a conflation of desire with death, a conflation of culmination with destruction. The buried realm of Eustacia's dreams is both conflicted and "prehistoric" in the indistinctions it suggests between polarities. Clym, according to this reading, becomes attractive not because he can satisfy her conscious desires but because he both invites and antagonizes those desires, representing both their object and their frustration in different elements of his character and experience.

One form of antagonism that may be necessary to Eustacia is that between her conscious and unconscious desires; another is evident between progressive and regressive elements of her experience. Neither antagonism is resolved. Eustacia eventually escapes Clym only to return to Wildeve, with whom she also dances, at a village celebration: "The dance had come like an irresistible attack upon whatever sense of social order there was in their minds, to drive them back into old paths which were now doubly irregular" (324). From this point on, Eustacia seems a backslider. More exactly, her condition is one of intensified irresolution toward the end of the novel. This is part of her regression. Even on the night she is to run away with Wildeve, she is struggling: "Can I go, can I go? . . . He's not *great* enough for me to give myself to—he does not suffice for my desire!" (421). Repeating the form of discontent that has characterized her throughout the novel, Eustacia remains in internal antagonism. It is because of this unresolved conflict that it is never clear whether she actually decides to run away and by accident falls into the weir or whether, deciding she cannot get away, she throws herself in. Hardy "ends" her life with an endlessly unresolved death.

Masculine High-Mindedness

Such a deconstructive reading is also invited by Clym Yeobright's experience. Desirous of progress, Clym has quit his profitable career in

Paris to start a school on Egdon Heath for local working people. One of his hopes in marrying Eustacia, a hope that seems particularly blind, is that she will help by teaching in the school. The greatest apparent obstacle to this plan is, at least initially, Clym's mother, who wants him to be conventionally successful, "to push straight on, as other men do — all who deserve the name" (233). Yet Mrs. Yeobright's antagonism seems necessary to Clym, as is clear when she begins to give in to him:

> His theory and his wishes about devoting his future to teaching had made an impression on Mrs. Yeobright. Indeed, how could it be otherwise when he was a part of her. . . . He had despaired of reaching her by argument; and it was almost as a discovery to him that he could reach her by a magnetism which was as superior to words as words are to yells.
>
> Strangely enough he began to feel now that it would not be so hard to persuade her who was his best friend that comparative poverty was essentially the higher course for him, as to reconcile to his feelings the act of persuading her. From every provident point of view his mother was so undoubtedly right, that he was not without a sickness of heart in finding he could shake her. (247–48)

Here, as with Eustacia, a realm of indistinctions — "he was a part of her" — and antagonism is glimpsed beneath Clym's conscious feelings. On the surface, his apparent respect for his mother's good judgment and independence seems to cause him disappointment, because he sees her compromised when she becomes supportive of him. But beneath this rational, and suspect, desire for distance from her may lie a deeper desire for separation.

Thus it may be to remain in antagonism that Clym marries Eustacia, of whom Mrs. Yeobright disapproves. Like Eustacia, Clym seems to court conflicting emotions:

> Sometimes he wished that he had never known Eustacia, immediately to retract the wish as brutal. . . . Though his love was as chaste as that of Petrarch for his Laura, it had made fetters of what previously was only a difficulty. . . . Just when his mother was beginning to tolerate one scheme he had introduced another still bitterer than the first, and the combination was more than she could bear. (260)

Here it seems possible that Eustacia's desirability to Clym is due to her undesirability to his mother. Such unconscious antagonism is most evident in the dream Clym dreams while Mrs. Yeobright is knocking at his door. It is because no one lets her in that she turns toward home again and dies on the heath. Eustacia is blamed for this, but Clym, too, seems to have heard his mother at the door. His dream, he explains, "was about my mother. I dreamt that I took you to her house to make up differences, and when we got there we couldn't get in, though she kept on crying to us for help" (353). At some level he is aware of his mother being refused entrance to his house. Yet he remains unconscious of it.

What is most important to the difference between Clym and Eustacia is that if such antagonisms do rule his behavior, Clym doesn't know it. Nor does Hardy do more than imply the importance of antagonism to Clym, whereas its importance to Eustacia is part of her consciousness and is emphasized in narrative descriptions of her. For Eustacia, conflicts that Clym represses occur on the surfaces of experience. She does not contain them but, on the contrary, experiences herself in conflicting terms, as a different person at different times and in different places.

The conflict between the surfaces and depths of Clym's feelings for his mother, whereby he both wants to be united with her and rejects her, remains in force throughout the novel. The last scene, after the deaths of both Eustacia and Mrs. Yeobright, depicts Clym as an itinerant preacher:

> He stated that his discourses to people were to be sometimes secular, and sometimes religious, but never dogmatic; and that his texts would be taken from all kinds of books. This afternoon the words were as follows:-
> " 'And the king rose up to meet her, and bowed himself unto her, and sat down on his throne, and caused a seat to be set for the king's mother; and she sat on his right hand. Then she said, I desire one small petition of thee; I pray thee say me not nay. And the king said unto her, Ask on, my mother: for I will not say thee nay.' " (474)

The incompleteness of Clym's biblical quotation suggests a hidden realm of unacknowledged conflict. The antagonism of conscious and unconscious experience, progress and regress, knowledge and reality, are in full force if not really evident.

On the evident level, Clym preaches that one should honor one's mother, try to improve things, do better in the future than one has done in the past, because Clym himself still suffers guilt about his mother's estrangement and death. But what is not evident here contradicts all of these good intentions, and the contradiction is increasingly apparent the more one knows. If one reads or remembers more of the biblical text Clym quotes, the relation of mother and son changes. Bathsheba has asked Solomon, her son, to allow Adonijah to marry Abishag. And although Solomon has agreed to grant her request, when he hears it he orders Adonijah's death (1 Kings 2: 19–25).

The effect of recognizing a "more complete" biblical text than Clym cites is to undermine even as it extends knowledge. Ending his novel with this scene, Hardy insists, again, on the irresolution rather than ends of experience. He suggests that beneath the surfaces of knowledge lies a vast and unknown realm of reality that confuses all the clarity of what people know, regressing toward primitive and destructive experience even as it progresses. To know more is to be thrown into uncertainty, to be faced with knowledge as uncertainty.

But no man in the novel cultivates uncertainty. Hardy does not call attention to such conflicts in Clym's experience; he leaves them beneath the surface of the narrative. Only Eustacia, it appears, in her desire to extract from experience as much sensation as she can, brings conflict to consciousness. When she goes to the Yeobrights' in disguise as a mummer, for example, she produces conflicts for her emotions. First she becomes jealous of Thomasin; then she feels insulted:

> "Nobody here respects me," she said. She had overlooked the fact that, in coming as a boy among other boys, she would be treated as a boy. The slight, though of her own causing, and self-explanatory, she was unable to dismiss as unwittingly shown, so sensitive had the situation made her. (200–1)

Eustacia produces a hyperconscious world where everything has an emotional and personal valence. Raising the pitch of emotional intensity by cultivating difference as antagonism, she has no capacity to repress or control conflict.

Gendering Commodity Culture

Hardy's society on Egdon Heath, where few commodities are available, replicates patterns of behavior identifiable as part of commodity culture. I discussed in chapter 3 fragmentations of experience in Dickens's

The Old Curiosity Shop as early evidence of the processes that William Leiss has identified with commodification. Leiss emphasizes the partial character of both subjects and objects as exchange values. Subjects and objects are represented in terms of attributes, partial characteristics that can be assigned to other subjects and objects. Floating free of material referents, the attributes of objects are subject to endless displacement and can be transferred to other objects, to subjects, to different places. As with the menthol cigarette advertised in pictures of rural beauty, the commodity can pick up attributes from other objects, subjects, and places, because none has a stable identity of its own.[8] What results is, as Jean-Christophe Agnew says, "seemingly random movement of detached and fragmentary motives and goods through a radically defamiliarized material and symbolic landscape."[9]

Such systematic fragmentations or dissolutions of subjects and objects occur repeatedly in *The Return of the Native* because of the detachment of any particular human mind from the surrounding world. For Hardy, the human mind is the locus and means of displacements and fragmentations that for critics of commodity culture are social processes. Moreover, the mind, in its perpetual fragmentation of experience, is always divided between experiences of symbolic displacement and the recurrent idealization of wholeness and stability: both fragments and wholes are abstractions.

Yet men seem able to find more stability in their representations of experience than do women. In the first of two scenes I will look at as evidence of a consumer mentality in *The Return of the Native,* Diggory Venn watches from a distance a landscape markedly "defamiliarized" as it becomes the scene of the bonfire building. At first the figure who appears on the barrow, only later identified as Eustacia Vye, appears as part of a unified and satisfying scene. As the scene dissolves, however, the observer must negotiate unfamiliar territory:

> As the resting man looked at the barrow he became aware that its summit, hitherto the highest object in the whole prospect round, was surmounted by something higher. It rose from the semi-globular mound like a spike from a helmet. The first instinct of an imaginative stranger might have been to suppose it the person of one of the Celts who built the barrow, so far had all of modern date withdrawn from the scene. . . .

... Such a perfect, delicate, and necessary finish did the figure give to the dark pile of hills that it seemed to be the only obvious justification of their outline. Without it, there was the dome without the lantern; with it the architectural demands of the mass were satisfied. The scene was strangely homogeneous, in that the vale, the upland, the barrow, and the figure above it amounted only to unity. ...

The form was so much like an organic part of the entire motionless structure that to see it move would have impressed the mind of a strange phenomenon. Immobility being the chief characteristic of that whole which the person formed portion of, the discontinuance of immobility in any quarter suggested confusion.

Yet that is what happened. The figure perceptibly gave up its fixity, shifted a step or two, and turned round. As if alarmed, it descended on the right side of the barrow. ... The movement had been sufficient to show more clearly the characteristics of the figure, and that it was a woman's.

The reason of her sudden displacement now appeared. With her dropping out of sight on the right side, a new-comer, bearing a burden, protruded into the sky on the left side. ... A second followed, ... and ultimately the whole barrow was peopled with burdened figures.

The only intelligible meaning in this sky-backed pantomime of silhouettes was that the woman had no relation to the forms who had taken her place. ... The imagination of the observer clung by preference to that vanished, solitary figure, as to something more interesting, more important, more likely to have a history worth knowing than these new-comers, and unconsciously regarded them as intruders. (62–64)

What Diggory Venn "sees" here is mostly a series of invisible, imagined relations of much more value than the objects observed (the barrow, the figure) because they are what satisfy aesthetic, formal demands. According to the ideals of aesthetic unity, certain attributes of the scene — finish, homogeneity, unity, immobility — take precedence over objective characteristics.

To attribute unity and homogeneity to the scene, however, is to identify it only partially. For one thing, from a different perspective the values attributed to it might be inappropriate; thus the partial perspective of the observer is responsible for much of the scene's character. For another thing, the elements of the scene are not perceived in their actual wholeness. The "figure" seen is Eustacia Vye but is recognized only as an abstract and symbolic form, so emptied of individual identity as to be seen as representative of the ancient Celts. Homogeneity and unity are attributed only to objects already associated with parts. The observer is unable to sense Eustacia's wholeness because the apparent unity of the scene as a whole makes any particular element seem only a fraction of a thing. Even the landscape that seems a whole is partial, and the parts of it are also wholes.

The illusion of the scene's unity dissolves when something happens. Partiality takes over when change occurs and a narrative begins. As Venn watches, the elements of the scene disperse, and when this happens, the scene suggests only confusion — a confusion that appears, however, only in relation to the illusion of unity that has come before. But a new evaluation follows the movements of the figures of the scene, according to which the observer's imagination clings to the displaced figure, attributing to it a number of new characteristics — originality, interest, importance — that are derived *from* its displacement. Such attributes constitute a set of values with no referent whatever in the experience of the persons observed. By this point the observer is utterly deluded about the figure, who, in relation to those who succeed her on the barrow, seems to have come first (although Eustacia has only lately come to Egdon) and to be pushed out by intruders (who are in fact "natives").

Diggory is abstracted in time and space from the spectacle he observes. His spatial distance enables him not to see certain details that would particularize the scene; it enables him enough scope to compose his spectacle of many ingredients, so that the scene becomes comprehensive; and it enables him to use space to organize relations among the parts of the scene. Moreover, he values the elements he sees in spatial terms; their organization in space meets aesthetic standards, as does his "aesthetic" distance from them. Space here is used to provide order, and time is reordered to correspond to the spatial order. History collapses as Eustacia is identified as a Celt. Then, because her figure stands out in space, Diggory assumes that hers and no other's has "a history worth knowing." And although what he actually sees is "confusion," he nevertheless begins to make up a history about a solitary person driven from her place by "intruders."

What Hardy emphasizes is the abstract, formal character of ideals, ideas, and desires, which are thereby disconnected from their physical environment. Diggory's and Hardy's aesthetic "demand" here is as separated from natural and actual things — and the values it assigns are as alien to natural and actual things — as are demands for commodities in late-nineteenth-century society. In Hardy's view, both demands and the alienation they require are due to a "natural" disjunction between the human mind and the world as it exists outside the human mind.

In another landscape later in the novel, a different exchange occurs when Eustacia Vye goes "out to seek pleasure" at a country dance (322). Like Diggory, abstracted from the objects around her, Eustacia is nevertheless a consumer of a different sort. She meets Wildeve and begins to dance:

> Through the length of five-and-twenty couples they threaded their giddy way, and a new vitality entered her form. The pale ray of evening lent a fascination to the experience. There is a certain degree and tone of light which tends to disturb the equilibrium of the senses, and to promote dangerously the tenderer moods; added to movement, it drives the emotions to rankness, the reason becoming sleepy and unperceiving in inverse proportion; and this light fell now upon these two from the disk of the moon. All the dancing girls felt the symptoms, but Eustacia most of all. . . . The air became quite still; the flag above the waggon which held the musicians clung to the pole, and the players appeared in outline against the sky. . . . Eustacia floated round and round on Wildeve's arm, her face rapt and statuesque; her soul had passed away from and forgotten her features, which were left empty and quiescent, as they always are when feeling goes beyond their register.
>
> How near she was to Wildeve! . . . Wildeve by himself would have been merely an agitation; Wildeve added to the dance, and the moonlight, and the secrecy, began to be a delight. Whether his personality supplied the greater part of this sweetly compounded feeling, or whether the dance and the scene weighed the more therein, was a nice point upon which Eustacia herself was entirely in a cloud. (322–23)

Rather than seeking pleasure in objects of desire, Eustacia is carried away from the objective world altogether, and from herself too. Like Diggory in the earlier scene, she is in the presence of figures who appear, because of the light, as "outlines against the sky." But Eustacia doesn't notice them. She does not perceive fragmented objects so much as she experiences an inner fragmentation, with her soul passing out of her features and her feeling moving "beyond their register."

The scene in which Diggory watches the figure on the barrow is described mostly in terms external to him. His perceptions, moreover, identify the objects he perceives according to "aesthetic demands," which are wholly conventional and impersonal and are ordered according to rules of aesthetic unity. Eustacia's experience of pleasure is confused. Her reason is "sleepy," and she is "entirely in a cloud" when it comes to distinguishing the elements of her experience. She experiences "delight" and "compounded feeling," but her perceptions are neither directed at nor differentiated in their objects; nor do they correspond to any conventional standard of judgment. What is external and what is internal to her are in confusion.

Diggory's pleasure is a matter of record, coded and conventionalized in its demands; but Eustacia's pleasure is beyond even the register of her own features. Her experience is registered here only as spectacle, in which she is the central figure. Unlike Diggory, whose perceptions as a subject anchor the description of his pleasure, Eustacia is not differentiated as a subject from objects, nor does she seem capable of making such differentiations. Her pleasure lies in this among other confusions; she takes pleasure in being "taken" by emotion.

If Eustacia exists more as object than subject even in the scene of her own pleasure, this indicates that she is represented little differently as a subject than she is in the earlier scene in which she is watched by Diggory. In the earlier scene she is empty and still, a figure resembling a statue; in the later scene her face is "empty and quiescent," "statuesque," and she is a form "entered" by vitality, which emphasizes her status as object. In both scenes she is identified with disintegration, first in the dissolution of the earlier scene's aesthetic unity, and later in the split of body and soul. First she disappears bodily, to become a missing object of desire; later she is carried away internally.

Represented as an empty figure, Eustacia lacks means of representation, means even of recording or reading experience. She is embodied as object and figured as object; but as subject she is neither aware of objects nor able to figure. She does not seem to have the space or time needed for such distinctions. Even as she is identified out in the open in both scenes, and even as she seems dispersed in space by the splitting she experiences, her own feelings are "compounded" and things fuse together in her perception. Moreover, Hardy identifies Eustacia's dancing as a confined activity: "A clear line of difference divided like a tangible fence her experience within this maze of motion from her experience without it. . . . She had entered the dance from the troubled hours of her late life as one might enter a brilliant chamber after a night walk in a wood" (323). Closed in yet carried away, Eustacia is depicted in this scene as she often appears in the novel: looking through her telescope, from a place that feels like a prison to her, at distant things and places. Like Isabel Vane in *East Lynne*, Eustacia's eyes look elsewhere, especially when she is looked at. But unlike the distances Diggory uses for purposes of ordering and understanding, Eustacia's telescope collapses space so that her eyes are drawn to points in space as if she were, immediately, there. In different places at the same time, she is split up in space. Moreover, because she does not sort out her experience, Eustacia doesn't know the difference between what she is now doing with Wildeve at the dance and what she used to do with him. Her history also collapses as she feels what she felt before and is driven "back into old paths" (324).

With differences in time and space collapsed, Eustacia corresponds to women who "lack lack," according to current theories of female desire: Eustacia seems to desire the distance that would enable desire.[10] With her object pleasure, she is difficult to identify as pleased or satisfied. Whereas Diggory Venn can identify pleasure according to objects, measures, and standards, Eustacia seems so confused in her emotional intensity that she can't tell pleasure from anything else. Diggory exhausts the potential of the scene he watches, pleased by it until it differs from his ideal; Eustacia exhausts herself. Immediately experiencing herself as object and subject of pleasure, her pleasure consumes her.

Yet she is a consumer, and she puts much heavier demands on the supply of the "commodities" she desires than do the men of the novel. Though Eustacia is not much of a purchaser, she is a consumer of culture like those Habermas identifies with a late-nineteenth-century public. But unlike Diggory or Clym, when Eustacia joins a public she is one of a mass. Seeking entertainment and excitement, she experiences these by joining a public group in which she hopes to be carried away from herself. Whereas early in the novel she is frustrated by the loss of status and recognition she experiences when disguised as one of the mummers, later she wishes to escape her status and recognition. It is in her loss of reason that Eustacia joins those persons who perform "unweetingly" the traditional rituals of the heath. The abstraction she and they experience in this public sphere is not the disinterested abstraction of logical men debating public policy or organizing public orders. Eustacia and the other dancers are abstracted from their surroundings by a "consuming" interest in pleasure that cuts subjects off from rational control of their experience. Grouped together in an undifferentiated mass, these consumers seem to be subject to control by others because of their unreasoning consumption.

Men above the Masses

Whereas Eustacia ends her life in a hole, by falling into Shadwater Weir and drowning, both Diggory Venn and Clym Yeobright are raised to heights of distinction. Both men are able to dominate space by means of distinguishing representations that Eustacia does not employ. Eustacia and the lower class of persons on Egdon Heath experience their own indistinction in the repetitive performances of mumming, dancing, and bonfire building. Diggory and Clym both experience returns at the end of the novel: Diggory returns to the life of a middle-class farmer; and Clym stages a comeback as a kind of teacher, preaching on the heath. But despite the repetitive character of these returns, both men represent comebacks in redemptive symbolics that identify them with mythical, biblical precursors whose distinction is transferred to them.

Diggory, as a reddleman, has been marked "unmistakably, as with the mark of Cain," by his reddle and has been treated by the people on the heath as a bogeyman or devil: "That blood-coloured figure was a sublimation of all the horrid dreams which had afflicted the juvenile spirit since imagination began" (131). But Diggory reappears late in the novel as his white self, in a change that seems "supernatural" (450). As if transformed from devil to god, his reincarnation as a white man implies his ability to control and manipulate not only representations but also bodies, and this is in fact how he has lived for some time. Selling the dye that marks sheep as private property, Diggory is identified with the ability to monitor bodies as they move through space and to signal where they belong. His social life is also focused on policing, specifically on tracking the movements of Eustacia and Wildeve;

he follows Wildeve around and even shoots at him to keep him away from Eustacia. Acting as a go-between, Diggory also carries objects, letters, and information from various characters to others. In effect, he is able to distinguish bodies not only by marking them but also by marking the spaces between them, covering and enforcing distances that keep them distinct.

Whereas Diggory exercises the apparently disinterested power of the police, Clym exercises the apparently distinterested power of a public leader who goes through the forms of a representative publicity such as Habermas identifies with twentieth-century public figures. Discussing "public relations" as the cultivation of representative publicity in modern life, Habermas argues that "[t]he aura of personally represented authority returns as an aspect of publicity" to the extent that "modern publicity indeed has affinity with feudal publicity." The medieval public sphere "was entailed by the position of the carriers of representation and was also safeguarded in its continuity through a firm traditional symbolism." Hardy identifies a public sphere in *The Return of the Native* in which the public figure of a male character takes a position and "mobilizes a potential of inarticulate readiness to assent" in ways resembling feudal power.[11]

Clym Yeobright experiences a less conscious but more powerful social rise than Diggory when he is identified with Christ. Taking the dominating position at the top of Rainbarrow that Eustacia was forced to give up early in the novel, Clym appears like her lone figure. But he

> was not really alone. Round him upon the slopes of the Barrow a number of heathmen and women were reclining or sitting at their ease. They listened to the words of the man in their midst, who was preaching, while they abstractedly pulled heather, stripped ferns, or tossed pebbles down the slope. This was the first of a series of moral lectures or Sermons on the Mount....
> ... The speaker was bareheaded, and the breeze at each waft gently lifted and lowered his hair, somewhat too thin for a man of his years, these still numbering less than thirty-three.... He stated that his discourses to people were to be sometimes secular, and sometimes religious, but never dogmatic; and that his texts would be taken from all kinds of books. (473–74)

Identified, but only implicitly, with Christ, Clym can never be alone; he always carries another identity, which gives him public significance.

As someone whom people look up to and listen to, Clym claims no power to dictate and no interest in dogma. His discourses are listened to by people who barely pay attention; he assumes his "commanding" position (473) not before a thoughtful public but before an audience that listens to him without thinking. Tolerant, broad-minded, appealing, he is in a position whose power is underwritten by his repetition of traditional signs of powerful humility, apparently both produced and consumed unconsciously.

Hardy's spectacular depiction of power here suggests a shift from an abstracted to an embodied public authority in specific terms of a return to a set of beliefs held in common and assigning ultimate power to God. It is a return to the idea of a medieval prince, "[t]he image of the body that informed monarchical society" and that "was underpinned by that of Christ," Claude Lefort argues. The medieval prince, Lefort says, was "*supposed* to obey a superior power," and "declared himself to be both above the law and subjected to the law, to be both the father and the son of justice." In this the prince differs from the modern totalitarian leader.[12] Lefort's distinction is made in terms that identify the prince with Foucault's doubled man, an identification particularly appropriate to Hardy's princely Clym. In keeping with this image, Clym denies dogma, claims to take "all kinds" of ideas and books into consideration, and exercises power on the basis of his representation of a figure of religious dogma.

The Return of the Native

If Hardy returns to the feudal in this novel, he does so as part of his return to "native" elements of experience. Significantly, he locates his novel in a setting so natural that it is recognized as impervious to culture:

> The untameable, Ishmaelitish thing that Egdon now was it always had been. Civilization was its enemy; and ever since the beginning of vegetation its soul had worn the same antique brown dress. (56)

This inviolate and unchanging place indicates a realm of natural existence unimagined in the earlier novels I have discussed. It comes closer than does Mrs. Henry Wood's depiction of women to the various late-nineteenth-century conceptions of prehistoric, elemental depths I have mentioned in my discussion of *East Lynne*: Freud's unconscious, Nietzsche's Dionysian unity of nature and culture, Darwin's primordial past. But like Mrs. Henry Wood's undifferentiated mass of women, Hardy's nature is placed in both space and time so as to be averse to history.

According to G. M. Young, the past claimed so much attention among thinkers in England in the 1870s because history was taking the place of space as the frontier of discovery:

> Such a change as had come over the human mind in the sixteenth century, when the earth expanded from Europe to a globe, was coming over it again. Now space was shrinking, time expanding.... [A]s the home of mankind grew smaller to the imagination, so the history of the race was perceived to stretch in longer and longer perspective.... [A] new age, not to be reckoned by the centuries of Europe or even the millennia of Egypt and Babylon, was thrown open to explorers, and close on the discovery of primitive man followed the discovery how much of man, not least his religion and his morality, was still primitive.
>
> We are passing from the statistical to the historical age, where the ground and explanation of ideas, as of institutions, is looked for in their origins: their future calculated by observation of the historical curve. As Early Victorian thought is regulated by the conception of progress, so the late Victorian mind is overshadowed by the doctrine of evolution.[13]

This may seem a "historical" development, but, as Young notes, the sense of history looks for certain changeless characteristics of "man" and culture. Aimed "backward," this sense of history discovers backwardness rather than any history of social change. And the spatial dimensions of this "discovery" make social history itself difficult to discover.

Searches into the past, unlike searches into unknown parts of the world, are necessarily regressive according to a progressive historical perspective. As part of what was a clear courting of regression toward the end of the nineteenth century, British imperialist ideology, in which expansion and discovery remained primarily spatial, shifted from a progressive to a regressive posture. In his *Rule of Darkness,* Patrick Brantlinger contrasts the "reform optimism" of evangelical imperialists early in the century, when colonies were often treated as future civilized nations, with a later recognition of primitivism and brutality, in both colonized and colonizers, as unchanging and unchangeable attributes of human nature.[14] Such a shift clearly served to justify increasingly "brutal" imperialist exploitation, as Brantlinger emphasizes.

The identification of regressive, "prehistoric" spaces in the world allowed colonial appropriation to occur as a return to some elemental place of belonging. Moreover, such a return balanced progress: it suspended the forward impetus of progress, and it could seem "fulfilling" because it provided a return of what progress left behind. A century earlier, the Gothic novel claimed a return to nature for its sensitive, contemplative characters but effected a more compelling psychic return in its reconception of desire. Displacing nostalgia for the past by identifying progressive desire with a return to the past, Walpole's hero and heroine are moved backward toward lost objects, as well as forward to substitutions for lost objects. Hardy's *Return* returns human experience to its "native" elements by identifying the human condition in a similar suspension between regression and progression. Invoking, moreover, a supposedly natural economy in which only middle-class men are productive, like Smollett in *Humphry Clinker,* Hardy stages a replay of class distinctions that Smollett thought were disappearing forever from the public scene.

These distinctions respond to a new sense of confusion in Victorian society, confusion that can be identified with the increasing relativism of knowledge. Opposite ends of experience begin to run into each other when scientific knowledge and colonial appropriation identify progress as a move toward a prehistoric realm. It is characteristic of *The Return of the Native* that what seem to be various extremes from one perspective, are from another perspective repetitions of each other. Clym ends the novel in the image of Christ, in one kind of repetition. The behavior of middle-class consumers mimics the indifference of lower-class consumers, in another kind of repetition. Progression resembles regression. Yet this kind of confusion produces the need for a spatial order to sort it out. What G. M. Young does not consider, but what has been considered by current postcolonial theorists, is that if space was limited for colonial exploration and exploitation, practices of domination could nevertheless be progressively refined by a spatialized order that never runs out of potential or resources, because it is a matter of representation.

Conclusion

In the preceding chapters I have traced a history of representations of public and private life in British novels and, much more briefly, works of social theory written between the later eighteenth and the later nineteenth centuries. I have not focused solely on one line of development in these works, but have tried to indicate that the contents of public and private realms have shifted around in different representations and at different times. Trollope, for example, puts emotional depths into the public domain as part of the order of social class, whereas both earlier and later writers confine emotion to private experience. Dickens identifies a production of obscurity as the work of both reproductive bureaucratic orders and social snobbery; Mrs. Henry Wood internalizes a reproduction of obscurity in women's private lives; then Hardy moves the cultivation of obscurity back into the public domain as a characteristic of all knowledge.

These novels clearly indicate that public and private, as Leonore Davidoff says, "have become a basic part of the way our whole social and psychic worlds are ordered, but an order that is constantly shifting, being made and remade."[1] Such remaking is a matter not only of reconceiving public and private experience but also of ordering many changing concepts and changing circumstances. Shifts occur even to the extent that what first appear as threats to stability later appear as securities, what at one time is known as artificial is known at another time as natural. Even the idea of restoration, which seems a safely conservative process in the eighteenth century, becomes, in Hardy's work, a threat to whatever security is possible, as "depths" of old, prehistoric, or backward behavior are identified with disorder.

At the same time that writers disagree about exactly what constitutes public and private life, however, there are recognizable lines of thought carried through and developed in the course of this hundred-year period. The lines of development on which I have focused have the effect of stabilizing and securing various kinds of economic and political behavior. One clear example of this is the focus of my last chapter. When Hardy insists that the "nature" of human knowledge is relativism, patterns of individual frustration and social fragmentation that Dickens located in bureaucratic processes, and therefore understood as changeable, become necessary and inevitable.

Also evident in Hardy's fiction is an unusually secure separation of public from private life along gender lines. Most clearly in the late works I have discussed, *East Lynne* and *The Return of the Native,* gender distinctions are used to sort out various kinds of political and economic experience that don't fit together as parts of a stable public order. Various kinds of knowledge are distributed among men and women so as to separate contradictions within modern experience. Self-knowledge that represses emotional confusion characterizes men of the middle class; knowledge of the self as emotionally confused and insecure characterizes women. This distinction not only keeps public order distinct from private confusion, it also maintains both public order and consumer demand. It is a distinction useful, therefore, both to public order and to economic growth as it keeps separate the independence and rationality required of orderly persons from the emotional dependence and insecurity that fuel consumption.

The usefulness of gender to the reorderings I have identified is emphatic, even though the particular terms in which genders are distinguished are inconsistent. Trollope identifies women with repressive representation and men with depths of feeling, putting the genders into unusual categories of experience. Yet like Mrs. Henry Wood and Thomas Hardy, Trollope uses gender as a primary ordering device in his depiction of community life. His gendering of repression allows him to represent his ruling class of gentlemen as free of repressive tactics.

Knowledge is repeatedly and increasingly depicted in nineteenth-century novels as a gendered phenomenon, and knowledge and gender work together as means of distinguishing and ordering public and private experience. That different kinds and practices of knowledge are distributed among men and women means that no single theory of knowledge is adequate to understanding the experience of both genders. I have argued in particular that the "empirico-transcendental" tension that for Michel Foucault characterizes nineteenth-century knowledge can account for only half the story, if that. Foucault identifies contradictions between surfaces and depths, both within structures of institutional knowledge and within the male individual's psyche. Beneath its surfaces, the production of knowledge turns against itself, confounded by knowledge of nature just as the individual psyche is confounded by knowledge of death.

Foucault's distribution of knowledge depends on a structural containment that becomes, in the novels I have discussed, a primarily male and primarily public capacity. Women, in private life, experience little containment of their contradictory experiences and indeed seem to distribute, to openly elaborate the contradictions that men keep within limits so secure as to obscure them. Male characters ignore the reproductive effect of the progress they produce, an effect belonging to the depths of Foucauldian knowledge. But female characters know themselves to be reproductive and reproduced. Women, therefore, experience much confusion in their lives, whereas men bury confusion beneath the surfaces of their experience.

In effect, these distinctions mean that the kinds of experience Foucault identifies beneath the surfaces of knowledge become inhabited depths. "Depths" of confusion, ignorance, and emotion and "depths" of waste become the provinces of certain groups of persons who are thereby marked off from the men who take part in reproductions of knowledge and public order. What Foucault identifies as a contradiction within structures of knowledge becomes a mechanism of social order.

Persons known to be disorderly are not merely located beneath others in the social order, they are understood to belong there naturally.

One strategy by which knowledge stabilizes experience is to represent various "man"-made phenomena as natural. Bourdieu's theory of the reproduction of social classes by means of naturalized experiences of taste and habitus points to such a practice. Dickens suspects a similar effect when he criticizes the cultivation of unknowable phenomena in the name of knowledge. Late-nineteenth-century theories of relativism claimed natural limits to knowledge, identifying necessary disparities between nature and culture. When women as well as lower-class "natives" are then identified with nature and natural reproduction and middle-class men are thought to participate in cultural reproduction, social repression seems to occur inevitably, as part of a necessary relation of nature and culture.

This strengthening of gender and class divisions is another form of what Jürgen Habermas has identified as a "refeudalized public sphere" in the late nineteenth century.[2] My attention to knowledge as well as gender is the source of the greatest differences between my readings of eighteenth- and nineteenth-century literature and Habermas's theory of public and private spheres through these centuries. I have argued that knowledge rather than reason became the primary medium of government in nineteenth-century Britain, and that this development, according to Dickens in *The Old Curiosity Shop,* could be understood to cause subjectivity to be emptied out. Habermas argues that a "surreptitious hollowing out of the family's intimate sphere" occurred later in the century as family life was reduced to a life of consumption.[3] But earlier reforms of knowledge, as well as patterns of consumption, seem to contribute to an internal emptiness.

Moreover, in the novels I have considered, subjective emptiness is increasingly linked to a female lack of self-knowledge. Emptied of any distinct sense of self, the female who mirrors others also reproduces a consumer mentality. She is understood to do so, moreover, not because patterns of consumption have restructured both private and public life, as Habermas argues, but because of some deep emotional need.

My revisions of the thinking of both Habermas and Foucault have allowed me to trace a more detailed series of revaluations and reforms of public and private experience, as well as a more intricate sense of trade-offs occurring between the two. Though I have proposed developments and distinctions that are inconsistent and at times indefinite, this arises, at least in part, from the shiftiness and indefinition of public and private realms in the works I have studied. These I hope I have represented so as to indicate both the ways in which public and private distinctions have been used to produce social order, and a variety of representations sufficient to mark those social orders as optional.

Notes

Introduction

1. See Joyce Appleby, *Capitalism and a New Social Order: The Republican Vision of the 1790s* (New York: New York University Press, 1984), pp. 25–33. In *The Passions and the Interests: Political Arguments for Capitalism before Its Triumph* (Princeton: Princeton University Press, 1977), Albert O. Hirschman traces a history of changing ideas of passion and interest that served capitalism (see especially part 1).

2. McKendrick discusses the new "world where fashion was being deliberately designed to encourage social imitation, social emulation and emulative spending, a world which blurred rather than reinforced class divisions and allowed the conspicuous lead of the fashion leaders to be quickly copied by the rest of society." See his introduction to *The Birth of a Consumer Society: The Commercialization of Eighteenth-Century England,* by Neil McKendrick, John Brewer, and J. H. Plumb (Bloomington: Indiana University Press, 1985), p. 43.

3. One recent critic of bureaucracy, Claude Lefort, suggests how systematic self-production is built into the bureaucratic institution. See his "What Is Bureaucracy?" in *The Political Forms of Modern Society: Bureaucracy, Democracy, Totalitarianism,* ed. John B. Thompson (Cambridge: MIT Press, 1986), especially p. 108.

4. I discuss Pierre Bourdieu's *Distinction: A Social Critique of the Judgement of Taste,* trans. Richard Nice (Cambridge: Harvard University Press, 1984), in chapters 4 and 6 especially.

5. A similar pattern of displacement is suggested by Nancy Armstrong's argument that eighteenth-century conduct books provided a nonpartisan and nonviolent mediation, in domestic life, of conflicts enacted in public political struggles. See her *Desire and Domestic Fiction: A Political History of the Novel* (New York: Oxford University Press, 1987), p. 69.

6. Ibid., p. 20.

7. In *The Disorder of Women: Democracy, Feminism, and Political Theory* (Cambridge: Polity Press, 1989), Carole Pateman argues that "beliefs about women [have] become an acute, though not always acknowledged, problem in social and political theory and practice" since "about the seventeenth century" (18). My readings of novels suggest that the identification of women with subversion and disorder occurs with particular emphasis in the later nineteenth century. In her discussion "Feminist Critiques of the Public/Private Dichotomy" (chapter 6), Pateman also discusses the gendered identity of the public and private spheres of liberal theorists, including Habermas.

8. Michael McKeon, *The Origins of the English Novel, 1600–1740* (Baltimore: Johns Hopkins University Press, 1987), p. 155.

9. Ibid., pp. 174–75.

10. Armstrong, *Desire and Domestic Fiction*, p. 73.

11. Ibid., p. 81.

12. Jürgen Habermas, *The Structural Transformation of the Public Sphere: An Inquiry into a Category of Bourgeois Society*, trans. Thomas Burger (Cambridge: MIT Press, 1989), pp. 7–8. All subsequent references are to this edition; page numbers are cited in the text.

13. Particularly useful is Leonore Davidoff's discussion, in *Worlds Between: Historical Perspectives on Gender and Class* (New York: Routledge, 1995), pp. 255–59, of "multiple publics" in nineteenth- and twentieth-century Britain. Davidoff's analysis provides a clear sense of the historical variety and complexity of relations of gender, class, and public/private distinctions (see chapter 8, pp. 227–76).

14. Nancy Fraser, "Rethinking the Public Sphere: A Contribution to the Critique of Actually Existing Democracy," in *Habermas and the Public Sphere*, ed. Craig Calhoun (Cambridge: MIT Press, 1992), p. 115.

15. I can note here one sense of a public that I do not consider much, and that is a reading public. In *The Letters of the Republic: Publication and the Public Sphere in Eighteenth-Century America* (Cambridge: Harvard University Press, 1990), Michael Warner emphasizes particularly the importance Habermas assigns to reading — of newspapers, criticism, novels — in the identification of a critical, debating public of rational men. In Warner's historically specific explanation of a "public sphere," the republican "culture of print" enables a reader to "imagine oneself, in the act of reading, becoming part of an arena of the national people that cannot be realized except through such mediated imaginings" (xiii). A somewhat parallel analysis of an English reading public is offered by Jon P. Klancher in *The Making of English Reading Audiences, 1790–1832* (Madison: University of Wisconsin Press, 1987). Klancher's emphasis is on the formation more of a middle class than of a national public. Klancher argues that the English middle class was characterized as a readership by its critical capacity to balance various perspectives and to remain detached while multiply entertaining them.

Several of the novelists I discuss identify "culture-consuming" publics in terms of the personal detachment necessary to Warner's and Klancher's reading publics. But fairly early on, public spheres are identified with knowledge rather than critical acumen, and through the nineteenth century consumption becomes increasingly identified with fragmented private lives of women rather than with a coherent male public.

16. See Fraser, "Rethinking the Public Sphere," pp. 110–11.

17. Michel Foucault, *The Order of Things: An Archaeology of the Human Sciences* (New York: Vintage, 1994), pp. 238–39.

18. Ibid., p. 256.

19. Ibid., p. 257.

20. Alan Liu, *Wordsworth: The Sense of History* (Stanford: Stanford University Press, 1989), pp. 304–5.

21. Such internalizations and abstractions of social relations are evident in the work not only of McKeon and Armstrong but also of a number of other critics. David Marshall, discussing Adam Smith's theory of sympathy in *The Theory of Moral Sentiments*, emphasizes that Smith's "impartial spectator" is ideal, so that no second person is actually necessary to "sympathy." See Marshall's *The Figure of Theater: Shaftesbury, Defoe, Adam Smith, and George Eliot* (New York: Columbia University Press, 1986), pp. 172–90. John Bender, in *Imagining the Penitentiary: Fiction and the Architecture of Mind in Eighteenth-Century England* (Chicago: University of Chicago Press, 1987), discusses an internalization of otherness in the eighteenth-century subject (see especially pp. 221–27). Terry Castle discusses the dematerialized character of memory and desire that detaches subjects from the world around them in the Gothic novel. See her "The Spectralization of the Other in *The Mysteries of Udolpho*," in *The New Eighteenth Century: Theory, Politics, English Literature*, ed. Felicity Nussbaum and Laura Brown (New York: Methuen, 1987), pp. 231–53.

22. Foucault, *Order of Things*, p. 312. See also Foucault's discussion of "man" as "empirico-transcendental doublet" (pp. 318–22).

1. Models of Stability: Production and Consumption in *Humphry Clinker* and *The Castle of Otranto*

1. John Sekora, *Luxury: The Concept in Western Thought, Eden to Smollett* (Baltimore: Johns Hopkins University Press, 1977), p. 64.

2. Jürgen Habermas, *The Structural Transformation of the Public Sphere: An Inquiry into a Category of Bourgeois Society*, trans. Thomas Burger (Cambridge: MIT Press, 1989), p. 27.

3. Tobias Smollett, *Humphry Clinker* (1771; reprint, ed. Angus Ross, Harmondsworth, England: Penguin, 1967), pp. 133–34, 136. All further references are to this edition; page numbers are cited in the text.

4. Habermas, *Structural Transformation*, p. 47.

5. Horace Walpole, *The Castle of Otranto: A Gothic Story* (1764; reprint, ed. W. S. Lewis, Oxford: Oxford University Press, 1964), p. 3. All further references are to this edition; page numbers are cited in the text.

6. Joyce Appleby, "Ideology and Theory: The Tension between Political and Economic Liberalism in Seventeenth-Century England," *American Historical Review* 81 (1976): 509.

7. Ibid., pp. 514, 513, 515.

8. Ibid., p. 514.

9. J. G. A. Pocock, *The Machiavellian Moment: Florentine Political Thought and the Atlantic Republican Tradition* (Princeton: Princeton University Press, 1975), pp. 486–87.

10. Ibid., p. 487.

11. Daniel Defoe, *An Essay Upon the Publick Credit* being an Enquiry How the Publick Credit Comes to Depend Upon the Change of the Ministry or the Dissolution of Parliaments (London, 1710). The passage is cited by Isaac Kramnick in *Bolingbroke and His Circle: The Politics of Nostalgia in the Age of Walpole* (Cambridge: Harvard University Press, 1968), p. 40.

12. Michel Foucault, *The Order of Things: An Archaeology of the Human Sciences* (New York: Vintage, 1994), pp. 238–39.

13. Ibid., p 239.

14. Adam Smith, *An Inquiry into the Nature and Causes of the Wealth of Nations* (1776; reprint, ed. R. H. Campbell, A. S. Skinner, and W. B. Todd, Oxford: Clarendon Press, 1976), p. 456.

15. See James H. Bunn's discussion of how the "poetic garden" of the eighteenth century indicated an increasing groundlessness of works of art, in "The Aesthetics of British Mercantilism," *New Literary History* 11 (1980): 309–11.

16. See Appleby's discussion, in "Ideology and Theory," of seventeenth-century balance-of-trade economists, who were "[b]locked from appreciating the role of domestic consumption," which they treated as "a necessary evil" (500).

17. Adam Smith, *The Theory of Moral Sentiments* (1759; reprint, ed. D. D. Raphael and A. L. Macfie, Oxford: Clarendon Press, 1976), p. 22, quoted in David Marshall, *The Figure of Theater: Shaftesbury, Defoe, Adam Smith, and George Eliot* (New York: Columbia University Press, 1986), p. 172. Marshall discusses this relation as "theatricality," thereby suggesting a self-division of conscious compromise between subject and object: "The mirror of sympathy in which the spectator represents to himself the feelings of the other person and places himself in the position and person of the other is itself mirrored in the experience of the person who knows he is being viewed" (172). Moreover, the desire for agreement between self and other causes suffering to be adjusted so that it accords with what others see: "Thus sympathy has a social function: it forces us to moderate our passions in order to create a 'harmony and concord with the emotions' of those who are watching us" (173).

18. Marshall, *Figure of Theater*, pp. 189–90. In *Imagining the Penitentiary: Fiction and the Architecture of Mind in Eighteenth-Century England* (Chicago: University of Chicago Press, 1987), John Bender also emphasizes the abstract character of spectatorship in Smith's moral theory, in that no second person is really necessary for the presence of the "impartial spectator." Bender points to this production of otherness within the self as evidence of the gradual internalization of punishment in the eighteenth century (see especially pp. 221–27).

19. Recent critics of *Tristram Shandy*, which began publication in 1759, have analyzed Sterne's cultivation of curiosity and detachment. As Carol Kay says of *Tristram Shandy*, "Curiosity in Sterne is not the dangerous political passion that we read about in Hobbes. . . . Sterne's curiosity is agreeable; it is not only a source of pleasure in itself, it is also an attitude that enhances social agreement." The enhanced "agreement" Kay points to is not an agreement on moral or rational standards but an inclusiveness

made possible by the inconsequential and detached character of eccentric individuals who have less and less in common. See Kay's *Political Constructions: Defoe, Richardson, and Sterne in Relation to Hobbes, Hume, and Burke* (Ithaca: Cornell University Press, 1988), p. 214. John Mullan, in *Sentiment and Sociability: The Language of Feeling in the Eighteenth Century* (Oxford: Clarendon Press, 1988), pp. 163–83, also emphasizes Sterne's cultivation of social distance in his discussion of ways that "the text exploits rather than shares" the innocence of characters (174).

20. Nancy Armstrong, *Desire and Domestic Fiction: A Political History of the Novel* (New York: Oxford University Press, 1987), p. 75. See Armstrong's discussion of how eighteenth-century conduct books affect "the dismantling of the aristocratic body" (p. 77) and other forms of display by women (pp. 75–81).

21. Judith Wilt, *Ghosts of the Gothic: Austen, Eliot, and Lawrence* (Princeton: Princeton University Press, 1980), p. 25.

22. Ian Watt emphasizes the authentic detail and concrete particularity of the prose of Richardson and Defoe. See his discussion of formal realism in *The Rise of the Novel: Studies in Defoe, Richardson, and Fielding* (Berkeley: University of California Press, 1957), pp. 32–35.

23. Calling attention to the Gothic tendency toward mistaken identity, Eve Kosofsky Sedgwick has argued that misunderstandings occur because the social code is itself archaic, as if incomplete or only "halfway toward becoming a language, a code, a limited system of differentials that could cast a broad net of reference and interrelation." The many confusions of identity in Gothic novels, Sedgwick argues, result from the incompleteness of a differentiating code in conjunction with the weakness of any grounds more secure than a code, such as "the fiction of presence." "The noncode level of discriminations having been vitiated by the fascination of the code," personal identity is limited largely to signs that make individual identity extremely difficult to secure. (See Sedgwick's *The Coherence of Gothic Conventions* [New York: Methuen, 1986], pp. 158, 159, 160.) But what seems regressive here may also be progressive, since the very insecurity of referentiality leaves representation free to proliferate, to produce and reproduce representations and likenesses.

2. Productions of Knowledge: *Emma* and *Frankenstein*

1. Jürgen Habermas, *The Structural Transformation of the Public Sphere: An Inquiry into a Category of Bourgeois Society,* trans. Thomas Burger (Cambridge: MIT Press, 1989), p. 56. All subsequent references are to this edition; page numbers are cited in the text.

2. This shift of rational thought from a medium of public debate to a means of producing value had both public and private repercussions in the early nineteenth century. My reading of Austen's *Emma* follows a number of lines suggested by Nancy Armstrong, who argues that Austen's "novel helped to create the conditions theorized by Bentham—a world largely written, one in which even the difference between words and things was ultimately a function of discourse." See Armstrong's "The Self Contained: *Emma,*" in *Desire and Domestic Fiction: A Political History of the Novel* (New

York: Oxford University Press, 1987), pp 134–60; quotation on p. 156. I want to add to Armstrong's connections between Austen and Bentham specifically by identifying reconceptions of critical discourse as a productive social and psychological mechanism — productive of knowledge, productive of objects of desire, productive of desire itself.

3. Sidney and Beatrice Webb, *English Local Government: Statutory Authorities for Special Purposes* (London: Longmans, Green, 1922), p. 423.

4. Ibid., p 425.

5. Ibid., p. 426.

6. Claude Lefort analyzes the self-productive character of modern bureaucracy:

[I]t is essential to grasp the movement by which the bureaucracy creates its order. *The more that activities are fragmented, departments are diversified, specialized and compartmentalized, structural levels are multiplied and authority is delegated at each level, the more the instances of co-ordination and supervision proliferate, by virtue of this very dispersion, and the more bureaucracy flourishes* [Lefort's emphasis].

Rather than serving to carry out work assigned from outside itself, then, the bureaucracy works to perpetuate itself: "The more bureaucrats there are and the more complicated the system of personal dependence becomes, the more the bureaucracy as a whole is constituted as a rich and differentiated milieu and acquires an existence for itself." See Lefort's "What Is Bureaucracy?" in *The Political Forms of Modern Society: Bureaucracy, Democracy, Totalitarianism,* ed. John B. Thompson (Cambridge: MIT Press, 1986), p. 108.

7. Michel Foucault, *Discipline and Punish: The Birth of the Prison,* trans. Alan Sheridan (New York: Pantheon, 1977), pp. 182–83.

8. Jane Austen, *Emma* (1816; reprint, ed. Stephen M. Parrish, New York: Norton, 1972), p. 23. All subsequent references are to this edition; page numbers are cited in the text.

9. Nancy Armstrong argues that in *Emma,* "signs of political distinction are transformed to point not to the object represented so much as to the person who uses the signs," and that Austen thereby creates a new grammar. See *Desire and Domestic Fiction,* p. 141.

10. Jane Austen, *Pride and Prejudice* (1813; reprint, ed. Donald Gray, New York: Norton, 1994), p. 135.

11. See particularly Judith Wilt's discussion of *Emma* in *Ghosts of the Gothic: Austen, Eliot, and Lawrence* (Princeton: Princeton University Press, 1980), pp. 163–72. Wilt emphasizes the Gothic dimensions of Emma's imagination and of the doubling of characters in the novel.

12. As Arthur W. Frank says in his discussion of "the mirroring body," the aim is less consumption of objects than the production of desires: "What counts is the endless producing and reproducing of desire, of the body in the world's image and the world in the body's image." See his "For a Sociology of the Body: An Analytical Review," in *The Body: Social Process and Cultural Theory,* ed. Mike Featherstone, Mike Hepworth, and Bryan S. Turner (London: Sage, 1991), p. 63. I will discuss consumption and "the mirroring body" at greater length in the next chapter.

13. Jon P. Klancher theorizes that the emerging middle class was formed by its reading and, as a readership, was characterized by its critical capacity to balance various perspectives and remain detached while entertaining them. See his *The Making of English Reading Audiences, 1790–1832* (Madison: University of Wisconsin Press, 1987), pp. 51–75.

14. Mary Shelley, *Frankenstein, or The Modern Prometheus* (1818; reprint, London: Penguin, 1985), pp. 116–18, 110. All subsequent references are to this edition; page numbers are cited in the text.

15. Gertrude Himmelfarb, *The Idea of Poverty: England in the Early Industrial Age* (New York: Knopf, 1984), p. 129.

16. Fred Botting, *Making Monstrous: "Frankenstein," Criticism, Theory* (Manchester: Manchester University Press, 1991), pp. 145–46.

17. Ibid., 147, 153.

18. Michel Foucault, *The Order of Things: An Archaeology of the Human Sciences* (New York: Vintage, 1994), pp. 318, 277.

19. See Homi K. Bhabha's argument, in *The Location of Culture* (London: Routledge, 1994), that Foucault spatializes history and so denies history to colonized people (pp. 196–97).

20. Joan Copjec, *Read My Desire: Lacan against the Historicists* (Cambridge: MIT Press, 1994), p. 128. Copjec discusses *Frankenstein* and vampire literature in the context of another issue in public debate at the end of the eighteenth century: mothering, specifically breast-feeding, which was advocated by Mary Wollstonecraft, among others. Focusing on the anxiety surrounding breast-feeding, Copjec argues that anxiety is caused by "a lack of lack, a failure of the symbolic reality wherein all alienable objects, objects that can be given or taken away, are constituted and circulate" (119). Vampire literature warns against "*the drying up of the breast*" (128; emphasis added) and the loss of the part-object as object of desire.

21. See the introduction to Chris Baldick's *In Frankenstein's Shadow: Myth, Monstrosity, and Nineteenth-Century Writing* (Oxford: Clarendon, 1987) for his initial discussion of myth and monsters, pp. 4–9.

22. Elisabeth Bronfen, in *Over Her Dead Body: Death, Femininity, and the Aesthetic* (New York: Routledge, 1992), traces representations of dead women in European novels of the eighteenth and nineteenth centuries. Bronfen argues that these representations have the effect of "appeasing the threat of real mortality, of sexual insufficiency, of lack of plenitude and wholeness" (xii). See her discussion of the dependence of male creativity on female death in *Frankenstein* (pp. 130–38).

3. The Emptied Subject of Public Knowledge: *The Old Curiosity Shop*

1. Charles Dickens, *The Old Curiosity Shop* (1840–41; reprint, ed. Angus Easson, Harmondsworth, England: Penguin, 1972), pp. 120–21. All further references are to this edition; page numbers are cited in the text.

2. See Jonathan Crary, *Techniques of the Observer: On Vision and Modernity in the Nineteenth Century* (Cambridge: MIT Press, 1992), p. 94, for a discussion of the nineteenth-century viewer as a "neutral conduit, one kind of relay among others." Crary analyzes how physiological reconceptions of vision early in the nineteenth century led in two directions: "toward the increasing standardization and regulation of the observer" and toward an increasing "sovereignty" of the observer (150).

3. Jürgen Habermas, *The Structural Transformation of the Public Sphere: An Inquiry into a Category of Bourgeois Society,* trans. Thomas Burger (Cambridge: MIT Press, 1989), pp. 131–32.

4. Benjamin Disraeli, *Coningsby* (1844; reprint, London: Longmans, 1906), p. 98.

5. David Roberts, *Victorian Origins of the British Welfare State* (New Haven: Yale University Press, 1960), pp. 100, 100–101. The phrase "presumptuous empiricism" is quoted from J. Toulmin Smith, *Government by Commissioners, Illegal and Pernicious* (London, 1849), p. 367.

6. Thomas Carlyle, "Signs of the Times" (1829), in *The Complete Works of Thomas Carlyle* (New York: Crowell, 1912), p. 472.

7. Ibid., p. 480.

8. John Stuart Mill, *Autobiography* (1869–70; reprint, ed. Jack Stillinger, London: Oxford, 1971), p. 162.

9. Alexander Welsh, *George Eliot and Blackmail* (Cambridge: Harvard University Press, 1985), pp. 33, 43–44.

10. Ibid., pp. 40–41.

11. Loren Eisley, *Darwin's Century: Evolution and the Men Who Discovered It* (New York: Anchor, 1961), p. 196.

12. Ibid., p. 199.

13. Crary, *Techniques of the Observer,* p. 81.

14. Ibid., especially pp. 94–96.

15. Michel Foucault, *The Order of Things: An Archaeology of the Human Sciences* (New York: Vintage, 1994), p. 257.

16. William Leiss, *The Limits to Satisfaction: An Essay on the Problem of Needs and Commodities* (Toronto: University of Toronto Press, 1976), pp. 88–89.

17. Jean-Christophe Agnew, "The Consuming Vision of Henry James," in *The Culture of Consumption: Critical Essays in American History, 1880–1980,* ed. Richard Wightman Fox and T. J. Jackson Lears (New York: Pantheon, 1983), p. 71.

18. Ibid.

19. Ibid., pp. 71–73. Thomas Richards also identifies a fluid field of consumption in his discussion of the transformation of the human body, in England at the end of the nineteenth century, into a "field for advertised commodities." Through this transformation, commodities sold for personal hygiene became characteristic of the body itself:

Patent medicine advertising laid the self completely open to commercial assault. It eroded the boundaries of the self by opening it up to various kinds of therapeutic intervention. Simultaneously it fragmented the self by reducing selfhood to a series of acts of consumption, and it told consumers that the only way they could sustain a secure sense of selfhood was to consume more and more commodities.

See Richards's *The Commodity Culture of Victorian England: Advertising and Spectacle, 1851–1914* (Stanford: Stanford University Press, 1990), p. 196.

20. Arthur W. Frank, "For a Sociology of the Body: An Analytical Review," in *The Body: Social Process and Cultural Theory,* ed. Mike Featherstone, Mike Hepworth, and Bryan S. Turner (London: Sage, 1991), pp. 62–63. Jean Baudrillard and Pierre Bourdieu are the principal theorists of consumption whose work Frank draws on in his discussion of a "mirroring body" (pp. 61–68).

21. Steven Marcus, *Dickens: From Pickwick to Dombey* (New York: Simon and Schuster, 1965), p. 151.

22. These theatrical productions of consistent and knowable public figures may be identified with what Audrey Jaffe calls "an anxiety about the theatricality of the social world, the susceptibility to manipulation of social identity" in later Victorian England. See Jaffe's "Detecting the Beggar: Arthur Conan Doyle, Henry Mayhew, and 'The Man with the Twisted Lip,'" *Representations* 31 (1990): p. 101.

23. Mary Ann Doane, *The Desire to Desire: The Woman's Film of the 1940s* (Bloomington: Indiana University Press, 1987), pp. 12–13.

24. See Elisabeth Bronfen's discussion of the ways in which Nell's deathbed scene presents a stabilizing image of death, in *Over Her Dead Body: Death, Femininity, and the Aesthetic* (New York: Routledge, 1992), pp. 88–90.

4. Public Knowledge, Common Knowledge, and Classifications of Will: *Barchester Towers* and *Little Dorrit*

1. Anthony Trollope, *Barchester Towers* (1857; reprint, Harmondsworth, England: Penguin, 1982), pp. 19, 23. All further references are to this edition; page numbers are cited in the text.

2. D. A. Miller, *The Novel and the Police* (Berkeley: University of California Press, 1988), p. 128.

3. Charles Dickens, *Little Dorrit* (1857; reprint, Harmondsworth, England: Penguin, 1967), pp. 157–58.

4. Jürgen Habermas, *The Structural Transformation of the Public Sphere: An Inquiry into a Category of Bourgeois Society,* trans. Thomas Burger (Cambridge: MIT Press, 1989), p. 133.

5. Ibid., p. 140; Habermas's emphasis.

6. Ibid., pp. 139–40, 137.

7. This is Miller's emphasis in his discussion of *Barchester Towers* in a chapter titled "The Novel as Usual." See *The Novel and the Police,* especially p. 145.

8. For discussion of how Trollope represents the gentleman as an internal phenomenon, see Shirley Robin Letwin, *The Gentleman in Trollope: Individuality and Moral Conduct* (Cambridge: Harvard University Press, 1982).

9. See Pierre Bourdieu, *Distinction: A Social Critique of the Judgement of Taste,* trans. Richard Nice (Cambridge: Harvard University Press, 1984), especially pp. 50–63.

10. Daniel Miller, *Material Culture and Mass Consumption* (Oxford: Basil Blackwell, 1987), pp. 149, 150.

11. Arthur W. Frank, "For a Sociology of the Body: An Analytical Review," in *The Body: Social Process and Cultural Theory*, ed. Mike Featherstone, Mike Hepworth, and Bryan S. Turner (London: Sage, 1991), p. 67.

12. Michel Foucault, *Discipline and Punish: The Birth of the Prison*, trans. Alan Sheridan (New York: Pantheon, 1977), pp. 179, 180.

13. Bruce Haley, *The Healthy Body and Victorian Culture* (Cambridge: Harvard University Press, 1978), p. 94.

14. Jonathan Crary, *Techniques of the Observer: On Vision and Modernity in the Nineteenth Century* (Cambridge: MIT Press, 1992), p. 147.

15. J. D. Y. Peel, *Herbert Spencer: The Evolution of a Sociologist* (London: Heinemann, 1971), p. 140. The quotation from Spencer is from *First Principles* (1862).

16. See Peel, *Herbert Spencer*, especially pp. 129–30, 165, on the relativism of Spencer's thought.

17. Spencer was influenced by Smith. See Peel's discussion of Spencer's relation both to Smith and to Malthus, in ibid., pp. 137–39.

18. Arthur even assigns to "nobody" his love for Pet Meagles: "Why should he be vexed or sore at heart? It was not his weakness that he had imagined. It was nobody's, nobody's within his knowledge; why should it trouble him?" (244).

19. Gillian Beer, in *Darwin's Plots: Evolutionary Narrative in Darwin, George Eliot, and Nineteenth-Century Fiction* (London: Routledge and Kegan Paul, 1983), suggests that "the organisation of *The Origin of Species* seems to owe a good deal to the example of one of Darwin's most frequently read authors, Charles Dickens, with its apparently unruly superfluity of material gradually and retrospectively revealing itself as order" (8). George Levine points out that "[d]istortion, excess, and clutter are the marks of Victorian design, of Dickens's novels, and of Darwin's world" in *Darwin and the Novelists: Patterns of Science in Victorian Fiction* (Cambridge: Harvard University Press, 1988), p. 150.

20. Levine reads this depiction of nature, among others, as evidence that *Little Dorrit* "impl[ies] a world coherent with that asserted by thermodynamics," in *Darwin and the Novelists*, p. 155.

21. Foucault, in *Discipline and Punish*, suggests the importance of shades of meaning to homogeneous and comprehensive normalizations of differences:

In a sense, the power of normalization imposes homogeneity; but it individualizes by making it possible to measure gaps, to determine levels, to fix specialities and to render the differences useful by fitting them one to another. It is easy to understand how the power of the norm functions within a system of formal equality, since within a homogeneity that is the rule, the norm introduces, as a useful imperative and as a result of measurement, all the shading of individual differences. (184)

5. Gender as Order in Public and Private: *East Lynne*

1. Mrs. Henry Wood, *East Lynne* (1861; reprint, intro. Stevie Davies, London: Dent, 1984), pp. 20–21. All further references are to this edition; page numbers are cited in the text.

2. Ann Cvetkovich's discussion of *East Lynne* in *Mixed Feelings: Feminism, Mass Culture, and Victorian Sensationalism* (New Brunswick: Rutgers University Press, 1992), pp. 97–127, focuses on the production of affect in sensation novels and the political meaning of such production. She argues, for example, that "the novel's sensationalism effaces the material causes of Isabel's suffering by representing it as the product of the repression of her feelings" (100).

3. Gillian Beer, *Darwin's Plots: Evolutionary Narrative in Darwin, George Eliot, and Nineteenth-Century Fiction* (London: Routledge and Kegan Paul, 1983), pp. 127–28.

4. Jonathan Loesberg, "The Ideology of Narrative Form in Sensation Fiction," *Representations* 13 (1986): pp. 115–38. Loesberg quotes Carlyle's prediction, in "Shooting the Niagara" (1867), that democracy was going "the full length of its course, towards the Bottomless or into it" (121). Loesberg argues that the loss of identity on which sensation novels focus "links up with a fear of a general loss of social identity as a result of the merging of the classes" that was part of the Victorian ideology of class (117).

5. See Matthew Arnold's argument in *Culture and Anarchy* (1869; reprint, ed. R. H. Super, Ann Arbor: University of Michigan Press, 1980) that "by our *best self* we are united, impersonal, at harmony," and that "this is the very self which culture, or the study of perfection, seeks to develop in us; at the expense of our old untransformed self, taking pleasure only in doing what it likes or is used to do, and exposing us to the risk of clashing with every one else who is doing the same!" (134–35).

6. Mary Ann Doane, *The Desire to Desire: The Woman's Film of the 1940s* (Bloomington: Indiana University Press, 1987), p. 141.

7. Anika Lemaire, *Jacques Lacan,* trans. David Macey (London: Routledge and Kegan Paul, 1977), p. 87.

8. In *Powers of Horror: An Essay on Abjection,* trans. Leon S. Roudiez (New York: Columbia University Press, 1982), Julia Kristeva theorizes the need to represent, differentiate, and get rid of a primary experience of undifferentiated "abjection." Kristeva theorizes that prior to the identification of self, the child experiences a territorial struggle with "the abject." This is a struggle for place in relation to, or in, the body of the mother: "'*Where* am I?' instead of '*Who* am I?'" (8). The struggle occurs without reference to representation, that is, not as a separation of subject from object but as a separation of the child, as a differentiable and differentiating being, from the undifferentiable, the abject that is without objects.

9. See Michelle A. Massé, *In the Name of Love: Women, Masochism, and the Gothic* (Ithaca: Cornell University Press, 1992), for the argument that masochism is a means of constituting a self. In her reading of beating fantasies, for example, Massé argues that "To be ignored—not to merit any kind of attention, no matter what form it takes—is to disappear as a self. To be beaten is proof of existence and even of lovableness for many protagonists" (105).

10. Ibid., p. 45.

11. My recognition of this distribution of Foucault's doubled man is similar to Homi K. Bhabha's argument, in *The Location of Culture* (London: Routledge, 1994), that Foucault is "spatializing the 'time' of history" in his "doubling of 'man'" (196). Bhabha clarifies how such a spatialization makes possible the erasure from history of

those groups of persons in the lower depths of Foucault's divide: "The invisible power that is invested in this dehistoricized figure of Man is gained at the cost of those 'others'—women, natives, the colonized, the indentured and enslaved—who, at the same time but in other spaces, were becoming the peoples without a history" (196–97). I am arguing that these "other" people are also deprived of space as a means of differentiation. Crowded by likenesses and repetition, such characters as Mrs. Henry Wood's women and Thomas Hardy's "natives" have neither time nor room to become different.

6. Naturalizing Class and Gender Distinctions: The Return of the Native

1. Thomas Hardy, *The Return of the Native* (1878; reprint, London: Penguin, 1985), p. 66. All further references are to this edition; page numbers are cited in the text.

2. Jürgen Habermas, *The Structural Transformation of the Public Sphere: An Inquiry into a Category of Bourgeois Society*, trans. Thomas Burger (Cambridge: MIT Press, 1989), p. 175.

3. Ibid., p. 176.

4. Ibid., p. 157.

5. Ibid., pp. 155–56.

6. Ibid., pp. 200, 201–2.

7. In Pierre Bourdieu's *Distinction: A Social Critique of the Judgement of Taste*, trans. Richard Nice (Cambridge: Harvard University Press, 1984), see the section "Distance from Necessity," pp. 53–56.

8. William Leiss, *The Limits to Satisfaction: An Essay on the Problem of Needs and Commodities* (Toronto: University of Toronto Press, 1976), pp. 88–89.

9. Jean-Christophe Agnew, "The Consuming Vision of Henry James," in *The Culture of Consumption: Critical Essays in American History, 1880–1980*, ed. Richard Wightman Fox and T. J. Jackson Lears (New York: Pantheon, 1983), p. 71.

10. See Mary Ann Doane's *The Desire to Desire: The Woman's Film of the 1940s* (Bloomington: Indiana University Press, 1987), especially p. 12.

11. Habermas, *Structural Transformation*, pp. 200, 201.

12. Claude Lefort differentiates the totalitarian leader as an "Egocrat" who "coincides with himself, as society is supposed to coincide with itself" in the totalitarian state. See his "The Image of the Body and Totalitarianism," in *The Political Forms of Modern Society: Bureaucracy, Democracy, Totalitarianism*, ed. John B. Thompson (Cambridge: MIT Press, 1986), pp. 305–6. Lefort's discussion is cited by Michael Warner in his analysis of the image of the body of public figures in the twentieth century, "The Mass Public and the Mass Subject," in *Habermas and the Public Sphere*, ed. Craig Calhoun (Cambridge: MIT Press, 1992), pp. 387–88. Warner argues that as the public life of twentieth-century Western nations has become increasingly visual and spatial in its dimensions, public political discourse has shifted from rational debate "toward the politics of identity." Political movements, therefore, "have been centrally about the personal identity formation of minoritized subjects" (399).

13. G. M. Young, *Victorian England: Portrait of an Age* (Oxford: Oxford University Press, 1964), pp. 107–8.

14. Patrick Brantlinger, *Rule of Darkness: British Literature and Imperialism, 1830–1914* (Ithaca: Cornell University Press, 1988), pp. 30, 34–45.

Conclusion

1. Leonore Davidoff, *Worlds Between: Historical Perspectives on Gender and Class* (New York: Routledge, 1995), p. 228.

2. Jürgen Habermas, *The Structural Transformation of the Public Sphere: An Inquiry into a Category of Bourgeois Society,* trans. Thomas Burger (Cambridge: MIT Press, 1989), p. 200.

3. Ibid., p. 157.

Index

Agnew, Jean-Christophe, 88, 106, 208
Appleby, Joyce, 1, 23–24, 228 n.16
Armstrong, Nancy, 4, 6, 14; on
domestic economy, 8, 225 n.5; on
Emma, 229–30 n.2, 230 n.9; on
women and display, 8, 35, 229 n.20
Arnold, Matthew, 166, 235 n.5
Austen, Jane, 5, 6, 72. *See also Emma;*
Pride and Prejudice

Baldick, Chris, 231 n.21
Barchester Towers, 148, 152, 155, 164,
165; bureaucratic process in, 113–15,
116, 120–21; community in, 130–31,
132–33, 220–21; integrity in, 122–23,
132; the press in, 119; social class in,
116–17, 119–20, 122–23, 125–27,
219; women in, 126–29, 131
Baudrillard, Jean, 233 n.20
Beer, Gillian, 145, 164, 234 n.19
Bender, John, 227 n.21, 228 n.18
Bentham, Jeremy, 80, 229–30 n.2; on
public administration, 49–50, 71; on
self-interest, 49–50, 57, 114
Bhabha, Homi K., 74, 231 n.19,
235–36 n.11

Body, 232 n.19, 236 n.12; and class,
173; female, 8, 74–75, 165; as
mirror, 62, 88–89, 157, 230 n.12,
233 n.20; monstrous, 72, 73, 74–75,
112
Botting, Fred, 71–72, 75
Bourdieu, Pierre, 2, 222, 233 n.20;
on reproduction, 173; on taste and
class, 124–25, 196–97
Brantlinger, Patrick, 217–18
Bronfen, Elisabeth, 231 n.22, 233 n.24
Bunn, James H., 29, 228 n.15
Bureaucracy, 119, 154; individual
interest in, 49–50, 120; procedures
of, 113–16, 141; productivity of,
115–16, 186, 230 n.6

Capitalism, 1–2, 6, 8, 23
Carlyle, Thomas, 80–81, 235 n.4
Castle of Otranto, The, 3, 52, 58, 62, 70,
75, 152; desire in, 23–25, 42–45, 46,
52–53, 218; detachment in, 39–42,
110; fragmentation in, 38–39;
irrationality of, 22–23; restoration in,
37–38, 46
Castle, Terry, 227 n.21

Patricia McKee is professor of English at Dartmouth College. She received her Ph.D. from Brandeis University. She is the author of *Heroic Commitment in Richardson, Eliot, and James* and of articles on James, Faulkner, and Morrison.